I Think ~
Therefore I Art

Reconnect with Your Artistic Self
And
Your Love Of Drawing

By

Gloria Miller Allen

DEDICATION

This book is dedicated to my many students.

ACKNOWLEDGEMENTS ~ TWO THANK YOU'S

First, to my friend Mary Noble, who read and re-read the book several times serving as editor and who helped me *think*. Mary never complained, always encouraged and was forever eager to have another look. Mary's very full and successful career was teaching journalism and English. She knows her stuff, and she taught me much. Thank you, Mary.

Second is my friend and husband Tony, who is not only my constant cheerleader, but was my constant computer guru. A thousand times during the process of creating this book, he rescued me with infinite patience and his wonderfully level head. His very successful career involved chemistry, physics and math at the Idaho National Laboratory. He is now and forever my hero and the love of my life. The book simply could not have happened without the two of us. Thank you, Mr. A.

All paintings and poems in this book are originals by the author/artist

Gloria Miller Allen

AWS, TWSA,WW, NWWS.

I Think ~ Therefore I Art

Reconnect with Your Artistic Self
And Your Love Of Drawing

An Introduction

I laid this book out like class work with planned progression – building from one chapter to the next. The assignments are aimed at developing fundamental skills we all want in order to put down on paper *what* we want, *how* we want, and *when* we want. A serious student can treat this book as a textbook or as a correspondence course complete with assignments and deadlines. Consequently, those students will graduate at the end of the chapters with more skill, awareness, and confidence than they previously had. On the other hand, if you flip from picture to poem to text, though hopefully enjoyable, it cannot possibly be the effective learning experience it could and should be.

It is my hope that you purposefully advance your artistic development by methodically going through it ~ start to finish.

Nearly 20 years ago, I went methodically through Betty Edwards' book *Drawing on the Right Side of Your Brain* It, too, is laid out like a textbook. I made a large drawing book and filled it with the assignments. At the end of that long process, I emerged as an artist who no longer experienced perplexing difficulties with drawing. I owe her my thanks. Although I've never met her, she helped me on my personal artistic journey. Certainly, I recommend her book to those who want to improve their drawing. She has inspired countless thousands.

Yes, I do believe in doing academic work. Perhaps it is partially because I never got to study art in college, but I've found great value and time well spent in giving myself academic exercises. In my workshops I hammer the basics perhaps to the point of fatigue, and I do it without apology. I believe discipline is integral to goal setting, and I know self-imposed academic work is rooted in self discipline. I believe we learn and grow with each other, and I believe that most humans love learning. These are my reasons for writing this book.

As a workshop instructor, my goal is to persuade you that academic knowledge and assignments have rich rewards for those who pursue them. I believe in hard work first and reaping the rewards later.

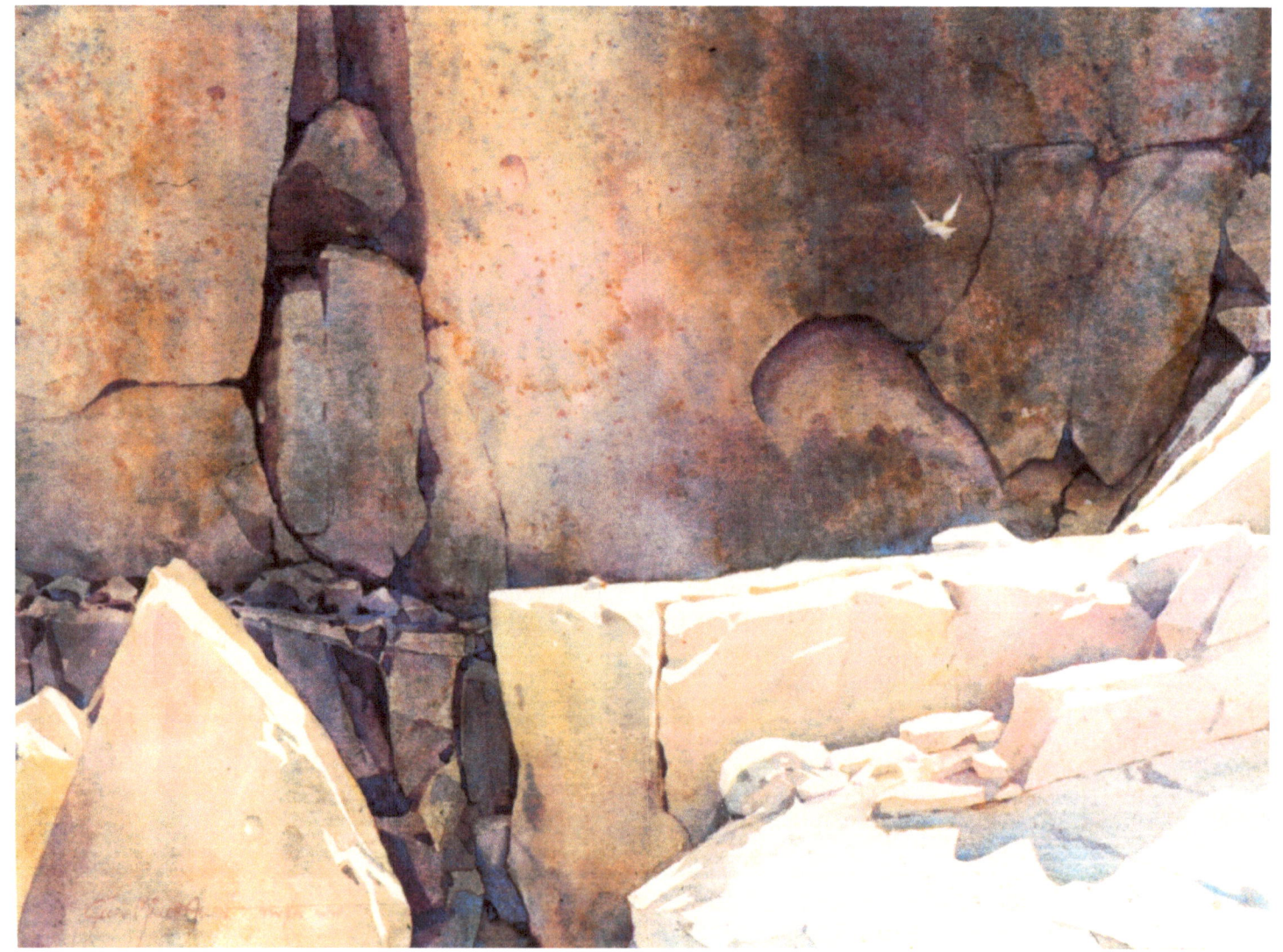

Out of the Darkness and into the Light   *watercolor*   *22 x 30*

So, get yourself a nice sketch book to use as a workbook. Get one with good enough paper to write, draw and paint in. Or choose a size of paper, both drawing, and painting paper and staple them together to make your own workbook. Either way, challenge yourself to do the assignments given here. Pretend you're working for a grade.

My expertise is in watercolor, but these fundamental lessons in drawing are usable in any medium: oil, pastel, colored pencil, acrylic, etc. Drawing is the basis for the vast majority of visual art. There simply is no substitute for sound knowledge and competence when it comes to drawing and perspective.

Thinking about these fundamentals, exploring what works and what doesn't work, and practicing some of the principles others have hammered out before us is a valuable process for all of us to work through, and I mean *work through for ourselves*. Over the years, I have come up with some homespun, down-to-earth, laymen's ideas, lessons, and practical thinking that have helped me. In these pages, I aim to share them with those who are searching.

Gloria Miller Allen

AWS
TWSA
WW
NWWS

I Think ~
Therefore I Art

Table of Contents:

TANGIBLE

I WAS THINKING ON SUNRISE TODAY,
HOW MANY MIRACLES COME TO STAY,
ONLY THEIR APPOINTED TIME.

BUD AND BLOOM,
GREAT HARVEST MOON,
SEASON AND GO AWAY.

A BABE COMES TO YOU
ONLY LATER TO
LEAVE YOU STILL HANGING ON,

LIKE LAST BITS OF TWINE
TRELLIS CLINGS TO VINE
AFTER THE PLANT DIES AWAY.

SO WHEN INSPIRATION FINDS YOU
DO ALL THAT YOU CAN DO
TO USE IT BEFORE IT FLIES.

WRITE IT, OR PLAY IT,
PAINT, SING, OR SAY IT.
UNDONE, IT'S AS AIR TO THE SKIES

BUT GRAB IT
AND HOLD IT,
WITH HAND AND MIND MOLD IT

FOR TANGIBLE
IT CAN STAY,
DON'T YOU SEE?

...IF IT'S TANGIBLE,
  IT CAN STAY

1970

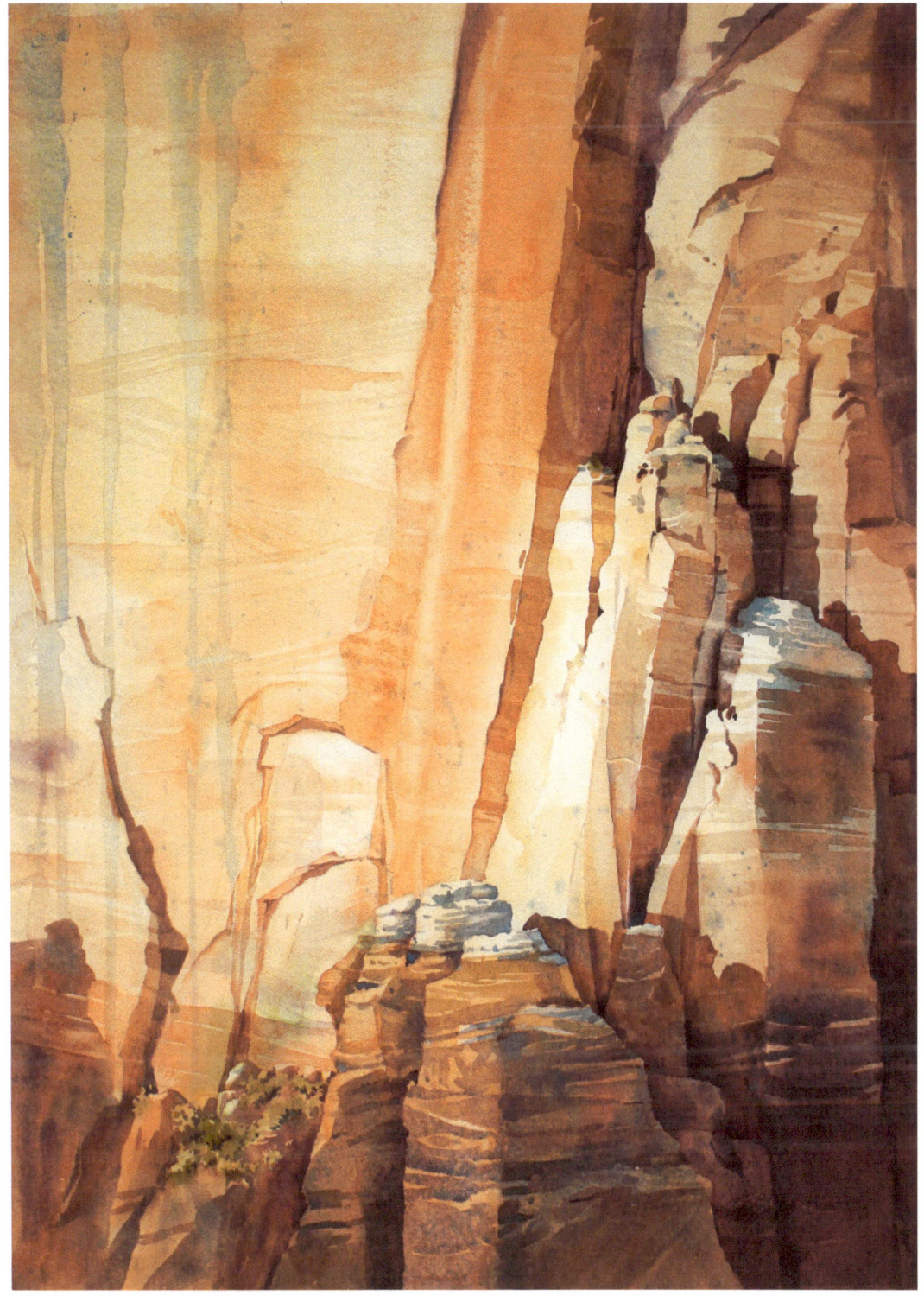

Ariella ~ *Zion National Park*   *watercolor*   *22 x 30*

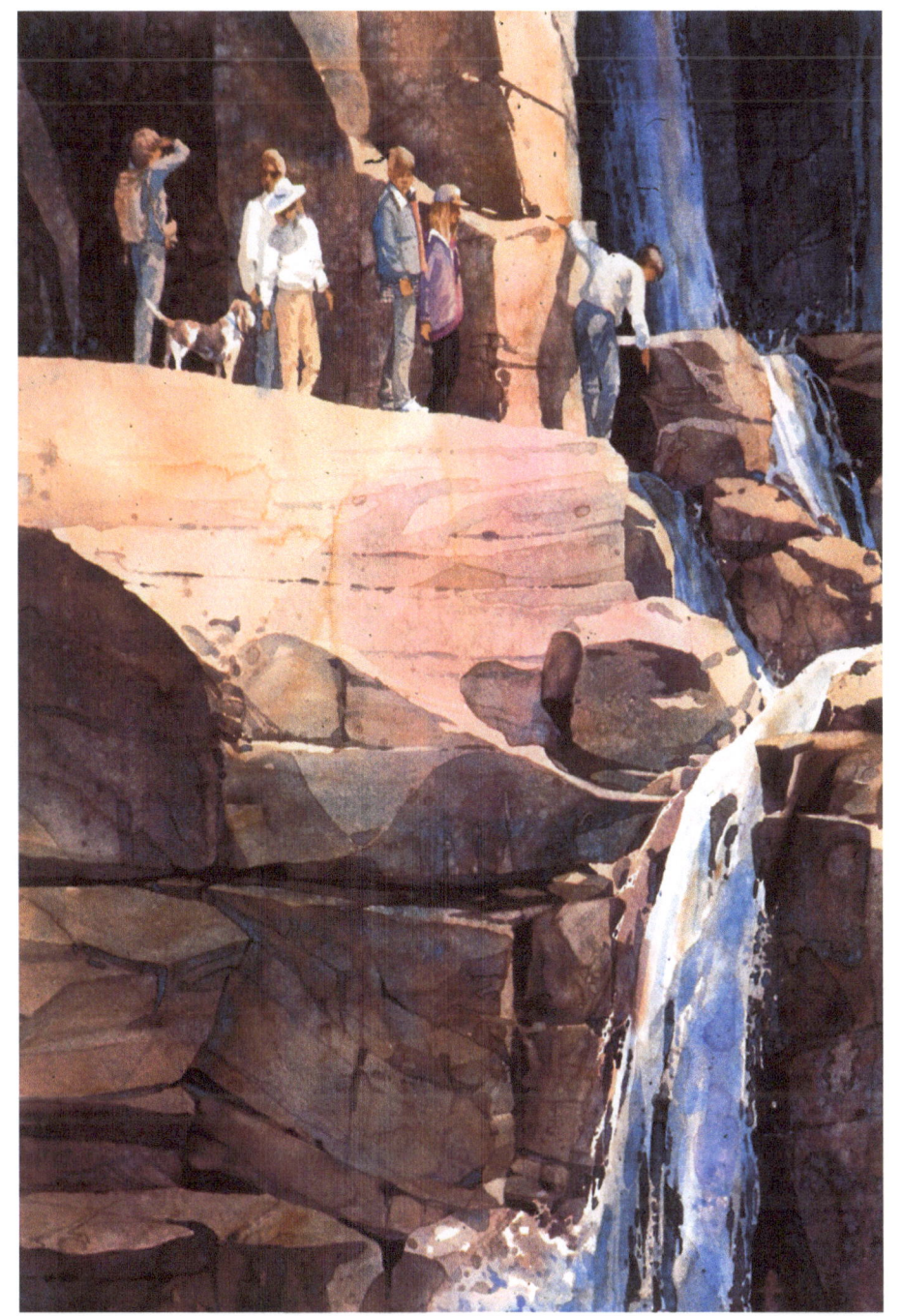

On a Lark   *watercolor*   *28 x22*

PART ONE

BEGINNING THOUGHTS AND SETTING THE STAGE

CHAPTER ONE
So, You Want To Be An Artist?

CHAPTER TWO
Tools You Bring To The Drawing Board

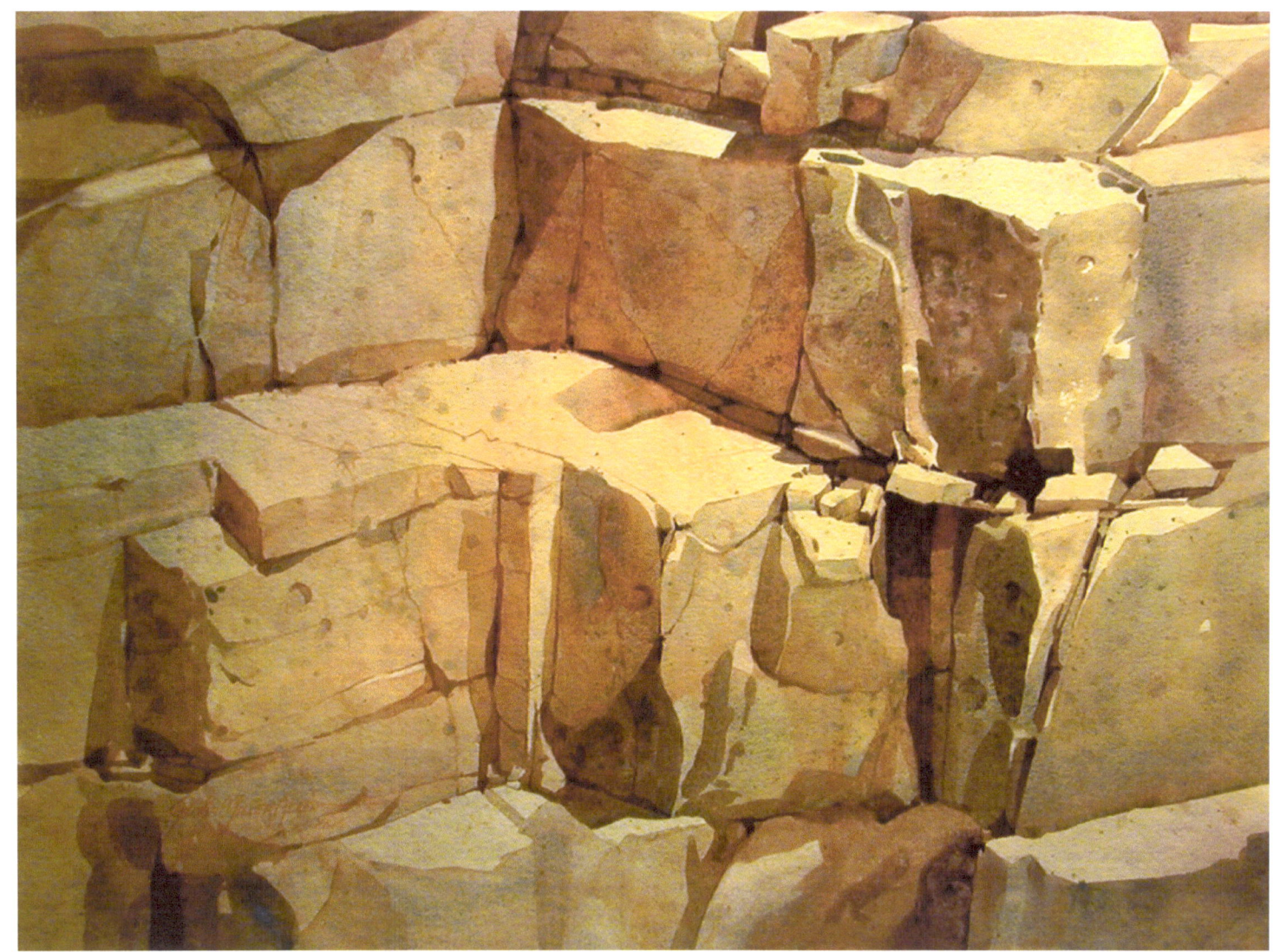

Canyon Steps   *watercolor AWS 2005*   *22 x 30*

SO, YOU WANT TO BE AN ARTIST?

FEATURING PAINTINGS FROM THE CANYON WALL SERIES

One of the biggest changes in our society over the past 100 years is the amount of free time we enjoy. It is true that we now have wonderful machinery to help with our day-to-day activities. Things such as dishwashers, computers, washing machines, airplanes, microwaves, power tools, all sorts of mechanical and electronic equipment, automobiles, and thousands of other modern marvels make our high standard of living easier to maintain. Our minutes, hours, and days are not spent so much in finding food and shelter as were the minutes, hours, and days of our ancestors. All this is to say that we live at a time in history when there is simply more leisure time. Because of that wonderful fact, the arts with all their rich diversity can be ours to explore with unprecedented luxury. Of course, we people do find ways to keep ourselves busy. But, as we know, we can and do make time for the things that are important to us.

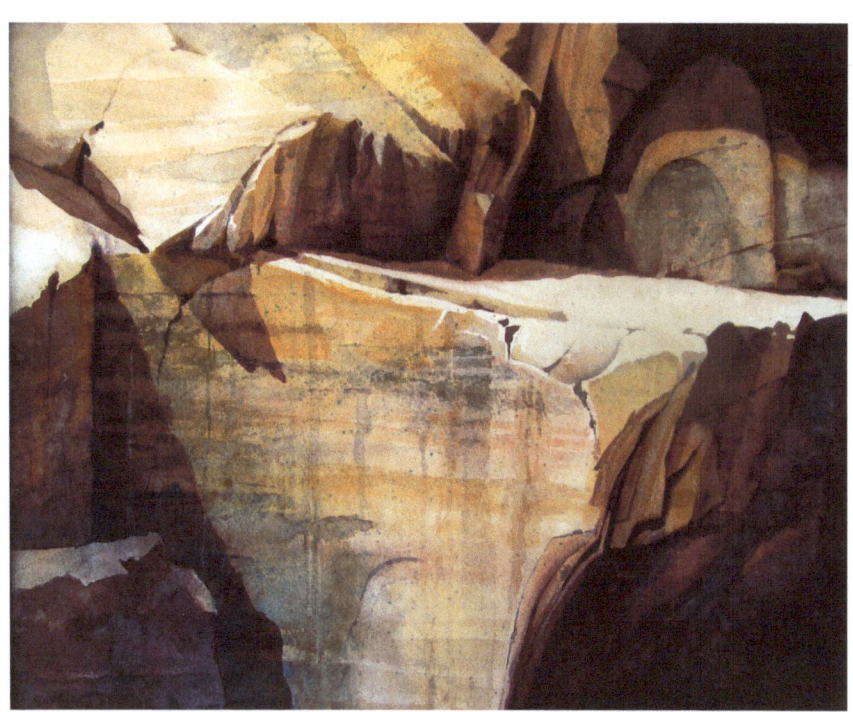

Safe Place To Land   *varnished watercolor*   *16 x 20*

I'd like to make a case for pursuing artistic avenues with some of that gifted time here and now.

There have always been people who pursued art no matter what, but these days artistic expression is enjoyed by more people than ever in history. It is a sign of our times, so why not join in? There are as many reasons to do so as you can think up reasons *not to do so*. None of

that matters, but what *does* matter, is that this great gift of time is yours. This is your life, and because you are reading this book, I must assume that you would like to play with the idea of being or becoming an artist. With that conclusion drawn, let's spend time *thinking* about that. Exactly what do you want your artistic *thinking* to bring to you? Where do you dream of it taking you? What are your thoughts about art in your life?

Obviously, art means different things to different people. Right now let's think about what it means to you—a person living right here, right now—an individual thinking about art and its role in your personal life. The choices are huge and varied.

Perhaps you want to

- create beautiful things for your home
- create cards or illustrate books
- write novels, or poetry, or plays
- film movies, write or direct them
- compose music, write lyrics, or sing
- dance, teach dancing, or choreography
- exhibit or sell paintings
- win a prize at the fair or a national competition

Obviously, this list can go on forever. Your own dreams will fit nicely into your list in one or more categories; but first, you *must know what they are*. Because you are reading this page, one of your choices is drawing and probably painting. Of course, this book focuses on the visual arts, yet we all know the same goal-setting principles apply no matter what particular art forms tempt you, and no mater what dreams and aspirations you hold for yourself in *non* artistic arenas. Goal setting simply works.

You can and do choose every day how you spend your gifted hours either consciously or unconsciously. Author, Lewis Carroll once said *"If you don't know where you're going, any road will get you there."* To put it another way, I'll quote from the movie *South Pacific* when Bloody Mary sang, *"You got to have a dream. If you don't have a dream, how you gonna have a dream come true?"* That is, of course how Rogers and Hammerstein put it, and I heartily concur.

At this time, take a few moments to list (in no particular order) your own dreams and ideas. What do you want to do with your gifted time? Be serious, be honest, keep it private, and *think*. Do it here in this book or in your workbook.

WHAT I WANT FROM MY ART

_____
_____
_____
_____
_____
_____
_____
_____
_____
_____
_____
_____
_____
_____
_____
_____
_____
_____
_____
_____
_____
_____
_____
_____

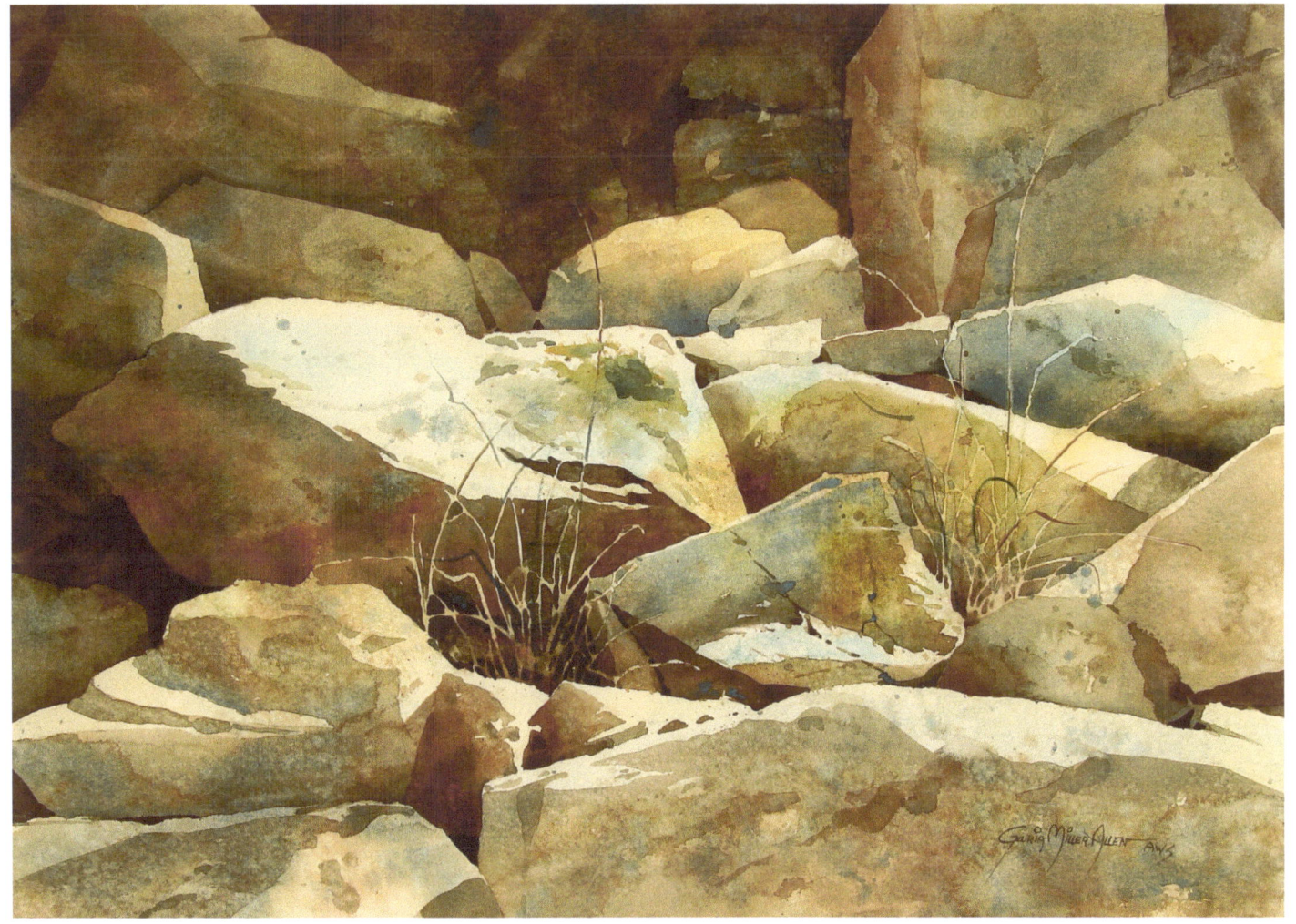

Among The Grasses II　　　　　　　　watercolor AWS 2009　　　　　　　　*22 x 28*

IN PURSUIT OF THINKING FIRST

As the title of this book indicates, I believe *Thinking* is huge. *Thinking* is simply everything. It's where things start, good or bad. It's the incubator where we hatch out our lives. We do it consciously, or unconsciously…but we do it. The goal is to get your dreams out of your subconscious and write them down in black and white. In tangible form, they are on their way to reality. That is so true of art. Making things tangible and concrete out of thought. That's it. Tiny simple or complex thoughts and dreams become a conscious day-to-day effort when one is seated at the drawing board or easel. Sometimes it seems my smallest fleeting thoughts turn out powerful in the end while some seemingly huge ones fizzle out. *Thinking* and brainstorming is fun and it's also something to build upon. It's an enormous part of painting. *Thinking* is first and foremost.

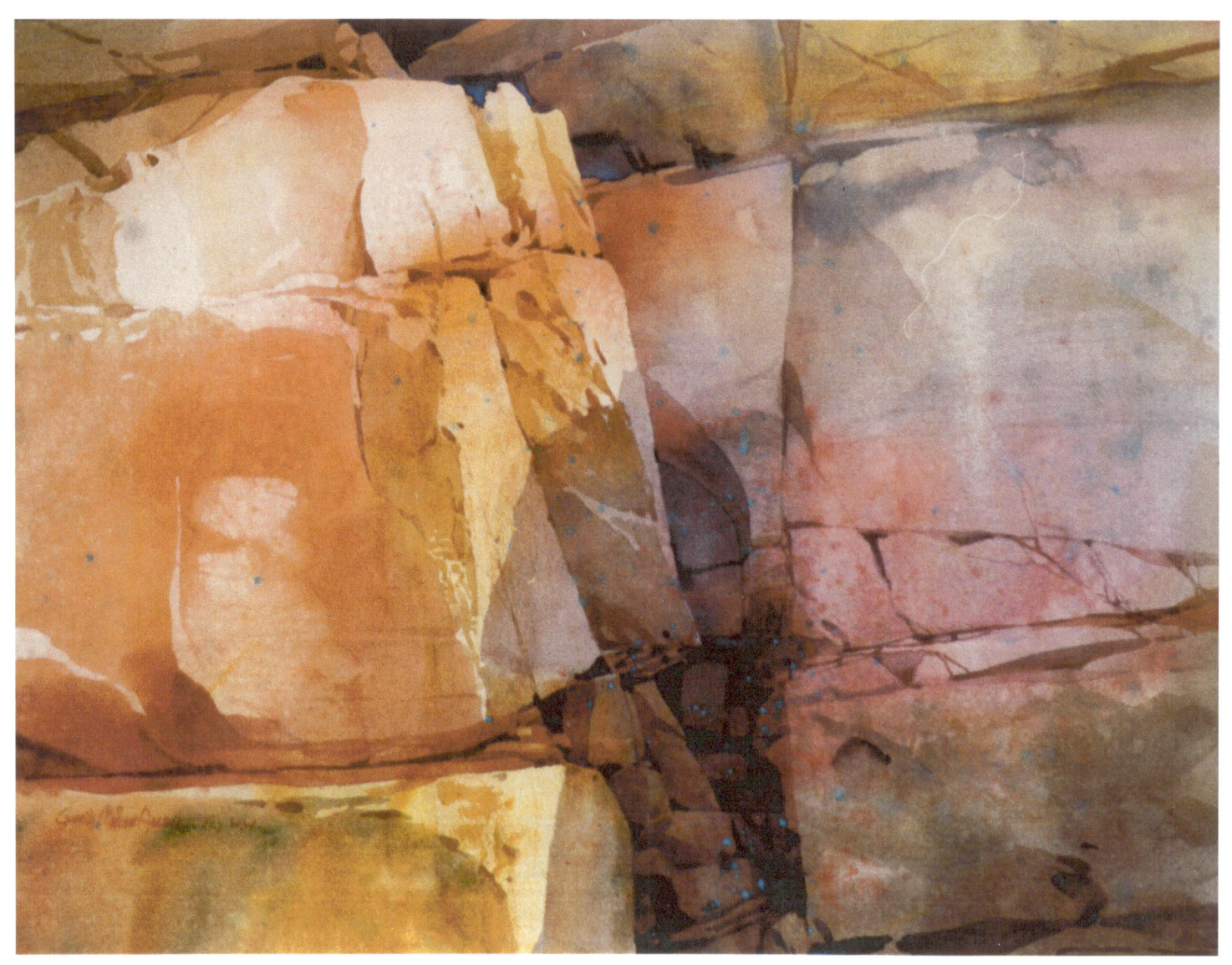

Purple and Gold   *watercolor*   *22 x 30*

Thinking, responding, and creating is part of our human experience. We cannot *help* but be creative. Artists get a lot of credit for it, but people all over the world are creative because we are creative creatures. We use our creative powers to do literally everything. If you have raised a child, you know you must be creative to handle the multitude of incidents every child will come up with and still manage to keep your balance between jobs, home, and the rest of life and all at the same time. Creative? I believe so. The scientist who delves into research, the plumber who fixes the leak, the boss who must fire or hire someone, the little two-year-old child who figures out whether or not tantrums have a chance with Mom or Dad—all exhibit great creativity. We *are* creative creatures. Never doubt that. Doubts can be pitfalls where we wallow endlessly. Doubts can stop our pursuits and dreams easier and quicker than just about anything else…including rejection slips. Why? I believe it is because our doubts are part of our own belief system. That's pretty potent stuff indeed.

CLAIM YOUR CREATIVE SELF

So right now, I want you to acknowledge your own creativity. Claim it. It is yours. You have all the native interest (talent) you need to pursue a personal artistic path—whatever that may mean to you. What if you have some insecure feelings? So what? Did you try drawing once and didn't like the outcome? Did you think artists drop onto planet earth as infants who know how to draw and paint?

That, of course, is worth a chuckle, but if there is one common thread that runs through the many work-shops I've taught over the years, it is just this one single thought:

Honestly, do I have the right, or the talent

to pursue my artistic dreams?

I believe if you are the possessor of an artistic dream, you not only have the right and the where-with-all to pursue it, but you also have the obligation. In fact, ignoring it will hurt you in one way or another. Doubts about ourselves and our ability put an end to many an artistic life before it can even begin. Overcoming doubt is always a worthy goal.

Any number of people say to me that someone once told them they didn't have what it takes to be an artist or some negative blockbuster like that. Words spoken carelessly by acquaintances or even loved ones can create such doubt that some people never quite get over it. Doubts are imagined, and we need to recognize them as such. In truth, *you* are the only person who can stop or start on any path - artistic or otherwise. That is a painful revelation for us to own.

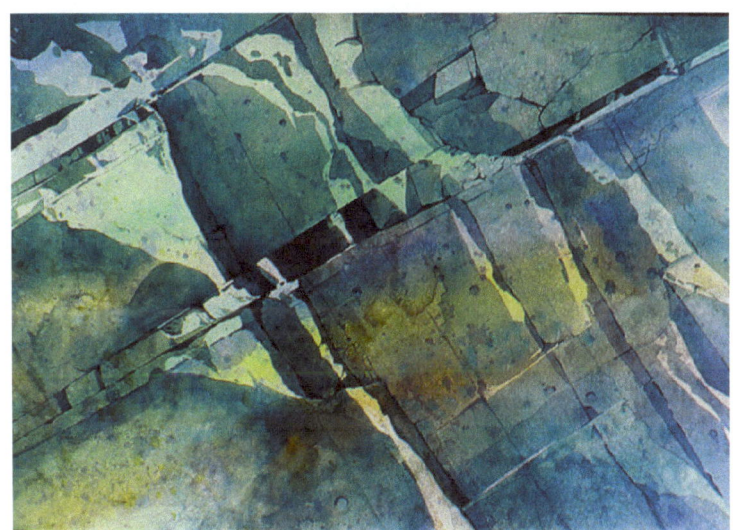

Canyon Verde　　　*oversized watercolor*　　　*27 x 39*

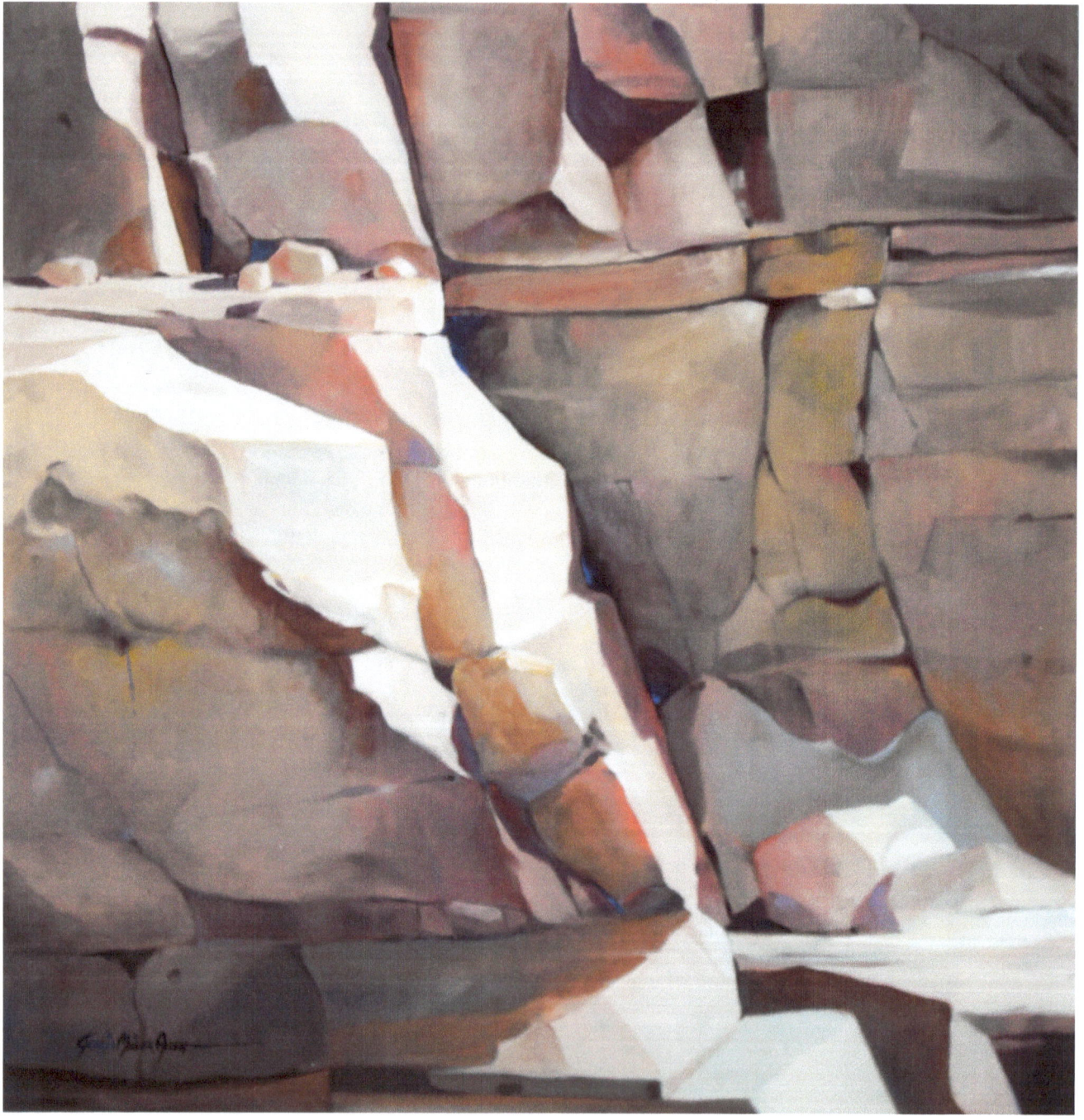

Steps of Stone ~ Rock of Ages Series   *36 x 36*

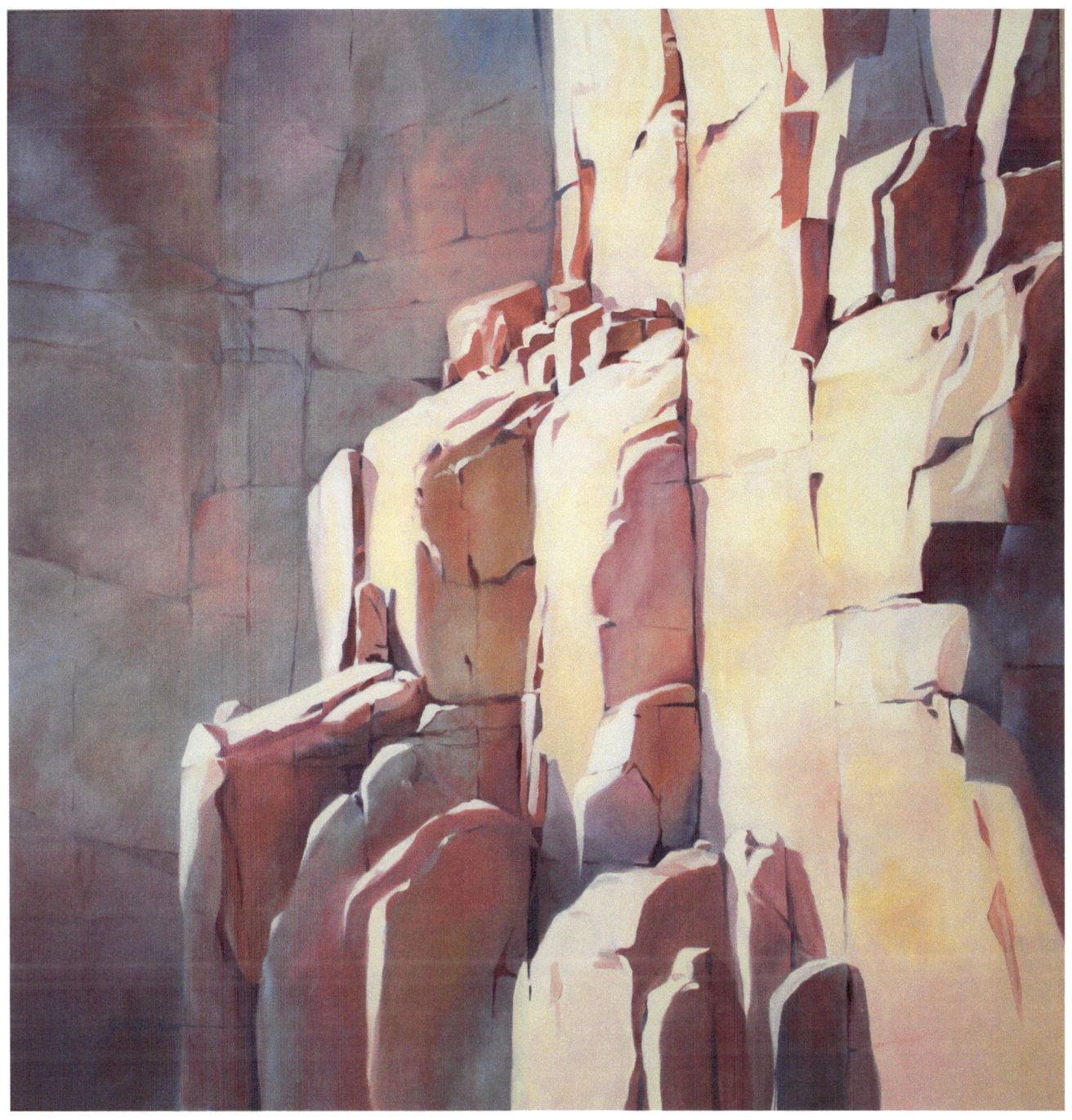

Alborado ~ Rock of Ages Series   *36 x 36*

WOULD THAT I WERE

WOULD THAT I WERE ALL I WILLED,
I COULD COME CLEAN WITH ME AND SAY,
THAT I HAVE CHANGED INSIDE OF ME,
ALL I WILLED TO CHANGE,
       ...BUT IT IS DIFFICULT TO DO..

SOME THINGS THAT I HAVE CHANGED
BECOME BETTER PARTS OF ME
BUT THEY MAY HIDE AWAY FROM ME
OTHER THINGS I SHOULD LET GO
       ...AND MUCH IS LEFT TO DO.

I'VE MANY PARTS INSIDE OF ME
EACH WITH GOALS THAT CHANGE IN TIME.
I'LL BE CONTENT TO LEARN AND GROW,
BUT NEVER STOP AND CLAIM TO BE
       ...COMPLETELY SATISFIED WITH ME.

1970

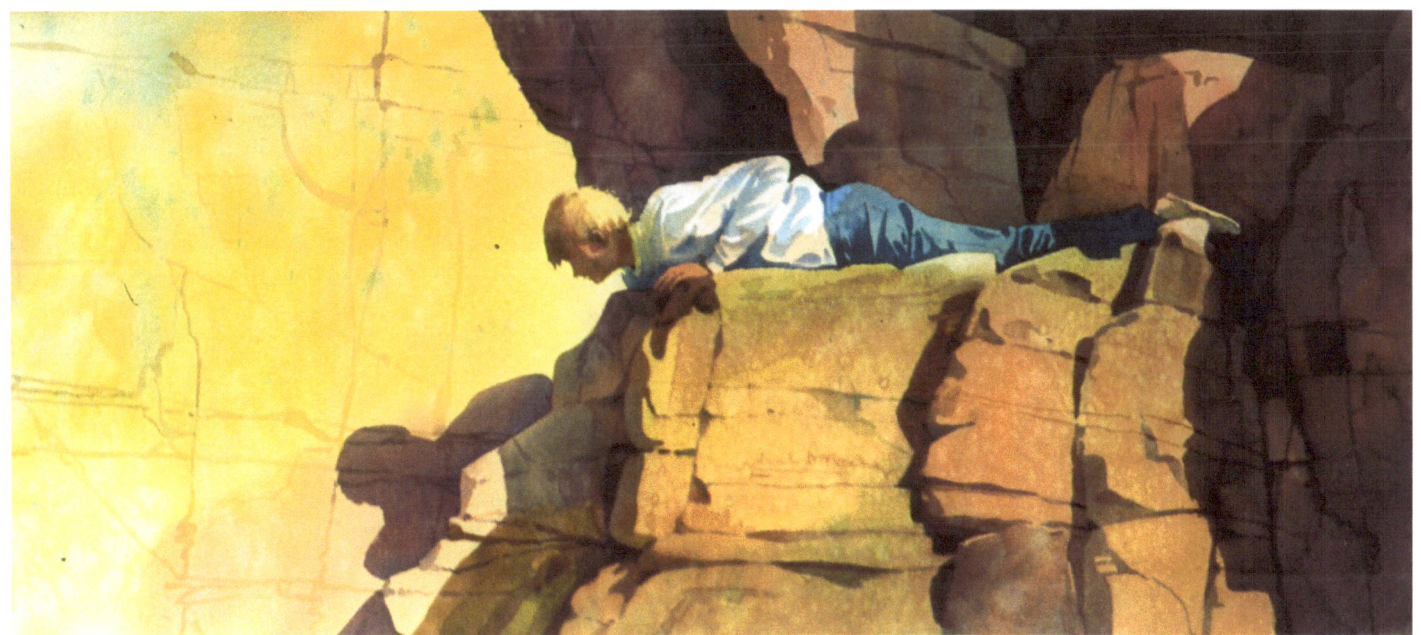

Shadows of Youth   *oversized watercolor*   *27 x 40*

Even though it is familiar and known to us, it is easily denied. Imagination and doubt get to us, and they are sneaky. It truly *must* be our goal to use the great gift of imagination to pursue our art, not to stop it. True, not everyone has nagging fears, yet many do. What about you? What part does all this play in your own pursuits? What are your fears? Do you know? Have you ever thought about it?

Now is a good time to put them down on paper in black and white and look at them. Who are your cheerleaders? Who are your critics? Which group are you yourself in? What makes you think you can't or shouldn't follow this art dream? Who or what makes you feel guilty about something that's incredibly good for you? What persistently sidetracks you? Never underestimate the power of self knowledge like this. You want to leap? This is a first step.

FEARS, DOUBTS & BUG-A-BOOS

_____

_____

_____

_____

_____

_____

_____

_____

_____

_____

_____

_____

_____

_____

We've now recognized and claimed that we are creative people and we've listed some doubts and fears on our papers. What next? If you want to take your artistic dreams closer to reality, you must give yourself permission. Now that sounds stupidly simple, but it's difficult for some. If it isn't for you, then you're lucky. As for the rest of us, it can be a hard-fought transition not easy to come by. Why? I won't attempt to answer that personal question for anyone else, but some of you might benefit from this little personal story of mine. I'll just call it:

GIVING MYSELF PERMISSION

When I was young, I had a silly almost worshipful idea of what an artist was. Artists were really special, and I'd put them on some perfect pedestal. They were somehow way above any images I had of myself. But I fanaticized about it anyway. I went to art shows, read library books, painted quite a lot, but not an artist by any stretch of my own imagination. I was beginning to show some of my work locally, but still, something kept me from claiming that word "artist." I couldn't actually say it out loud even to myself. Whenever someone off-handedly called me an artist, I was quick to correct them. "Oh, no, not really."

One day my artist friend, Marilyn Hoff Hansen and I were talking. I knew she confidently spoke of herself as an artist, and I was intrigued, curious, and a bit jealous. So I asked her when she began thinking of herself as an artist. She looked me in the eye and said, "Well, I always have...haven't you?"

That simply took me apart. Her words were so simple and heartfelt and just what I needed. While driving home, I gave myself permission once and for all to claim the title for myself and the next time I filled out a form that asked "occupation" I wrote "artist" in ink. I remember wondering at the time if lightning would strike. It did not, and I've never looked back. In truth, I was an artist even as a child. I was just an unconscious one. Marilyn woke me up.

After that, my whole view of my studio, my life, my efforts, my energies, my goals, and many of my choices changed—and would never be quite the same again. Of course, I had been an artist all along. Perhaps not a professional, perhaps not even a good one, but nevertheless, I was certainly an artist. After that, I had something to grow with, something to focus on, something to work at and to become.

It is my hope that Part I of this book titled *Beginning Thoughts* will help you begin or help you continue creating an artistic history of your own. You start by claiming your creative gift, and you continue by giving yourself permission. Oh, I repeat myself.

YOUR CREATIVE LICENSE

Here's a little idea. On the paper right in your workbook or on a separate sheet with crayon or marker, create your own "Artistic License." Make one to hang in the room where you paint. Many years ago an instructor had our class do just that. It was funny at the time, caused a lot of snickering, but still made its point very nicely. I dare you.

WHAT IS AN ARTIST ANYWAY?

Do you think you are one? Do you want to be? My early idea about artists has changed greatly over the years that I've been being one. First of all, there is no pedestal, no drum roll and no trumpet. Being an artist is simply a personal choice one makes to work or to play in the arts. I say work or play here very purposefully because some of the finest artists I know rarely show or sell their work. Surprised? It is true. A person can have the active heart and soul of an artist without ever wanting to make it into a business. Being an artist is something that comes into your life at various ages, but often it comes early on. It's rather like a perpetual habit that simply takes up residence and nags at you until you start to listen. Being an artist is far from appealing to everyone. The old stereotype of the starving artist has come into existence because it is not an easy way to earn a living. It is possible, but it is not easy. Art does not market itself, believe me, and without being marketed, there is no money. In the beginning money goes *out* much faster than it comes *in*. Do not do this expecting some easy money.

*O*nce upon a time there was a young man who went to his art professor and asked what he had to do to become a famous artist and make lots of money. The professor looked into the student's eager eyes and after a long pause said, " Go study business and marketing."

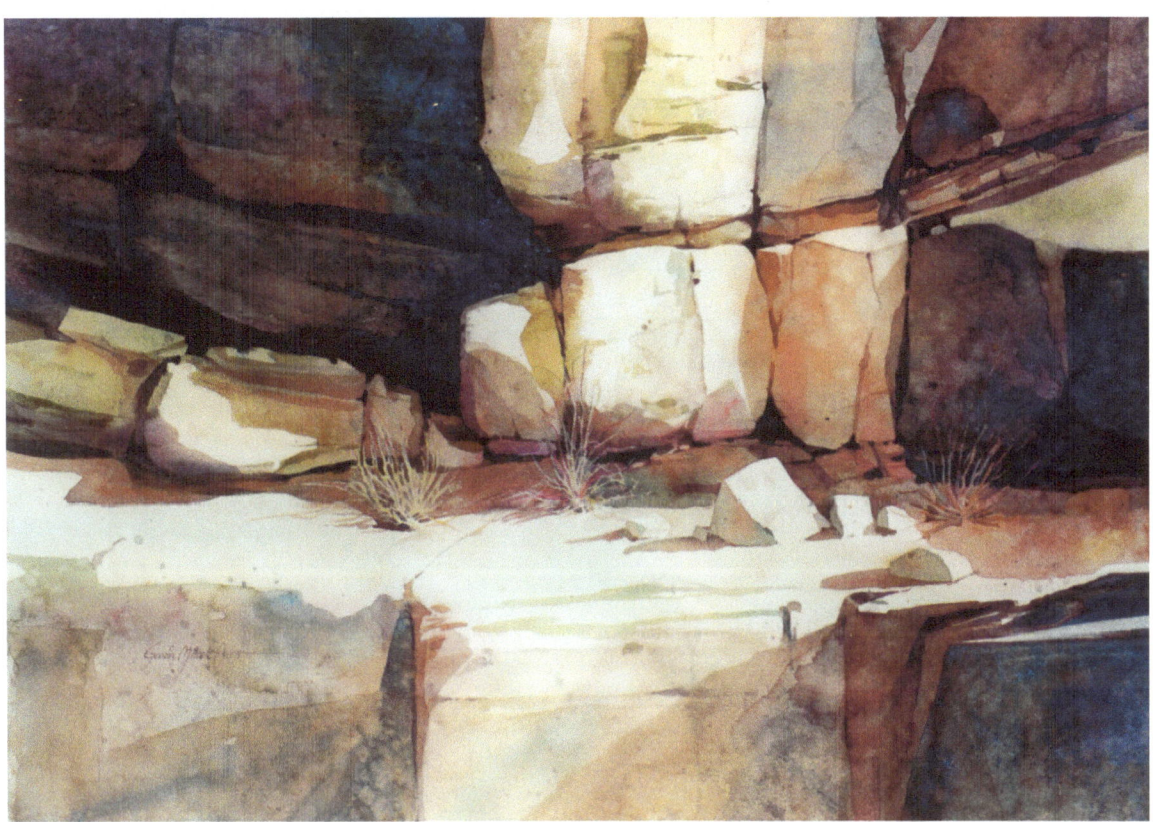

Taos Stone   *watercolor*   20 x 30

On the flip side of that coin, some people who sell their work have developed marketing skills far more than artistic skills. Some create fine products and sell them quite successfully. Many true dyed-in-the-wool, heart-and-soul artists finds themselves jealous of these marketers—right or wrong. An ability to market would be a blessing to any artist, but unfortunately it is not a pre-requisite. A large percentage of artistic people are lousy marketers. That's why many rely on commercial galleries for their sales. If you desire to be a professional, marketing skills are definitely something to work on, but I'm not the one to write that book.

To discover what being an artist is going to be for you personally, at least for now, let's go back to the first pages in this book. Look again at your first idea dream list and get some internal identifications started. Name it and claim it. That's a real power tool.

Art runs rich, varied, and deep in the veins connecting millions of people all over the world from the most primitive to the most sophisticated. There can be no actual defining of what an artist is. It is more a way of *thinking,* a way of seeing the world, a state of mind or a lifestyle than any attempt at identification will accomplish. In the first place, music, dance, theater, photography, sculpture, painting and others—so many venues create an endless list of possibilities. On top of that, the hobbyists, professionals and everyone in between—they all count too. If you dabble happily and contentedly, you are an artist. If you work in frustration and sweat, you are an artist. What we know for sure is that art can be a positive, beautiful, healthy and wholesome presence in your life. It *can* even be profitable. So, whether good, not so good, or somewhere in between, you have the right to pursue your artistic self and to grow. Art can be a way we can define purpose. Art is simply a way to live your life.

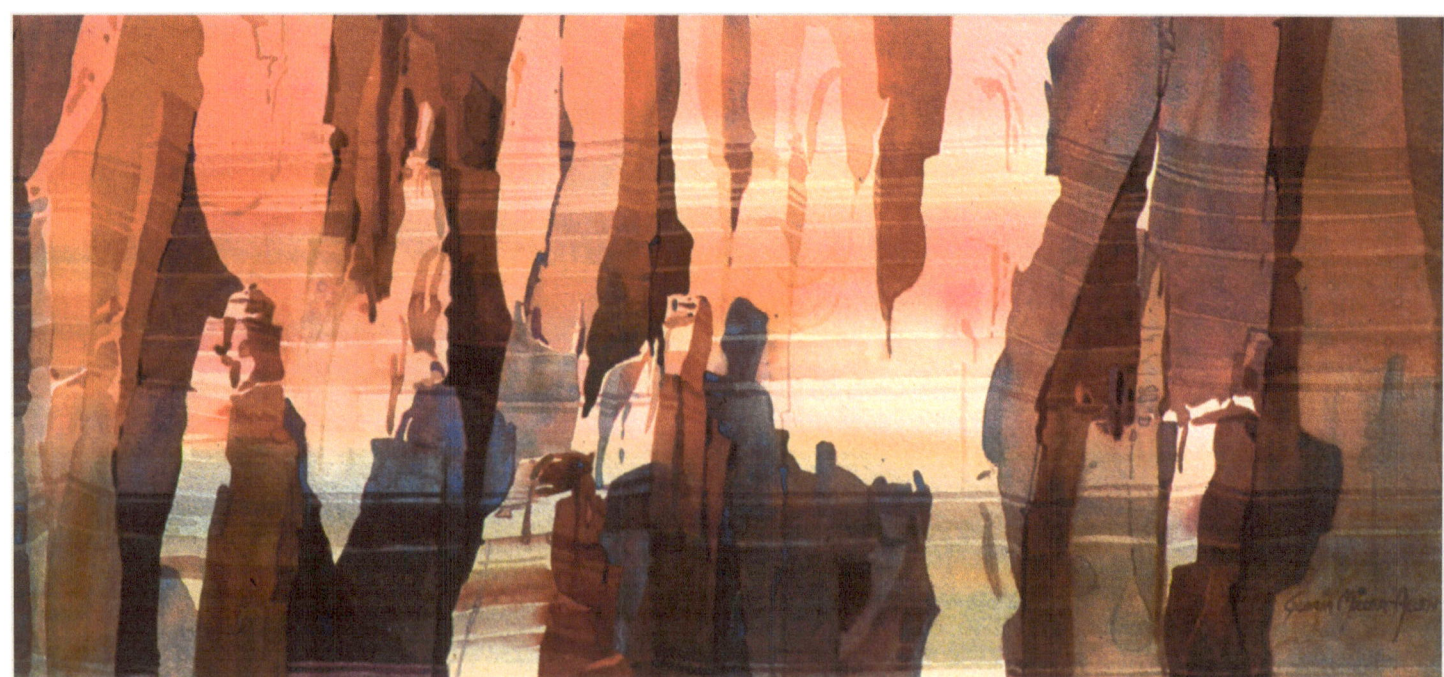

Zion Wall ~ *Zion National Park*   *watercolor*   *16 x 29*

PAPER-WEIGHTS
PAPER WAITS

SIT
RESTING
MIND
WATCHING
GUILTY
WASTING
TIME

TIME
HEAPED UPON US
BY THE GODS -
A GIFT
AN ANOINTMENT
SOMEHOW
BEYOND MY
USUAL ENDEAVOR
MY USUAL REACH
MY USUAL THRIFT
AND GATHERING

WHERE DID I PUT IT
THIS TIME?
AWAY
YES
AWAY
RESTING
WASTING
TIME.

WHAT DID IT BRING-
PARCHMENT?
INDEED,
SHADOWS
REFLECTIONS
OF THOUGHT
FRAGMENTS
ONLY.

I NEARLY TOUCHED
ONCE,
OR WAS IT TWICE?
I NEARLY
SAW MYSELF.

TRAINS LEAVE
WITHOUT ME
AND I WAS
ON TIME

BUT
PAPER
WAITS
QUIETLY
RESTING
EMPTY
BLANK
ANTICIPATING
NOTHING

THEN
UPON THE
PURE AND
VACANT WHITE
A
DARING HAND
DOTH MAKE
ITS MARK
AND
LO
FROM OUT
THE ETHER
A VISIBLE
REPLICA
OF THOUGHT
IS BORN

1983

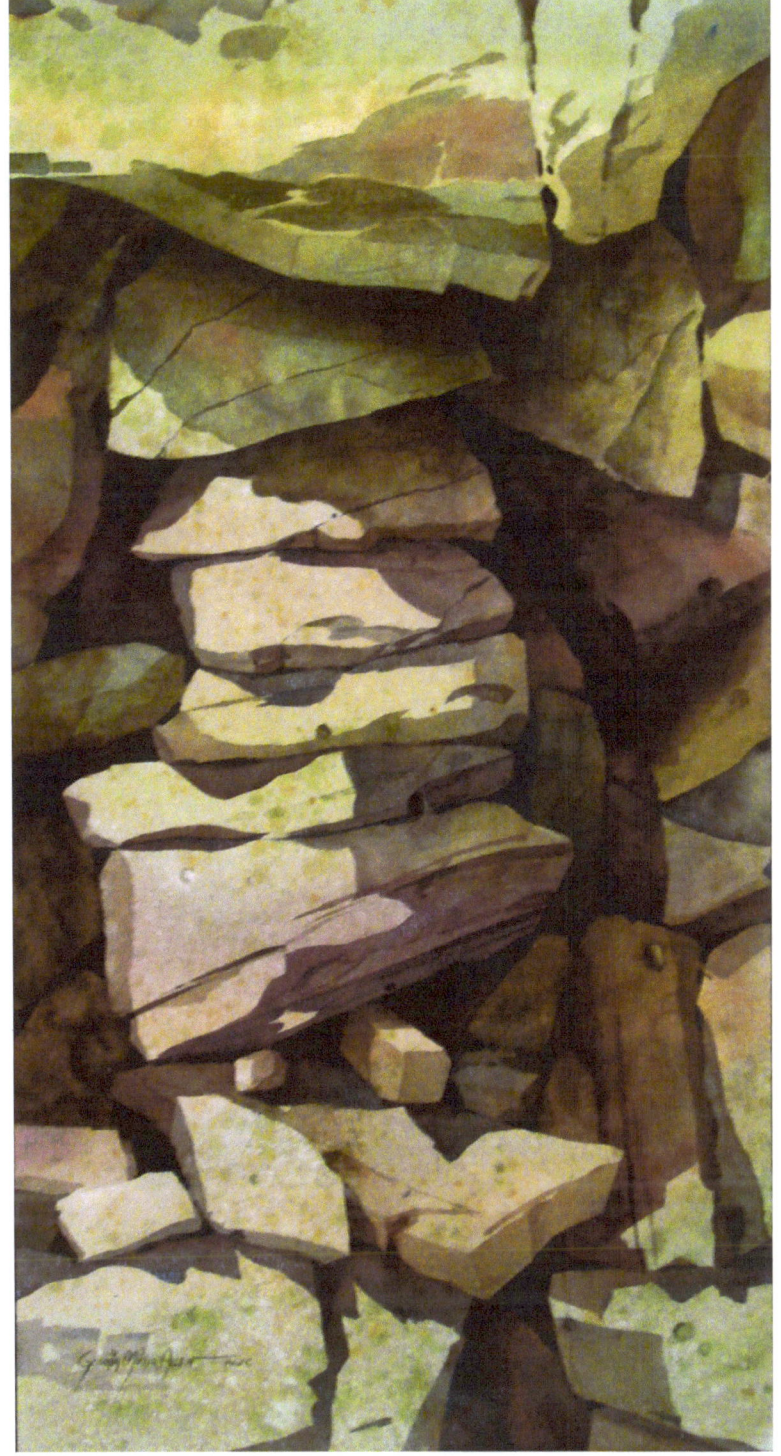

Still Standing   *watercolor*   *27 x 38*

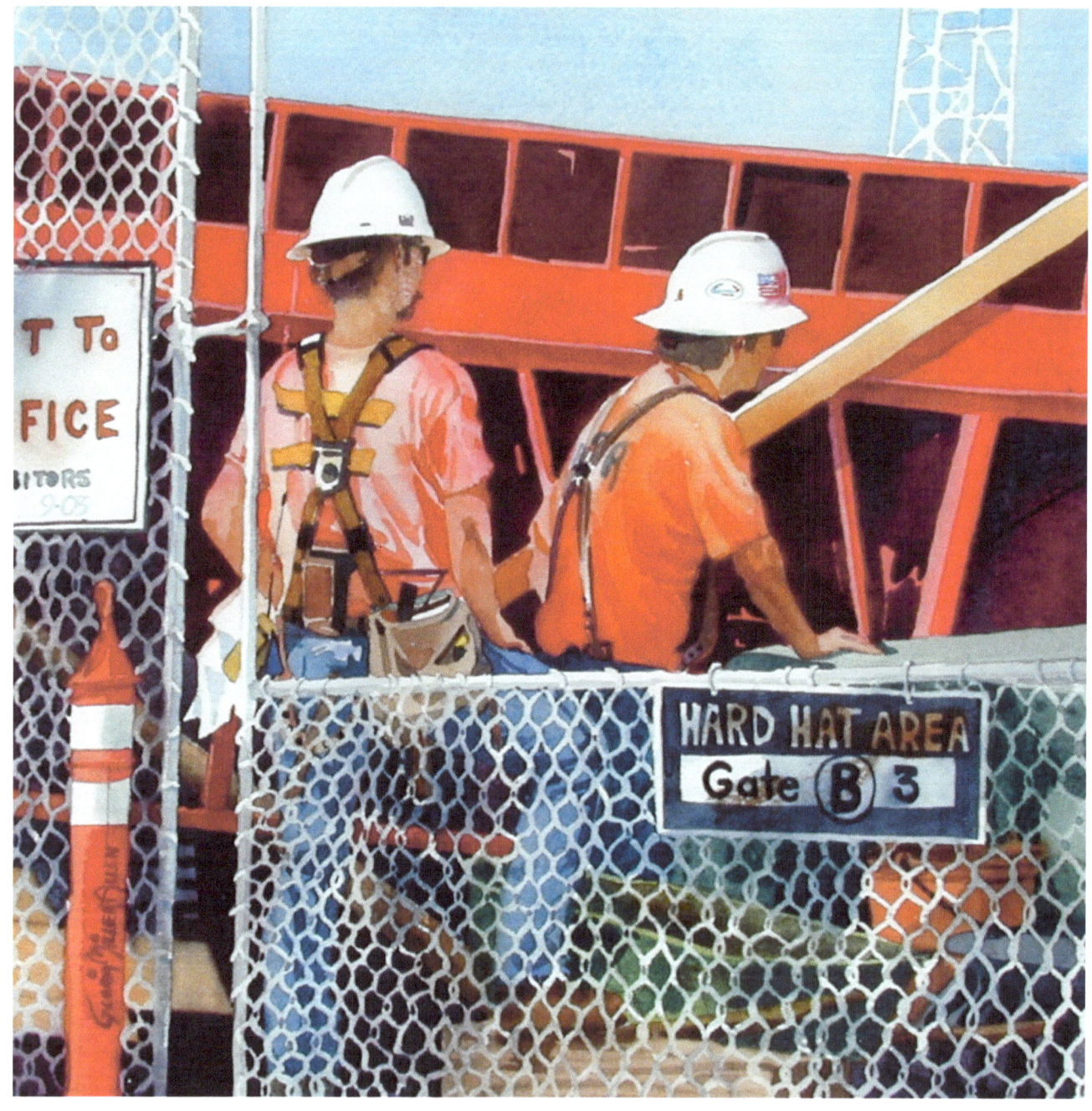

Gate B 3   *watercolor*   *10 x 10*

CHAPTER TWO

TOOLS YOU BRING TO THE DRAWING BOARD

FEATURING PAINTINGS OF AMERICANA BUILDINGS

And Street Scenes

So, you know you're creative. You know what your doubts and fears are. You have even given yourself permission to pursue this art dream. Now let's spend a few minutes *thinking* about this hunk of flesh that you reside in and just who it is, where it's been, and what history, tools and skills it already has. In other words, *just what are you bringing to the drawing board?* I might add here, "Ah shucks, not much" isn't a proper answer.

As artists we have many terrific tools at our disposal. Brushes, paper, paint, pencils, ink, erasers—all *tangible* tools. We basically have access to the same tools as every other artist. But right now I want you to become aware of some intangible tools. Sounds funny, doesn't it? How can tools be intangible? Perhaps you've never before thought of the following things as your tools, but I assure you—they are. I'm talking about such things as:

Your *thoughts*	Your wishes
Your preferences	Your sight/insight
Your history	Your beliefs
Your emotions	Your opinions
Your likes/dislikes	Your health
Your expressions	Your pain/joys
Your experiences	Your enthusiasm
Your temperament	Your struggles
Your vision/visions	*"Yourself"*

These intangibles are actually *power tools,* and though we may struggle through our entire artistic lives completely unaware of them, they are there for our use always. I suggest that very few things have any greater influence on our work. Let us resolve to be conscious of them and *never* underestimate their potential.

You possess personal qualities that nobody else can quite match. In other words, you are unique in all the world. I want to mention here that getting better acquainted with yourself is of immeasurable value. It is a huge part of each artist's journey and should *never* be neglected. Get curious about your intangible tools. It is amazing how once you look for them, you find them. They're always there, but unless you pay attention, they might as well not be.

THE PEBBLES WE WALK ON
COULD BE JASPER OR JADE,
YET KNOWING THEM NOT,
THEY LAY WHERE THEY LAID

1982

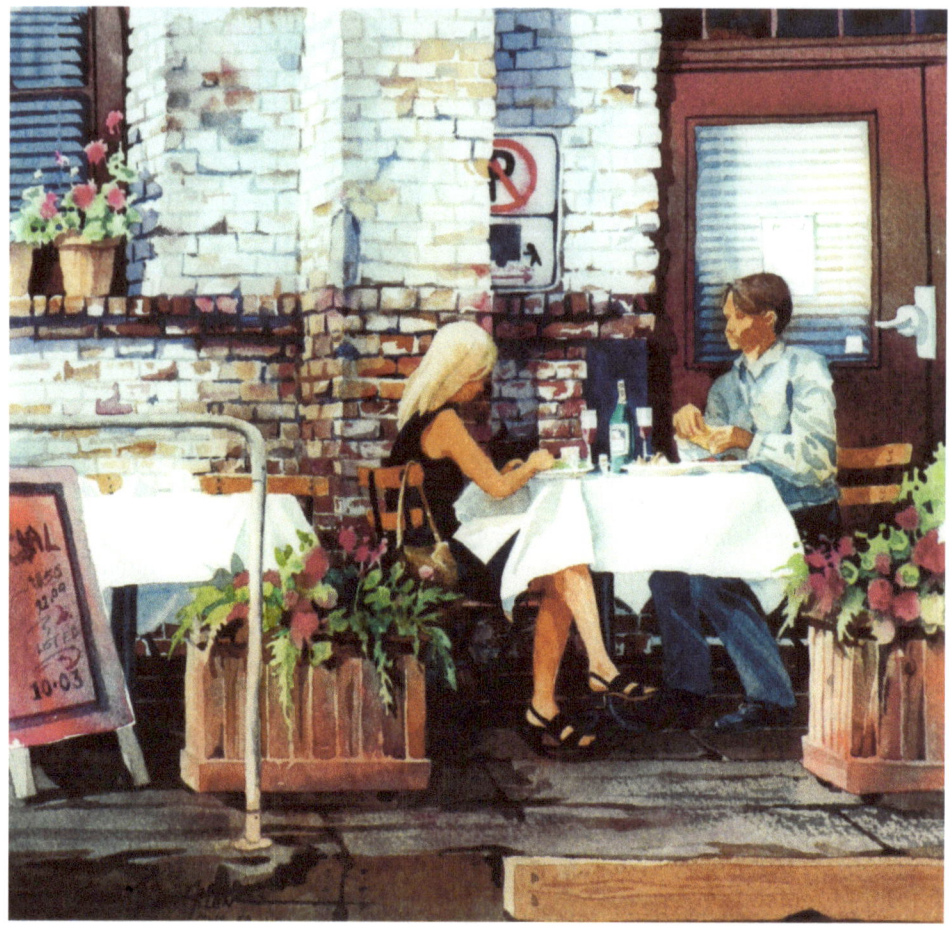

Dinner for Two at the Little Wing Café   *watercolor*   *10 x 10*

Paying attention is as much a tool as any brush. Awareness is intimate with observation—keen observation. Observing is crucial. Learn to observe yourself while you're observing everything else.

You *choose* things such as style, subject, technique, color, etc. in your work, and you make those choices from the list of intangible tools. Let's take *preference,* for example. Preferences make your choices. It's quite magical the possibilities presented by these tools. Like some part of your DNA, they're strange, miraculous and undeniably individual. Let yourself enjoy and grow in this part of your creativity. Art has many parts to play in our lives, in our communities, and in our world. Art can be anything— therapeutic, angry, joyful or sad. Art can mean one thing to its creator, and yet speak something altogether different to its observer. There is a kind of contentment that comes with playing your artistic part the best you can. So, no matter your history, the pain or the joy of it all…press it into your service.

Name it, claim it and use it.

Let's look at another intangible on the list. How about *sight*? How does your actual vision play a part? Here's an example: I used to paint with a friend who was far-sighted, and I am very near-sighted. You might guess that painting on location, my friend often painted the whole farm, while I might paint only the barn door. That's when I claimed the fact that I love close-ups. I still do. Every one of those intangible tools (and many more) have influence on your work. Recognize them, name them, claim them, and use them.

Have you ever noticed that the simple act of telling a friend something about yourself set it more firmly in your own mind as well? Once you make a good, true storyline about yourself, it can become yours...part of you. Something like: "*I think I'm really going to love going to this gym.*" Or what about these words: "*I find I'm painting more and more.*" This kind of positive self-talk can be a useful and a very powerful tool.

However:

Doubt-filled-negative storylines are just as powerful. They also may become part of our belief system. Be conscious and aware of that. *Minute-by-minute and day-by-day, our thinking has power.*

I'm going to digress briefly to mention something about the painting on the right, 'Work-A-Day'. This is an example of how one simple thought can rescue a painting. The large shadow on the right was not there originally. I thought the painting was finished, but I was not happy with it. It sat in the studio for quite a long time.

One morning I said, "Why doesn't this work"? The answer that popped into my head was... "It's blah...it has no drama." The gray brick wall was just too much the same all over. There could have been other solutions, but the one that came to me was to create a mysterious shadow to break up the sameness and add a little drama. It improved the piece.

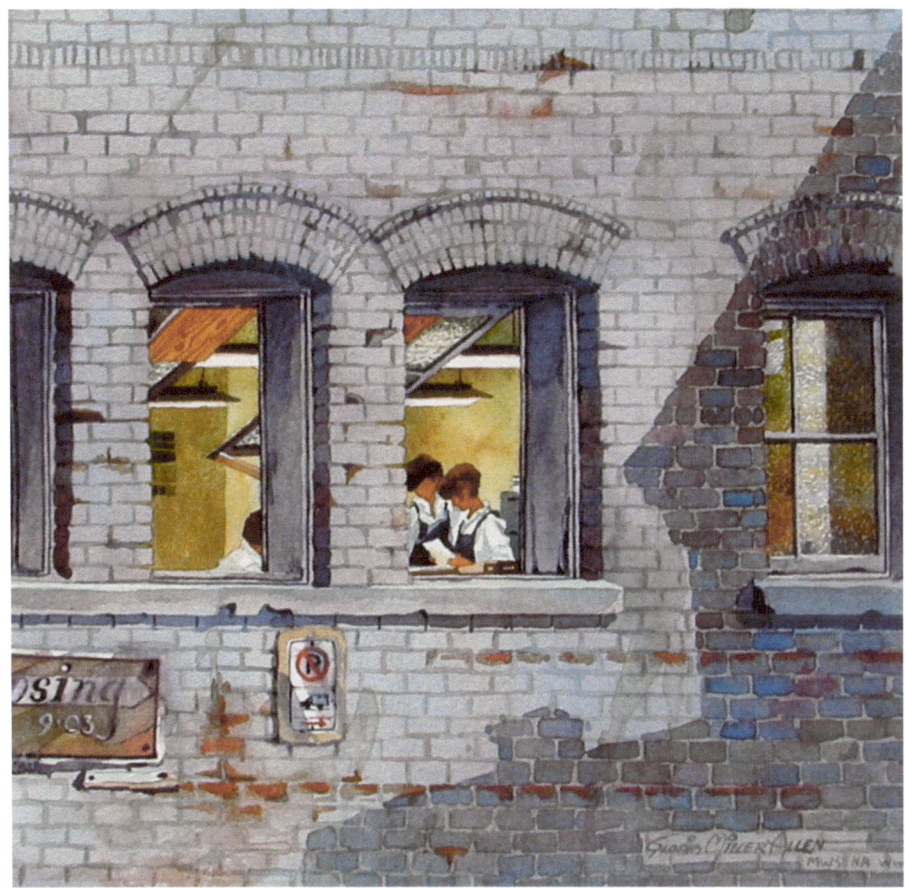

Work-A-Day   *watercolor*   *10 x 10*

BUT HOW DO I PUT MYSELF INTO MY DRAWINGS & PAINTINGS?

That's a great question with lots of answers, some of which we've already discussed. Here are just a few additional ideas to keep you *thinking* in that direction. They have to do with intangible-tool choices.

♦ Draw and paint subjects that interest you—not your spouse—you. Of course, you can paint some things for the spouse, but the best work will be of subjects that call to you. You might see a pile of bricks and find yourself intrigued by the abstract shapes they present. Walk around with a camera and pay attention where you aim.

♦ Try working in a series. Pick a favorite subject and continue to explore it year after year. Choosing a subject for a series means one choice yielding many paintings. For instance, my *Americana Street Series* and *Canyon Wall Series* continue through the years.

♦ What about telling stories with your paintings or making some social comments. Art has all kinds of reasons for being other than just being a picture. What do you want your art to be or to say? *Think.*

♦ You could capitalize on your love of animals, botany or trains. A friend of mine did a series about trains. They are wonderful. She is quite a feminine, lady but she *gave herself permission* to work with trains because they fascinated her. Think of your interests: sports, hiking, mushrooms, fashion, ships. Name them, claim them and use them..

♦ Maybe you really enjoy pattern, texture, line or color. Claim some of these preferences and create a whole series around them. A series simply about line could be a fascinating adventure taking you into many discoveries and much artistic growth.

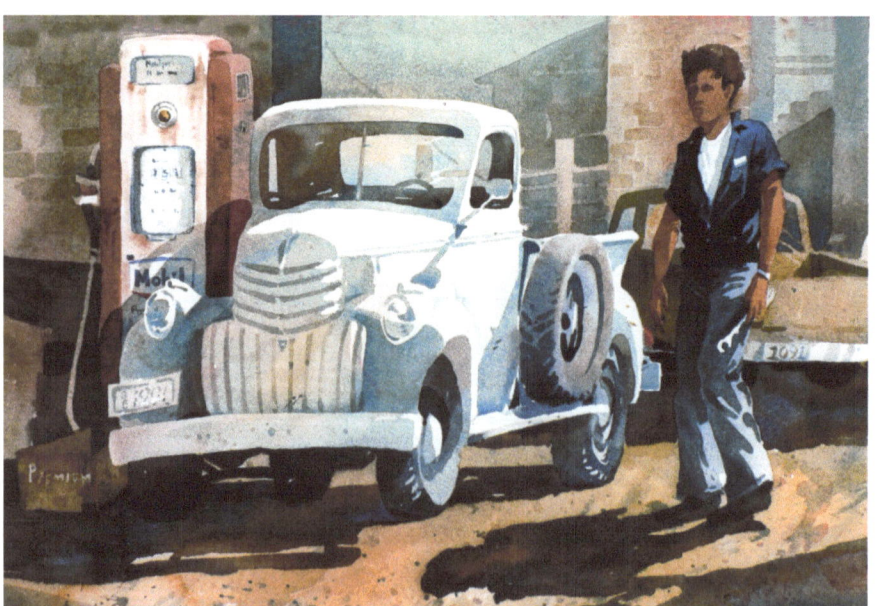

The Young Mechanic   *watercolor*   *10 x 14*

You'll be surprised just how far some simple ideas like these can go. You have ideas all the time. Become conscious of them, and the sky's the limit. No, actually, the limit is within ourselves. The point is to start consciously recognizing your preferences, and strengths as **power tools**. Name them, claim them, own and use them. They will become your most powerful works and most well-used tools.

However, when you're *unaware* of these power tools they're not animated and fall flat without the energy or passion to become something more than ideas tossed to the winds. I'll say again, *know thyself.*

SELF PORTRAIT

IN SUSPENSION
IN THE MIDDLE
UN-RESOLVED
UN-DISSOLVABLE
RESPONSIBILITY
BECKONS
BUT DREAMS
BECKON TOO

BOTH ARE HELD
IN SOLUTION
NEVER SET
NOR EVER GELLED

JUST HELD
FOR MY PURSUIT

POTENTIALS -
MY POTENTIALS
IN BOTH DIRECTIONS

HOLDING BACK
HOLDING ON
HOLDING

OUT OF THE DEPTHS
OF ESSENCE AND NEED
I MUST AND WILL
MEET RESPONSIBILITY
AND DREAMS
WITH WHATEVER
SKILL I FIND WITHIN

LIKE TWO COLORS
RED AND YELLOW
AND BRUSHES FULL
OF WATER SWIRLED
ON MY PALETTE
SUSPENDED
TRANSPARENT
WATERCOLOR

CHANGING IN HUE
TOWARD THE REDS
TOWARD THE YELLOWS
INTO MANY SHADES
OF DEEP
AND MYSTERIOUS
ORANGE

AS NECESSITY
DICTATES
AND AS TIME ALLOWS
MY PORTRAIT
FINDS ITS WAY
TO BE

1982

Mrs. McDermott's Porch   *watercolor*   *28 x 20*

*O*nce a woman asked a great chef for a recipe. He gave it without reservation. When the dish was prepared, it was not as wonderful as the lady had hoped. She confronted the chef and charged him with leaving out at least one important ingredient. "No," he replied, "I left nothing out. Did you remember to put yourself into it"?

29

*S*ometime back in the late '70s, a good art friend, Beth Griebenow, and I traveled to the little town of Florence, Oregon to take a workshop from the incredible Robert E. Wood. We were thoroughly immersed in his lessons for a full week. On one of those days, the assignment in the morning was to create designs using only geometric shapes and patterns. At lunch time as we drove to get some food, I said, "Wow, that was fun." Beth said, "Well, I don't know...it gave me kind of a headache." I clucked to myself and we continued on toward lunch. When we came back for the afternoon session—it was a completely different story. You see, the afternoon assignment was to design using only curvilinear shapes. You might guess who had the headache then. Curvilinear was difficult and not at all my cup of tea. Of course, Beth was feeling no pain and happy as a clam. Curves were within her grasp—not mine.

It wasn't until that very day that either one of us had ever thought about the fact that a person could have a definite design preference. Yet at this time in our artistic journeys, we were far from beginners. We were artists...just sort of unconscious artists, I guess. We started thinking and talking about all our past paintings. Sure enough, Beth's were largely of flowers, leaf patterns, etc. and all without a single straight line in them. And, of course, mine were extremely geometric. In fact, I had consistently used what I now call an axio-balance (kind of a cruciform) in the vast majority of my work. I'd painted many front porches, large canyon walls, and street scenes. Even my abstracts were geometric. We had a good laugh about the whole headache thing, but the lesson was indelibly imprinted in our history.

~

We were both able from that day on, to claim some of those intangible tools I've been talking about—some of our own preferences–of which we had previously been totally unconscious.

That was a giant discovery!

What do you do with a discovery like that? Well, I realized that geometric design was a preference of mine - kind of a long suit or comfort zone. I decided to work with curvilinear designs to increase my skills, but that very day I named and claimed geometric design as one of my *power tools* and began to capitalize on it. That awareness took me one giant step forward.

It added power and confidence to my work. It not only feels great to know what your strengths and personal tools are, it can also point up some areas that need work. Again, it's about knowing yourself deeper. When you are new to painting, *thinking* about something as abstract as design preference may be impossible because you don't have many paintings under your belt, and chances are your thoughts are more about developing drawing and painting skills. That is fine and—not to worry. For now, just be aware. You'll be ready to recognize them later.

After you have painted many paintings, you will start to pick out traits, tendencies and trends. Do you have a favorite subject, color, etc? In the meantime, be on the lookout for your wonderful intangible *power tools* that you bring with you. Some of them, I'll wager, you already know. Others may take a very long time to be identified. Either way, know they are yours, and yours alone. When you discover one, it can be very rewarding. Make it a treasure hunt to find some. Treasure hunts add greatly to the enjoyment of any trip, and this is going to be a very long and personal journey.

Are we there yet?

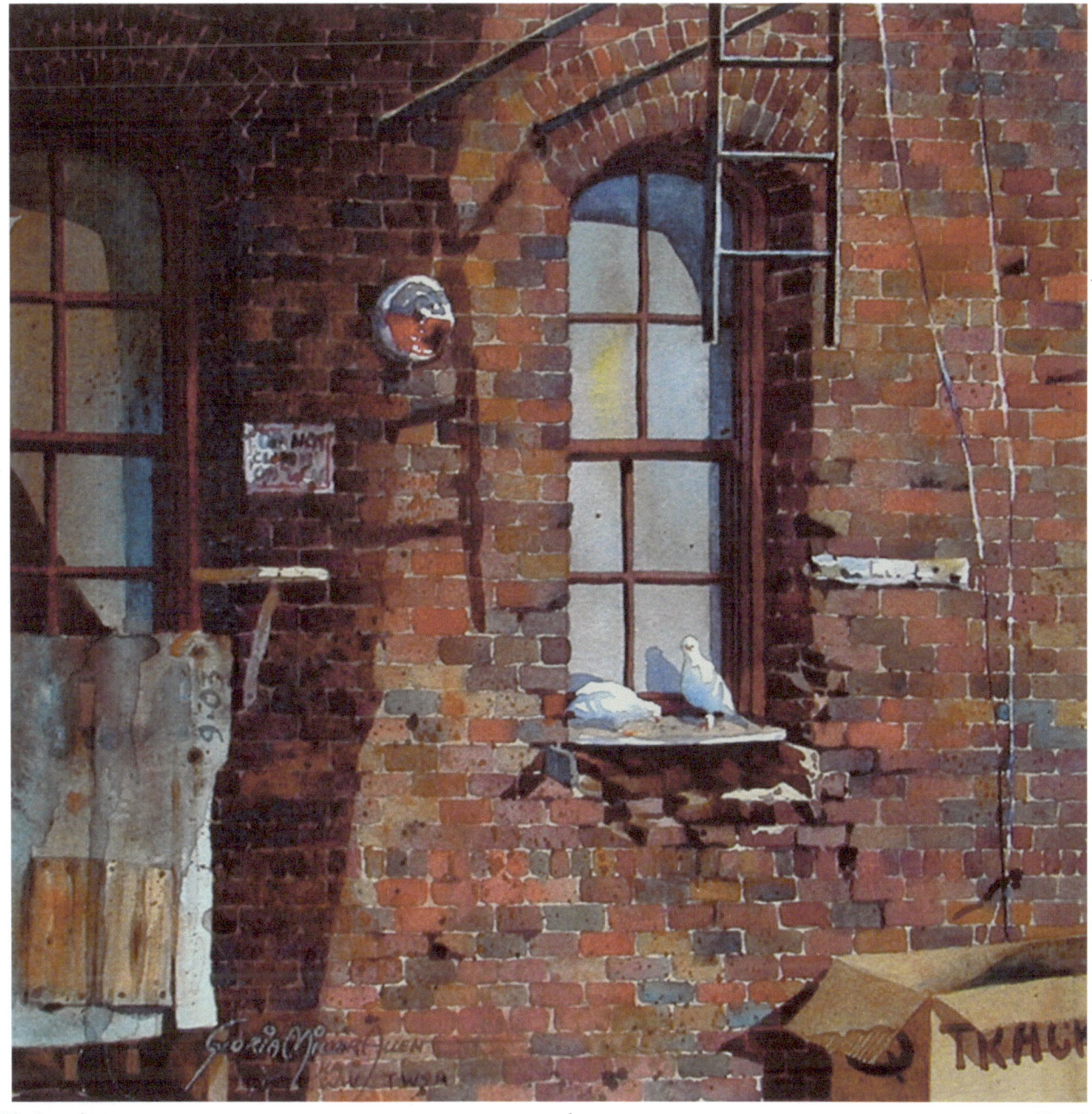

The Investigators   *watercolor*   *10 x 10*

HISTORY AND BEGINNINGS

*O*nce upon a time a small Kansas girl discovered mark making and loved it. She had seen her father drawing with a pencil and also watched him painting snow scenes with soap on their windows at Christmas time. Fascinated, she spent her own money on coloring books and would give herself assignments on different pages like, "I will color this page with only my purple crayon, and this page with only my orange." Of course, she had no earthly idea that she was actually learning about values. She only knew crayons were fun. Markers had not yet been invented.

Her studio was a large winged back chair in the living room with a table leaf spread over its arms like a desk top. That was a great place to be. She grew, she drew and she painted more. She could spend hours drawing flowers in her mother's flower garden. Her parents encouraged her but also thought she should spend more time in active play —which, of course, was true. By the time she was a senior in high school, she had her schedule planned so she could spend a full four hours a day in the art room. She didn't allow herself any actual conscious dreams of becoming an artist. It was just that she loved doing the work.

After graduation, she found employment in the litho-art department of Hallmark Cards in Kansas City. There she learned hand color separation (which is a totally obsolete skill in today's world of printing) but it was a great teacher of values. She married, had a family and painted as much as a young mother could—which wasn't much. During this time she went to local art shows, read many art books from the library, drew and painted a lot with her kids and came up with all sorts of art projects for her Cub Scout Den. Her focus was on her family. Art was just a lot of fun, and she loved doing the work.

Her children grew, her free time grew, and art became more of a focus. She started taking classes, and even exhibiting her work. Family finances were a little tight during those years.

One day her very supportive husband said, "You know,

Scout, if you sold even one painting, think of all the water-color paper you could buy"! Well, he had her there. Until then, she had never been able to even consider selling her work. After all, she was just an amateur. Her paintings were a bit too precious, they were her "artistic history." They were her creations, her children in a sense. However, at the next local art show, price tags appeared on some of her paintings, and one sold. Soon after that she had the fateful conversation with her friend Marilyn Hansen (as mentioned previously) and woke up. She gave herself permission to be an artist and still loves the work.

~

Important words in this story –
"She loved the work."

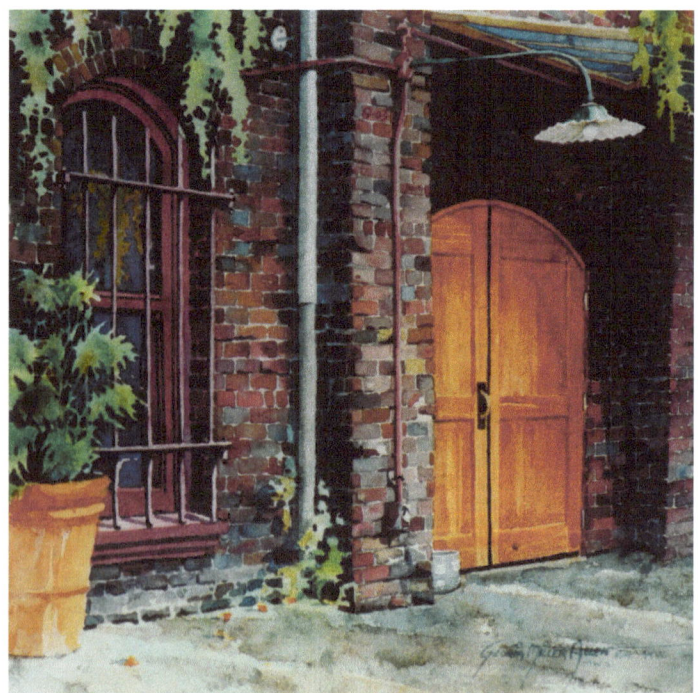

Door To The Bridgeport   watercolor   *10 x 10*

Pretty humble beginnings you will admit. Yet for me, very rich. The early seeds of artistic activities can be very tiny, unimpressive, sprouts with the capability of growing into a mighty oak in your life.

I wonder what you could learn about yourself and claim as a tangible history tool if you wrote just a few paragraphs about your early artistic dreams. You were there, you know. Quite possibly you are the only person who has an inkling about it. Your family may not even know. After all, they were busy with their own dreams. So what about it?

Take a few minutes and gift yourself a written beginning of your artistic self. Write it here on the next page or in your workbook, but do it.

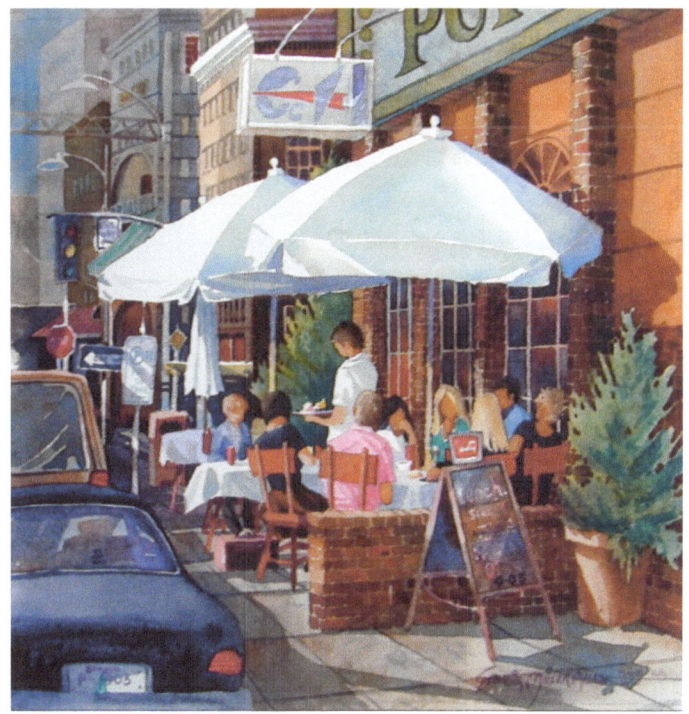

Lunch in the Pearl District   *watercolor*   *10 x 10*

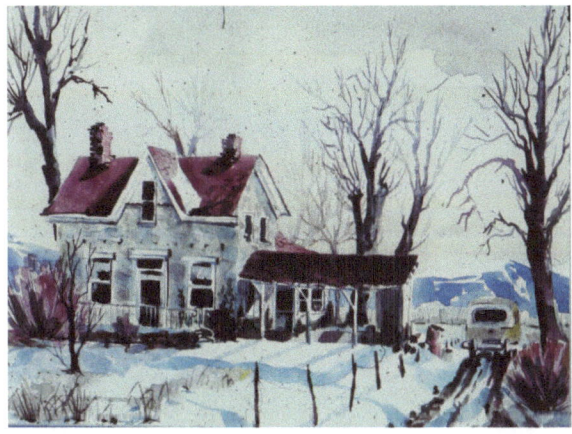

*T*his little painting was done in the late 1970s before I ever sold my art. I'd been working hard at painting for over ten years though. This little painting pleased me. It was painted in the car on location - yes, in the snow. I humbly include it here so you'll see what my paintings looked like about the time I decided to become professional. It was 8 x 10. At this time in my own artistic journey I was terrified of a full sheet of plain white watercolor paper. If this sounds familiar to you, push on.

WHAT SHALL I WRITE?
WHERE TO BEGIN?
HOW DO I START
REMEMBERING WHEN?

TO PEN A BRIEF STORY
I WANT TO BE NAMED.
MY HISTORY AND VISION
WILL NOW BE PROCLAIMED.

MY POSTPONED DREAMS
I NOW WISH TO SEE
BY BOLDLY DECLARING
WORDS THAT ARE ME

....WORDS THAT SIMPLY
   ARE ME.
                    2012

33

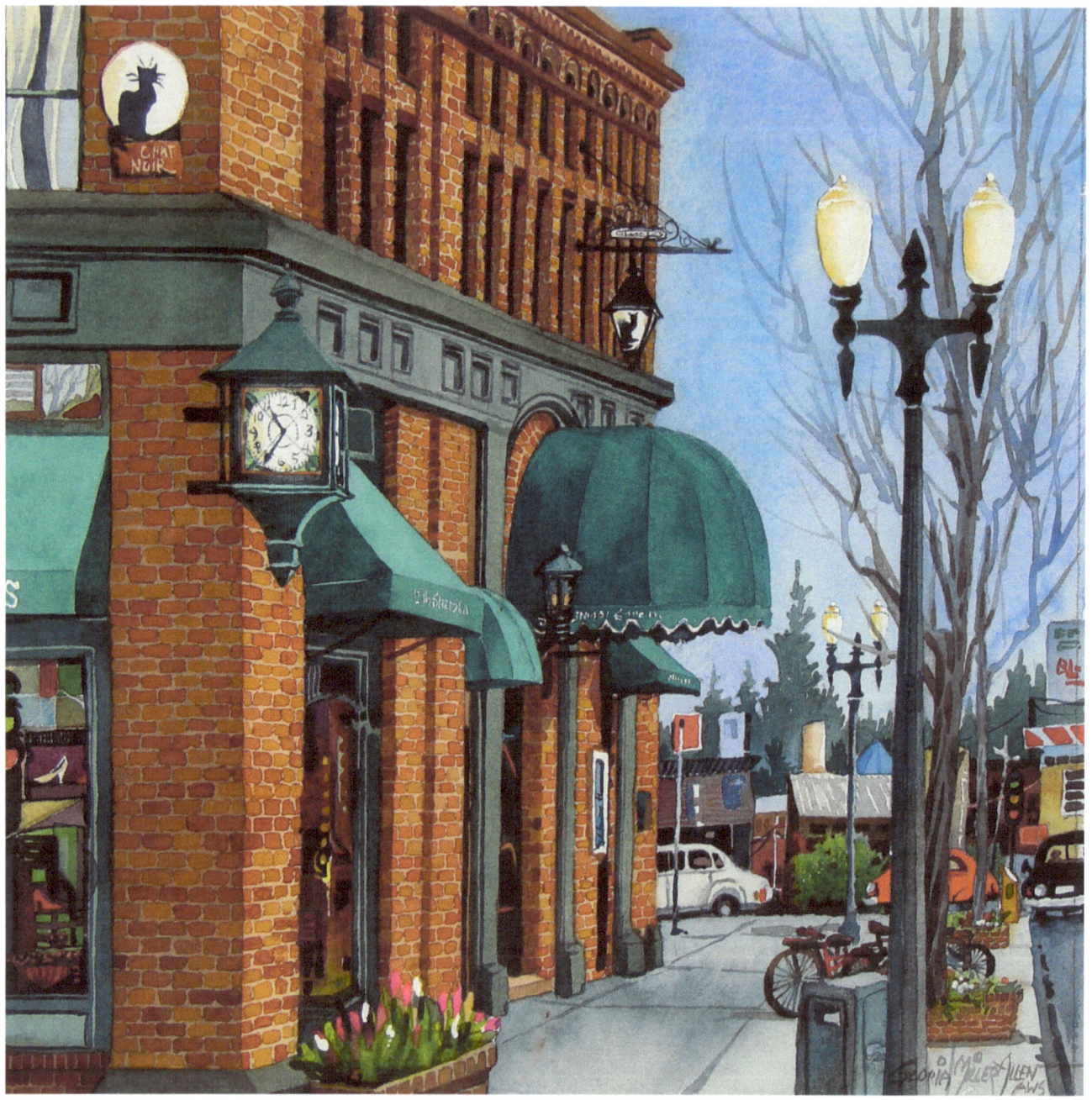

The Fairhaven Clock   *watercolor*   *10 x 10*

34

Once upon a time ~

CREATIVE TIME

IF IT'S TIME TO PAINT...PAINT.
WHEN IT'S TIME TO
CARE...CARE.
IF IT'S TIME TO WRITE...WRITE.
WHEN IT'S TIME TO
STARE...STARE.

TIME IS NO DEVIL.
TIME IS NO SAINT.
TIME SIMPLY PASSES.
TIME WILL NOT WAIT.

NOW IS YOUR TIME -
BE ALIVE AND AWARE.
BREATHE IN EACH MOMENT
EMPLOY TIME WITH CARE.

WHEN DID WE THINK
WE COULD EVER DECREE
BONDAGE OF TIME?
TIME IS TOTALLY FREE.

INTUITION IS USEFUL.
WITH TIME BE CLEVER.
CHOOSE WELL THE MOMENT
OR LOSE IT FOREVER.

1982

We've spent some time *thinking* about the many personal tools you are bringing to this effort, and haven't yet even mentioned your skill level (or perceived skill level) with the actual drawing and painting. Chances are you are already aware of these tools or skills and probably more concerned about them than the stuff I've been talking about. Most of us would rather skip right to the drawing and painting because that's the exciting, tantalizing and more obvious skills we desire to develop. We want to know how to draw and paint, and we want to know right now.

We are like kids in a candy store with money to burn who can't wait to satisfy our cravings. We flit around the delicious colors and supplies, and our eyes grow big in anticipation. We want someone to show us how to paint our masterpiece, and we want to paint it immediately.

Recognize this in part as the instant gratification era we live in, but also as being human. I must warn you though, when it comes to proficiency in drawing and painting you are going to have to *think* differently. There are few short cuts, few early enormous successes and no free lunch. Sorry. That is why I like to refer to the pursuit of art as a life journey—even a life style. No matter how many books you read, or how many workshops you take, this is a *long* journey.

If you are enjoying the journey, you will stick with it. On the other hand, if you're faced with too many frustrations, you will naturally have a difficult time keeping your momentum and enthusiasm up. Then you might tend to drop out and start up many times just spinning your wheels. That is precisely why keeping it fun and having an attitude of playing is so important for keeping you on this long journey. It has nothing to do with your drawing and painting skills as they exist today ~ nothing at all.

In this book I've been pushing the idea that each of us has the artistic capabilities and the absolute right to be an artist. I believe that, and I hope at this point you do too. Now, I'd like to take quite a different look at just what it really does take to pursue this art stuff. In reality, asking the question *"Do I have what it takes?"* hasn't much to do with skills or even talent. Artistic skills are learned and hammered out in time. The real issues involved in answering the question, *"Do I have what it takes?"* have much more to do with the intangibles I've been talking about.

What does that mean? What do you need to be an artist ~ no, really ~ what do you need?

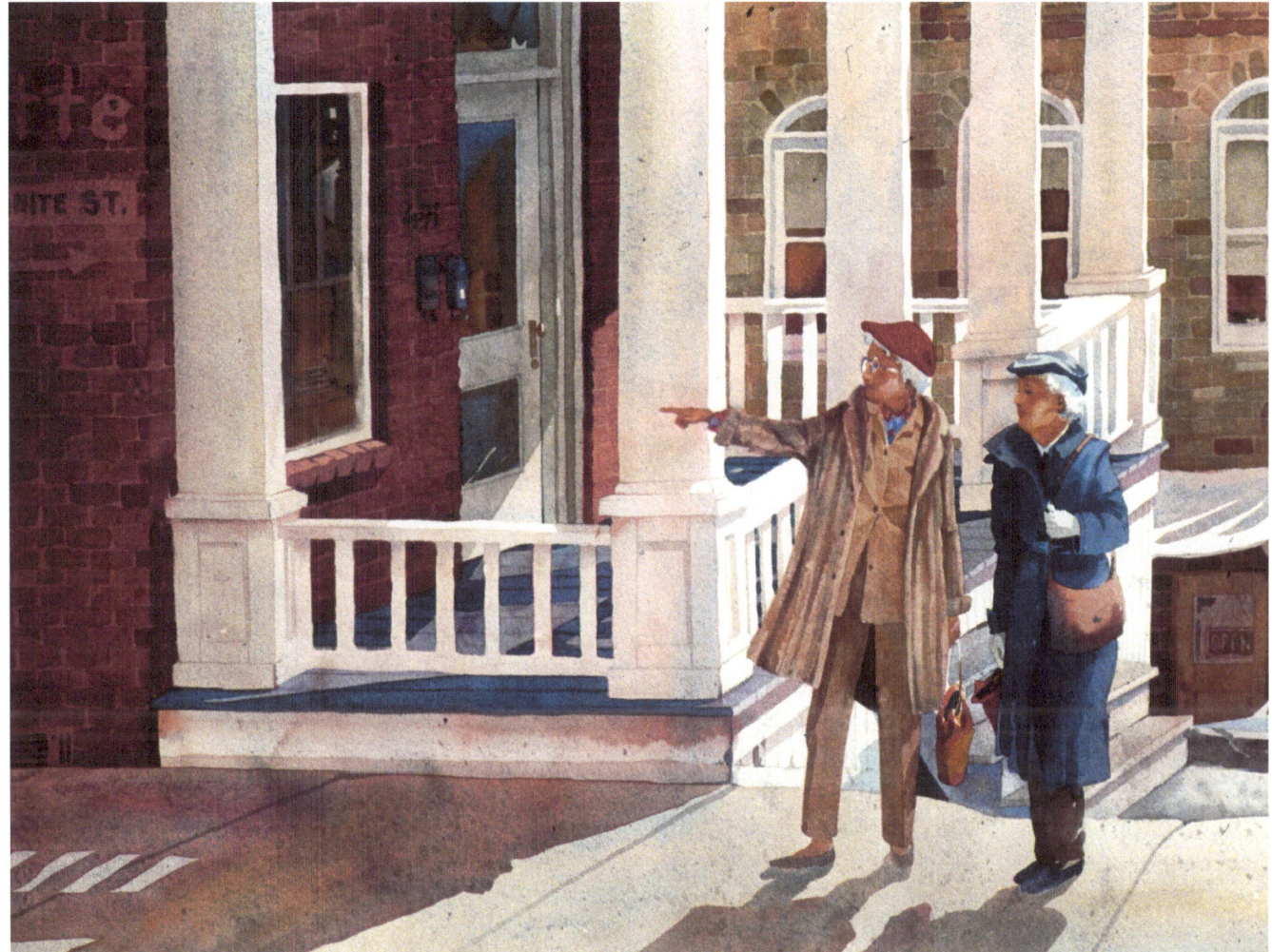

Pillars of Society   *watercolor*   *11 x 15*

Reading and digesting the bulk of this book will be much like taking a drawing workshop. As most of you know, whenever you take a workshop, you get a list of tools and supplies to bring to class with you. With that in mind, here is a list of things I would like you to bring with you into the rest of the book. *A great workshop supply list would not start with paints, brushes, and paper towels.* It would start with tools all artists need in their tool box.

GOLDEN POWER TOOL & SUPPLY LIST

The ability to budget time
A great deal of patience
A great belly laugh
Dogged persistence
Honest effort
An optimistic attitude
*Ability to predict weather
  (just checking)*
Self reliance
Self care
A sense of awe
Self respect
A great sense of humor
The willingness to make messes
   (*really, some can't stand messes*)
A self-starter button is critical

On the surface it looks like these things have little to do with drawing and painting; yet they have *everything* to do with living the life of an artist. Without some of these golden tools, you will have a difficult time continuing on your artistic journey. It most certainly does take quite a lot of your time, as well as patience, persistence, effort, and an undefeatable attitude.

You need to be an unsinkable Molly Brown.

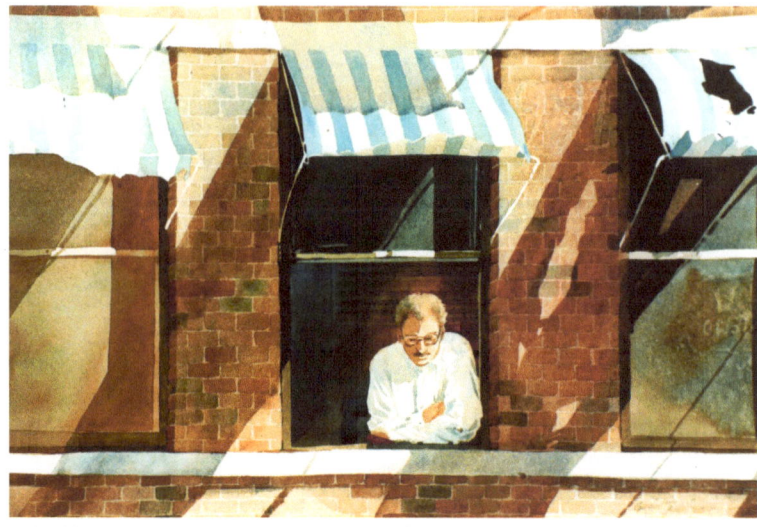

The Observer   watercolor   *14 x 22*

You will need to develop self reliance, self care, and self respect. These are not the tools that are usually mentioned on workshop supply lists; yet, their value is beyond words or money. These tools will carry you through to your goals. Do you have them? Some of you do, and some of you don't.

If you do not have them or are not willing to attain them, then I would answer the question as to whether or not you have what it takes as, "No, you do not."

You must be willing to pursue that power tool list right along with your art. Think about this. Do you have these tools? That is the real question to ask yourself. Searching for that answer helps bring into focus the manner in which you will claim your artistic self and all the subsequent goals you pursue.

Observe yourself.

Few of us ever thought about this type of a supply or tool list until late in our art career. If I had been aware of the big part these intangible tools played in the scheme of my own development, I would have been able to breeze through some of my harder times. I would have made better progress with the time I had. I wouldn't have allowed such things as what we used to call "artist's blocks." I'd have been more able just to plod on with *consciousness* of my persistence tool. But then again, that is all hypothetical nonsense for perhaps I'd still have gone through all the little nuances I went through anyway. After all, each of those little struggles are part of my own history, and that is what we were talking about on previous pages. Our own history does play into our work in all the wonderfully personal ways nothing else could ever do. Once you are aware, you can never be un-aware again.

Just as I was once unaware of my geometric design preferences, I was also unaware of my patience, persistence and attitude tools. At this time in my journey, I know those tools better in myself. When bogged down, I skip the artist block and dig out my golden power tools on my own supply list.

WHAT IF YOU FEEL YOU ARE LACKING?

It's been said that once you know the problem, you can start fixing it. Becoming conscious of yourself in these areas gives you a head start. Ignoring them will be frustrating. This is not the exciting glamorous part of what you want to learn about being an artist. We want to get to the fun and joy of the artwork itself; yet, acknowledging these unglamorous personal tools should be counted in your *thinking*. Unless you can call up some of them out of your own depths and face them squarely, you will not be able to progress at a pace that will be acceptable to your own expectations. That will land you right into a fine old "artist's block" where painting will be anything but fun and joy. The goal is to help yourself avoid discouragement and blocks by calling on your creative self to do a little conscientious and conscious *thinking*. That gets you into a great frame of mind to continue. *Thinking* is how we begin our dreams and how we discover ourselves in the process. *Thinking* is problem solving and so is drawing, painting and life.

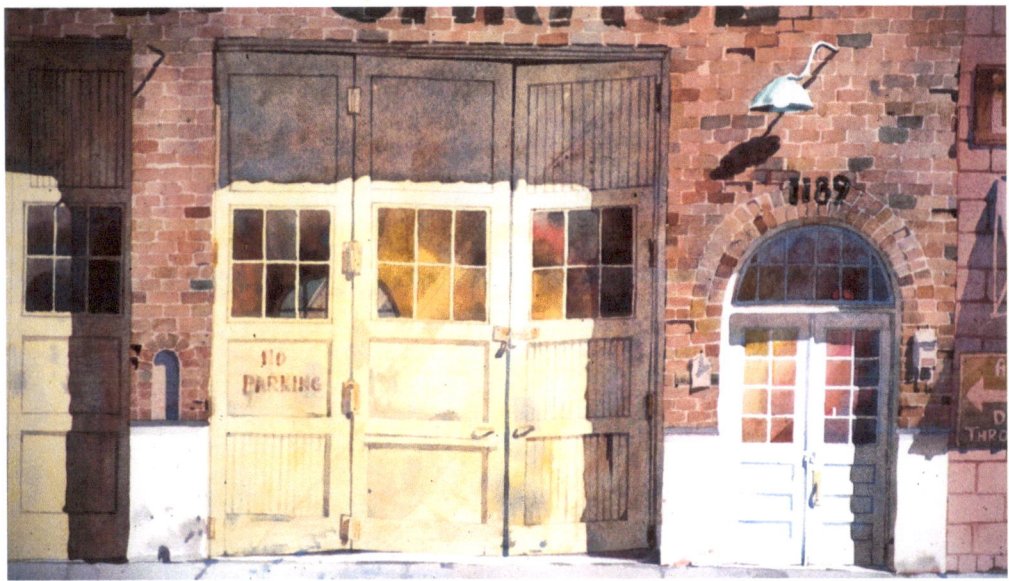

Joe's Garage   *watercolor*   *14 x 20*

JUST OUTSIDE
MYSELF

LOITERING
JUST OUTSIDE
DESIGNATED
BOUNDARIES
SEEING INVISIBLE
FENCES
INVISIBLE TRIP WIRES
INVISIBLE GATES

BOUNDARIES EVOLVE
SO EASILY
REMAIN IN PLACE SO
LONG
STOPPING
ANYONE WHO WOULD
OR COULD
DARE STUMBLE
THROUGH
FINDING A WAY

GRIPPING AND
CRIPPLING
BELIEF IN BOUNDARIES
LOITERING
JUST OUTSIDE
DESIGNATED WALLS
AND JUST OUTSIDE
OURSELVES

COULD I DARE
COULD I TRULY DARE
BE WHAT
I KNOW I AM?

COULD I?

REMINDERS COME
IN ENDLESS FORMS
FILLING OUR SENSES
BOTH WITH DREAMS
   AND WITH DOUBTS

MAYBE I BELONG -
THEN AGAIN -
MAYBE NOT

SO I LOITER
JUST OUTSIDE
THE WEALTHY
WORLDS WITHIN

I AM ONLY ONE
BUT—I AM ONE

INVISIBLE FENCES
AND INVISIBLE GATES
WHICH TO CHOOSE?

MUST I FOREVER BE
ON THE OUTSIDE
WITH ALL MY PAST
AND ALL MY FEAR
LOITERING ON THE
BRINK OF IDENTITY
ON THE EDGE
OF OCCASION
LOITERING
JUST OUTSIDE
MYSELF?

1991

THE PROCRASTINATION SYNDROME

Perhaps the *most* common problem that I hear about from artist friends and students is what I call the "procrastination syndrome." I am more than familiar with this malady. Years ago I suffered with it quite unconsciously until one day my husband said, *"Scout, why don't you go down to your studio? You know you want to."* At which time I said something like: *"Well, I have phone calls to make, laundry to fold, cooking to think about, because...well...er...a..."* You get the picture. Back then, my husband Tony smoked a pipe. He took a long contemplative puff on his pipe, sizing me up, grinned quietly, and said: *"You, my dear, are procrastinating."* After more sputtering, hemming and hawing, I had to admit he was right. Fortunately for me, I recognized that if my excuses didn't fool him, they shouldn't be fooling me either. It started me *thinking* (something my husband is extremely good at doing). I thought about my perpetual wish to paint more, and my equally perpetual ability to find excuses not to. It was an inner war. What was that all about—really? I honestly didn't know, but I thought I'd better find out. To repeat an earlier point, I had to get to know myself a little deeper and face another of my "bug-a-boos." If you are a fellow sufferer of this syndrome, it might help you to know what I learned about myself. Can you guess what it was? It was *fear*. It was plain old crippling fear— but of what?

Oh, I hammered out quite an impressive list of really scary things. I was afraid of failure, of ruining a lousy piece of paper, of not being able to paint as well next time as last time. I was afraid to face that great blank expanse of white. I could almost break out in a sweat thinking about it. I was afraid that inspiration would desert me...that the muse would not come...that I could never paint a masterpiece. Basically, I was afraid that I would not live up to my own expectations. My tiny ego was on the line, at least in my own mind. So I would do what hundreds of other people do in life:

I avoided failure by simply not trying.

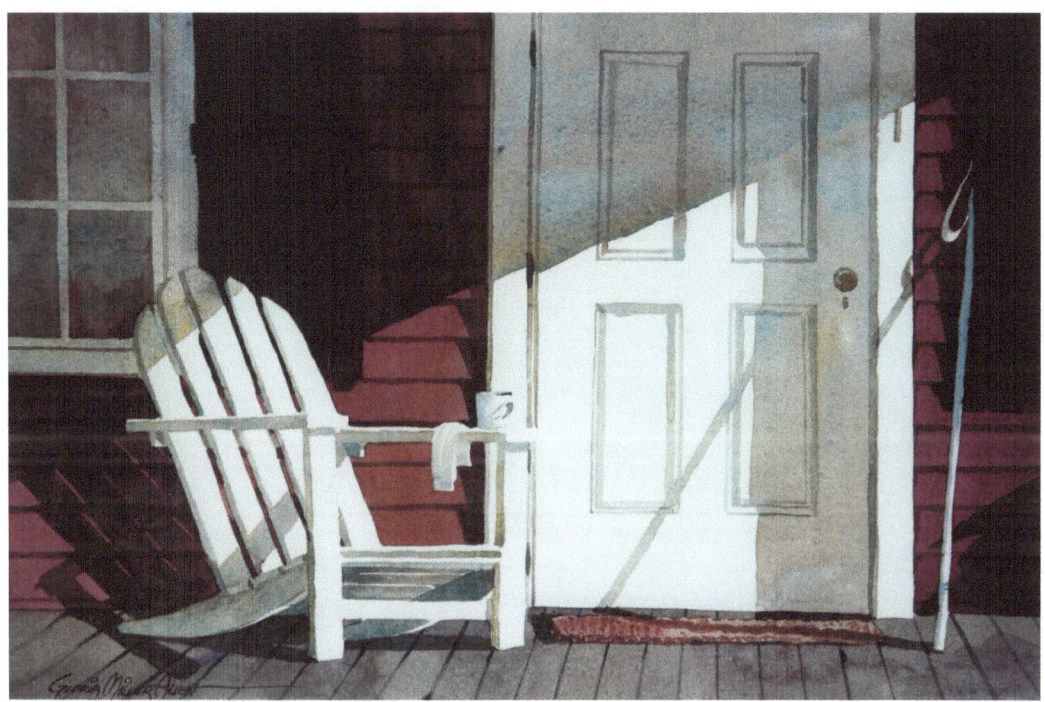

Little Red House   *watercolor*   *11 x 15*

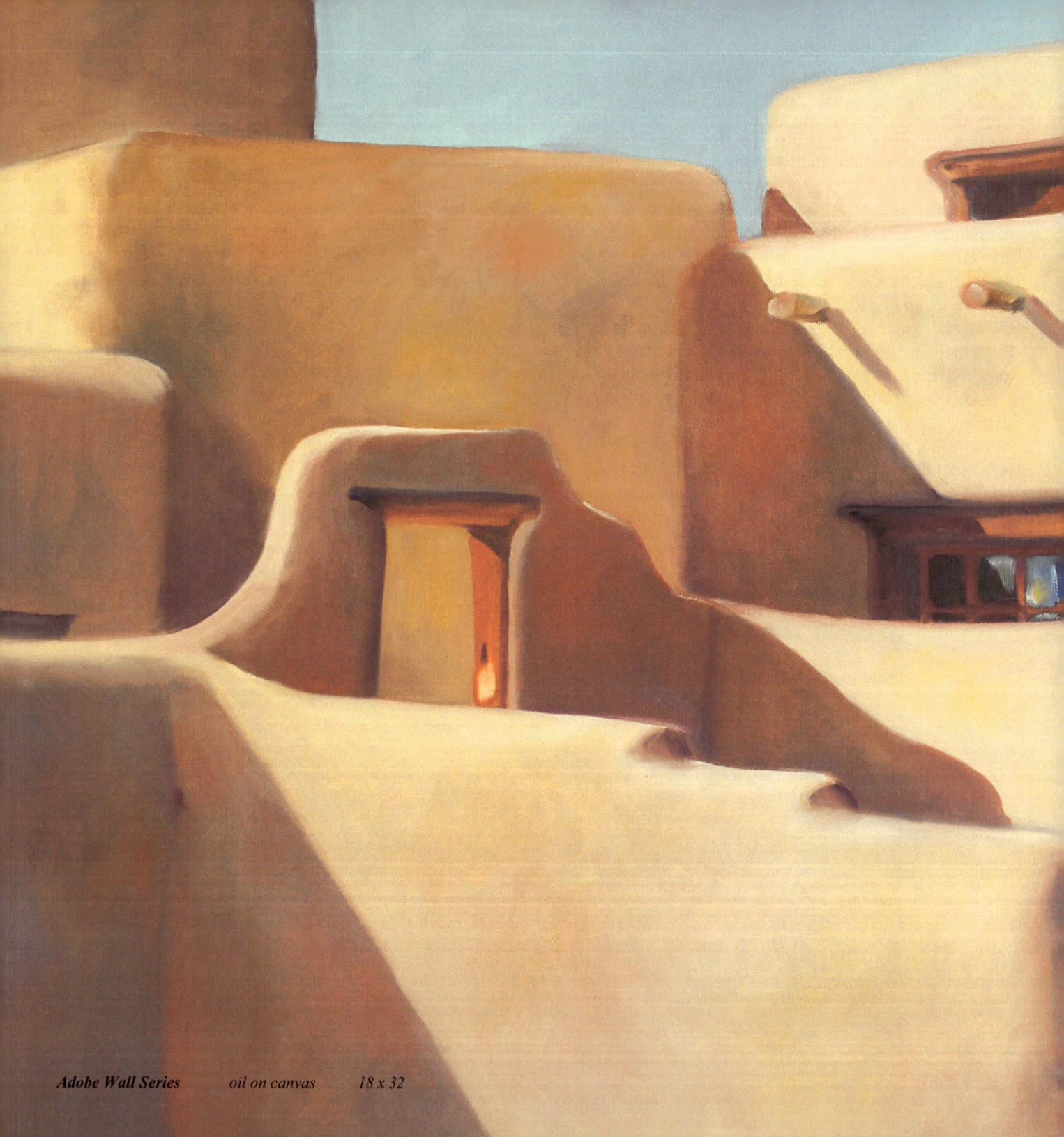

Adobe Wall Series   *oil on canvas*   *18 x 32*

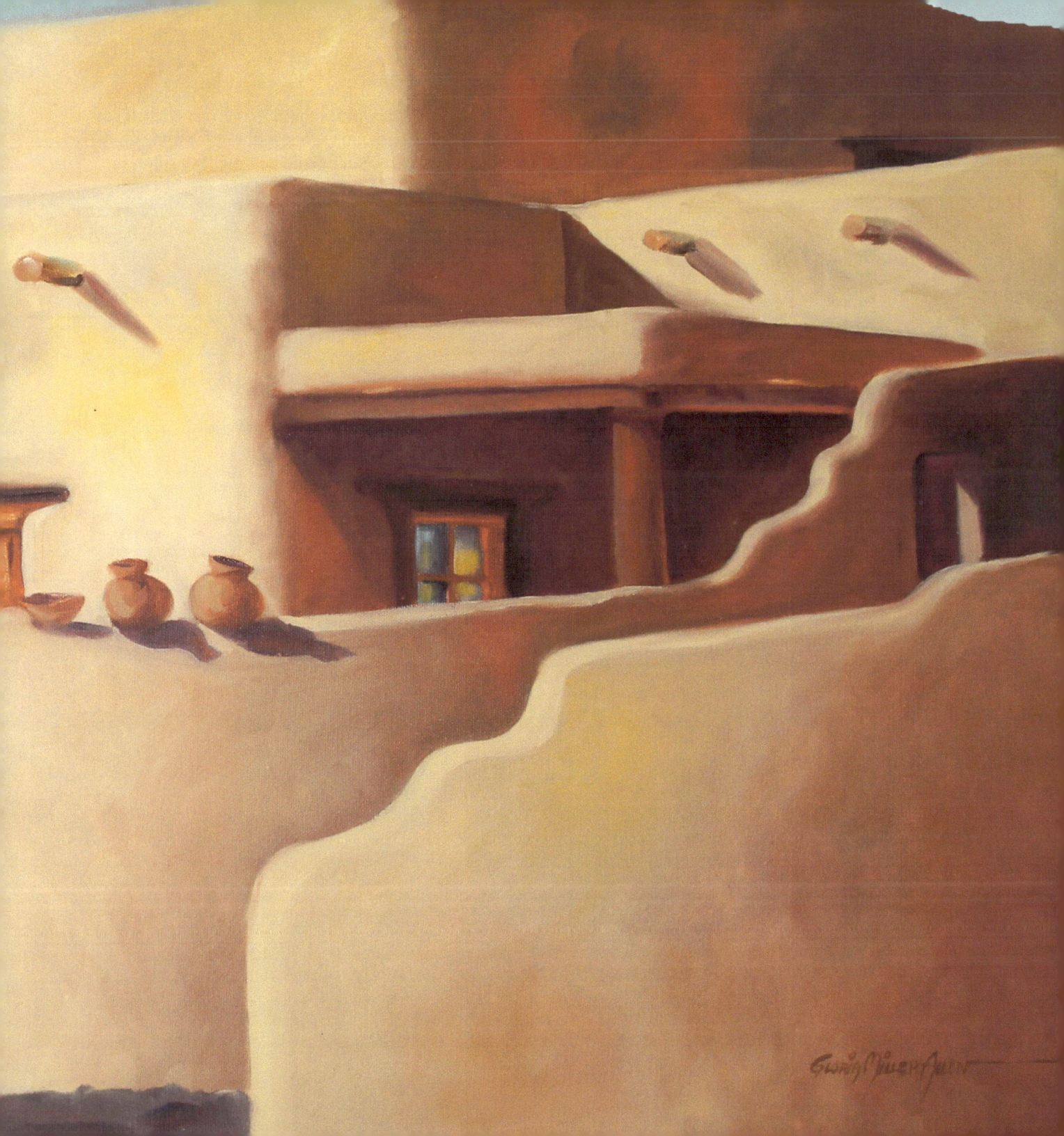

In other areas in my life, I felt competent. I decided that I wanted to feel competent about my art also. Once I could name my frivolous fears, I could recognize the "procrastination signs" Tony had noted in my behavior, and I could no longer hide behind them. Procrastination simply would not work any more. In fact, it became something we've both laughed at many times through the years. I still get caught in it sometimes, but it doesn't trip me up. I simply go to the studio and begin. Easy solution, isn't it? Hard to believe something that obvious could be so hard to figure out. When you recognize your own procrastination syndrome, you will be able to call it out in the open.

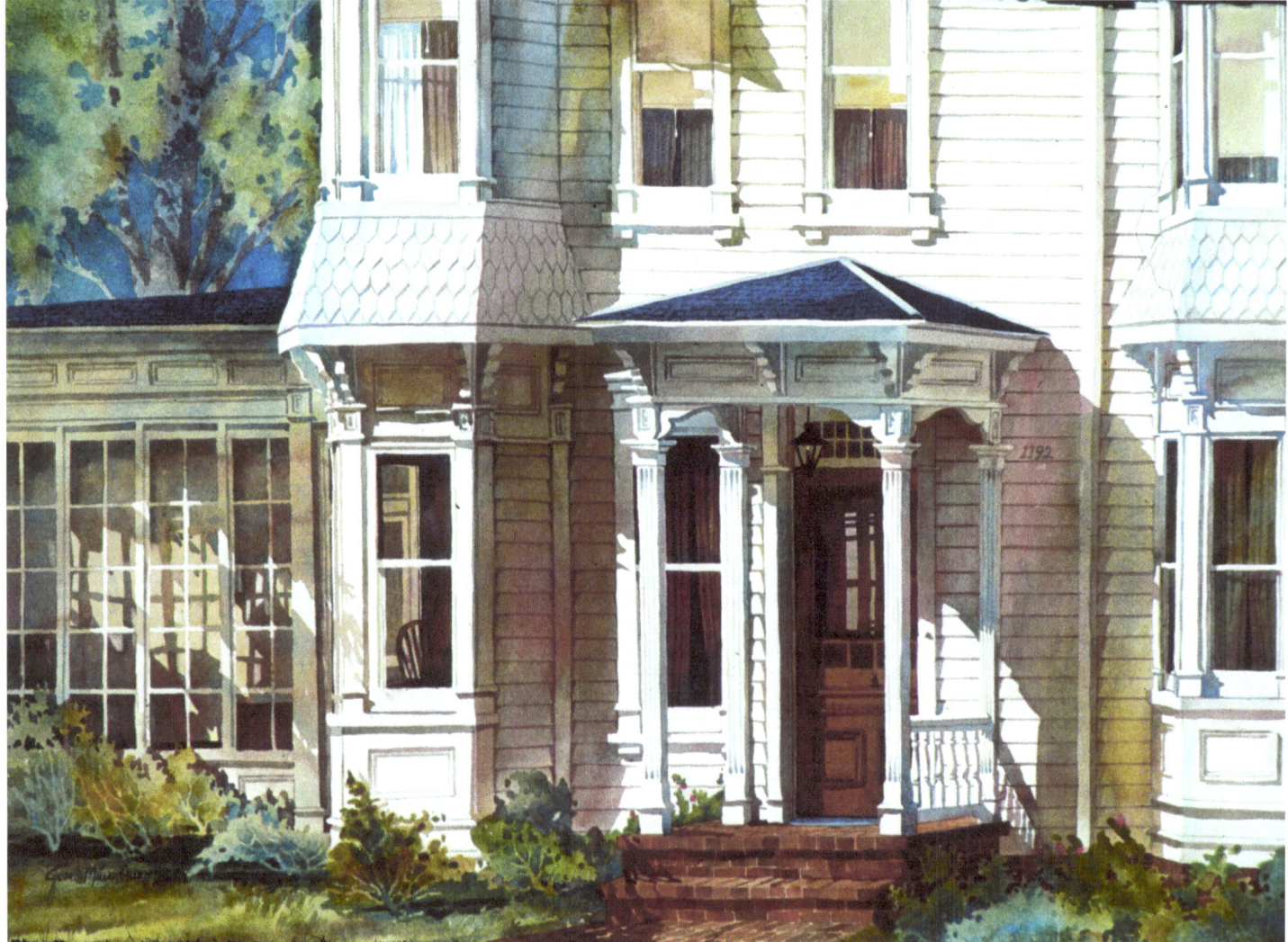

Port Townsend Mansion   *watercolor*   *22 x 30*

Once you know the answer to a riddle it almost always seems obvious. Also I've learned that ruining a piece of paper is not the end of the world. I've learned tomorrow's painting might *not* be as good as today's, and it doesn't matter one iota and there is a small chance it might actually be better.

When I'm in a period of dissatisfaction with my work, I've learned it means I'm making changes, taking a new tack, or on the brink of some discovery. When you can look at your dissatisfactions like that, it gives you courage to plow your way through. *Persistence* is definitely a golden intangible tool. I've learned that inspiration comes more easily and more often when I'm painting than when I'm waiting for it. I've come to believe the muse is inside me, not outside me. I've discovered that the mere act of going to the studio, flipping on the lights, turning on the music, and tying my smock or apron around me actually gives me a little shot of contentment. It makes me feel rich and excited about what will come to my paper today. Procrastination denies me those feelings and replaces them with anxiety and discontent. Learn to recognize this culprit.

If you are a self-employed artist, there is no time clock, (unless self imposed) and no weekly reward of pay. To be a professional artist, either full time, or part time, you *must* be a self-starter. You *must* be self driven. You *must* be able to depend upon yourself. Procrastination is a sworn enemy. If you were employed, you would be at work on time. Simply decide to employ yourself. Good move.

BALANCING DREAMS WITH REALITIES

I hope by now you realize that you're in this for the long haul. Depending upon your own goals, that could mean a plethora of things. If painting once a month with some special friends is a longed for hope, you should not beat yourself up about not painting every day. On the other hand, if you want to work professionally, don't imagine that you can progress without a large commitment of time. It is here that awareness of goals pays off. Knowing them right from the start gives you permission to claim the amount of time needed. It also gets rid of the guilt that many people feel for not spending as much time as some of their friends. I hear this all the time: "*I know I should paint more often, but... .*" Don't do that to yourself. Art is not a punishment. Your art should be what you *and you alone* want it to be. That simple awareness of what you really want helps fit it into your life comfortably and productively.

After all, life has many worthwhile dreams to pursue. One of yours is art. Set it up in a way that will be enjoyable for you. That's a good goal. *To be happy, know thyself and do not compare thyself to others for thou art unique.*

SOME GOOD NEWS

Art is something you need not retire from at age 65; in fact, you may just be getting started. The speed of your advancement will *always* have a great deal to do with the amount of time you spend on it. That is a given. After retirement, you may have a lot of time, and you can take giant steps on your path. If you have very little time, then it will be more like baby steps. Either way, your success is better assured by acknowledging goals and going in whatever direction that dictates. Goals will change with time, so can the *thinking*, plotting and planning. Balance your dreams and your reality. Keeping that balance puts you on track for contentment, fulfillment and success.

Is Watercolor Really Harder?

(For Those Who Are Interested)

INSPIRATION

DROPPED TONNAGE LIKE

BURYING ME IN

BEAUTIFUL DEBRIS.

IN THE

TWINKLING OF AN EYE,

THE SNAP OF A FINGER

SURPRISING POWER

IS GIVEN

FREELY

TO ALL WHO

DARE

TAKE IT.

HOW COULD I NOT

ACCEPT SUCH A GIFT?

EVERY TON,

YEA

EVERY SINGLE TON.

1985

Watercolor enjoys the reputation of being a difficult medium. You have heard that it is harder to fix, that you can't paint over, that you can't change anything. Well, all these statements have a grain of truth in them, but in real life, watercolor is no more difficult than any other medium. It is still basically making the color, the value, the design, and the subject all work together. By the way, that is my definition of a good painting. I do think with watercolor it is more difficult to get good early results from beginners. The paint seems unruly in the beginning. It flows and goes all over the place. It is easy to get muddy colors, and it seems to move with a mind of its own. But once you develop your technical skills with watercolor, it is no more difficult than any other medium. Give yourself time to acquire those skills and give yourself some patience. Look at it as fun, and laugh at the mishaps. I cannot over emphasize that. Set the stage for yourself to play, to discover, to anticipate, to grow, to make mistakes and to go on. I don't know who first said this, but I like it:

"The difference between a big shot and a little shot is that the big shot just keeps shootin'."

Also, I've heard that the great Babe Ruth sometimes held the record for strikeouts right along with the record for home runs. I've heard that Tiger Woods most likely hit more golf balls in his youth than most players hit in their entire lives. I once heard master painter, Cheng-Khee Chee say that once you have painted 1,000 trees, you have an un-purchasable knowledge of trees.

One of my sons has always been athletic. When he was quite a small boy, I found a little slip of paper in his room on which he had written:

"Practice is boring , but soon
you'll be scoring."

♦ Do you guess it pays simply to love the work?
♦ Would you say that practice counts?
♦ Would you say the amount of time spent pays off in the long haul?
♦ Would you agree having goals is useful?
♦ Could you dare argue with any of this?

It is my hope that the past two chapters have set the stage and the tone for you to plant both your feet firmly onto your own artistic path. It is also my hope that when the inevitable times come when the paint and paper just don't seem to cooperate you can brush discouragement off and not let it stop you from your path. Those times will come and you should expect them. In other words, you will never hit a home run every time at bat. The more years you paint, the easier it is to just accept the disasters when they come, pick up your brush, dip it in the paint, and keep working. It's simply part of your ebb and flow, part of your rhythm, part of your routine, part of your journey.

Learning to rejoice in your successes and not die with your failures will keep you happily on track.

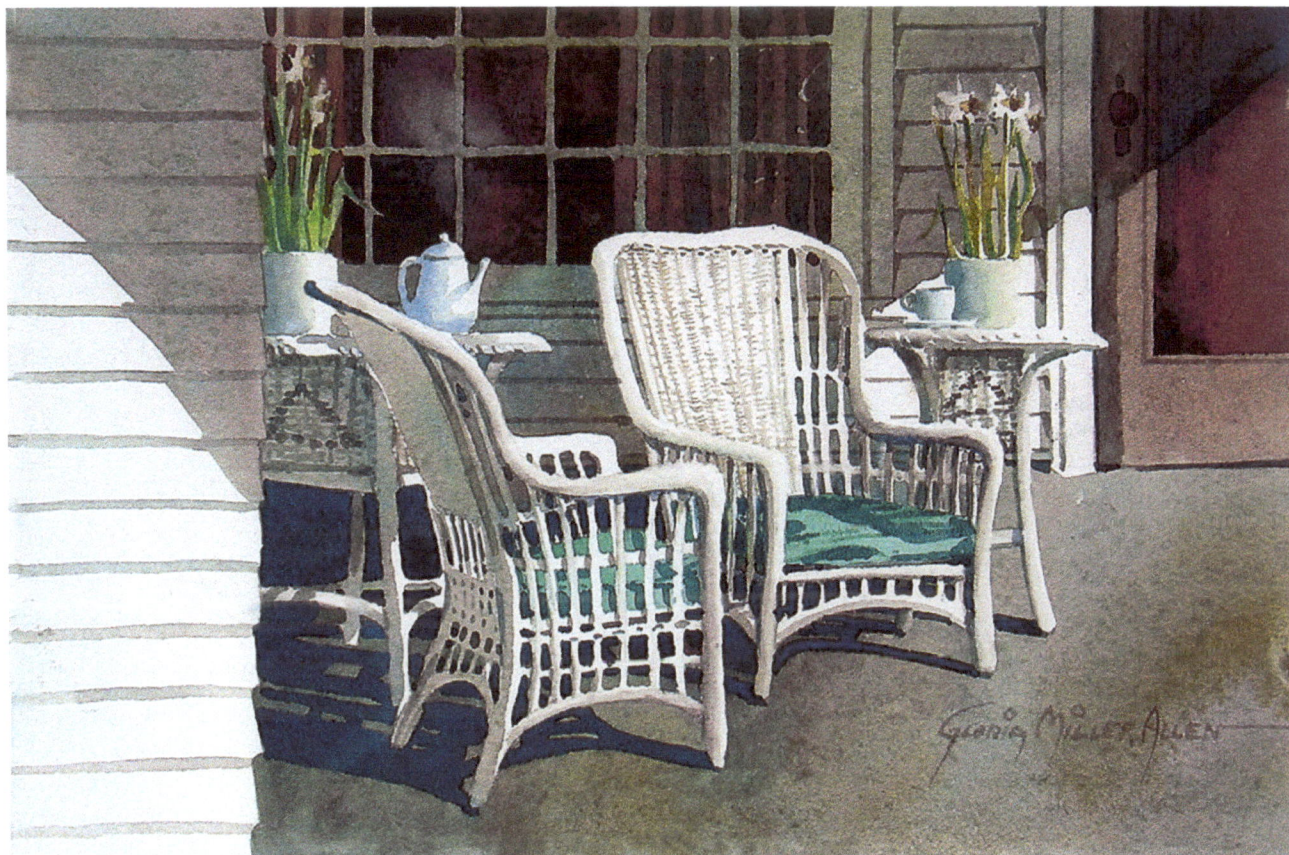

Tea For Two   *watercolor*   *10 x 14*

PART TWO

DRAWING ~
THE MAGIC
OF DEPICTION

CHAPTER 3
ACQUIRING REAL
CONFIDENCE IN DRAWING

CHAPTER 4
THE WIZARDRY OF PERSPECTIVE
AND THE TRICKS IT PLAYS

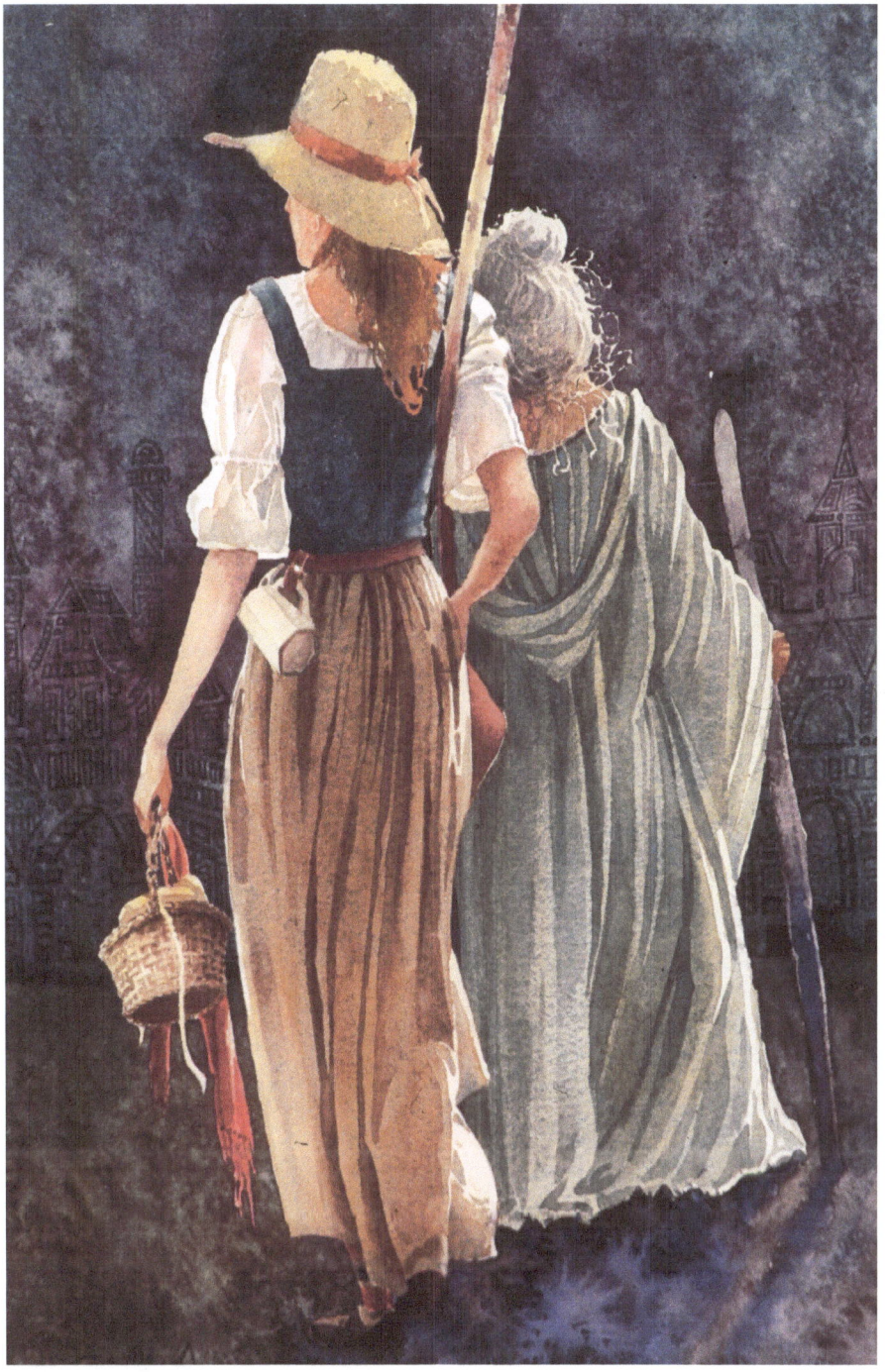

Into That Dark Night   *watercolor*   *14 x 11*

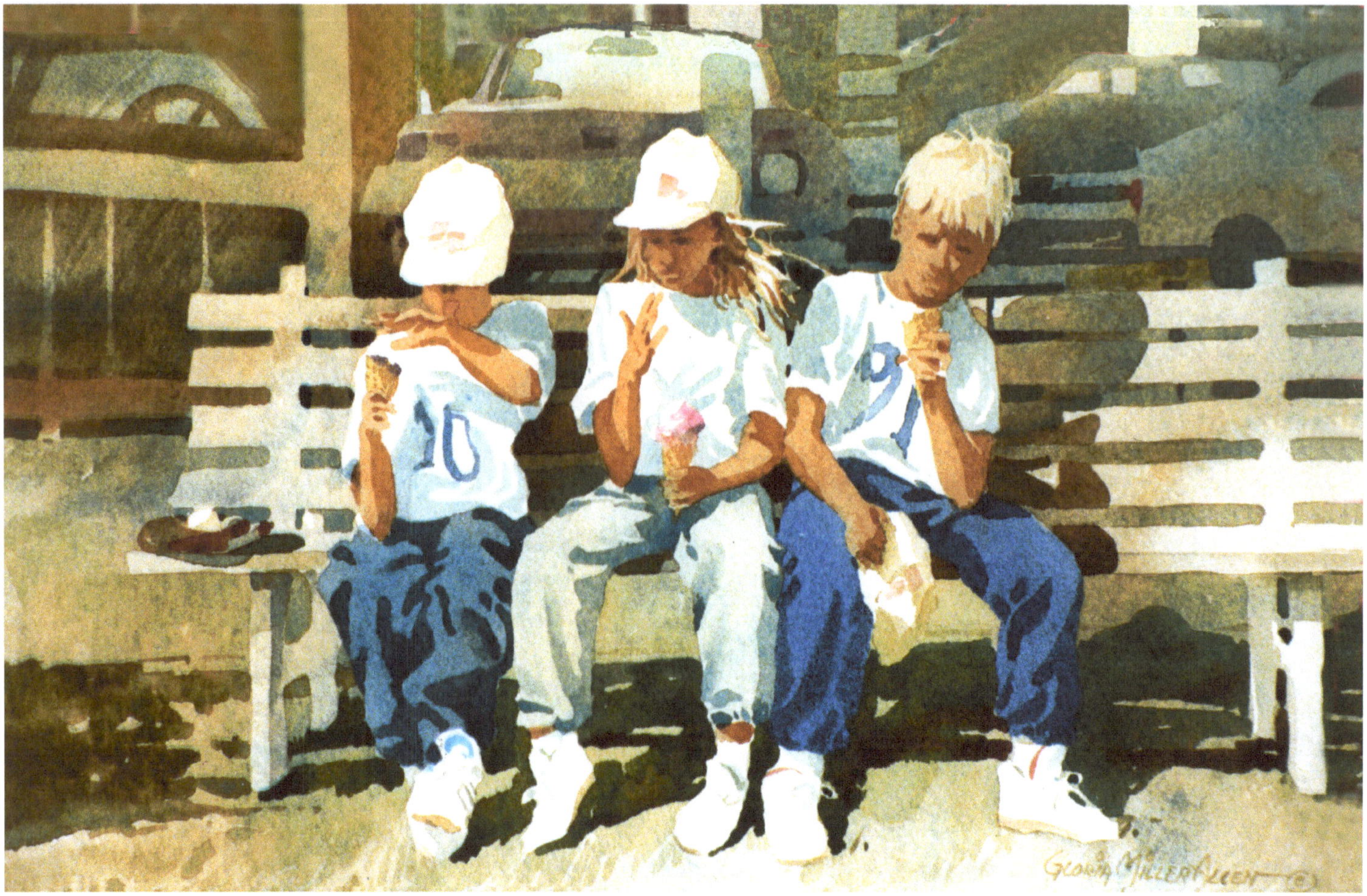

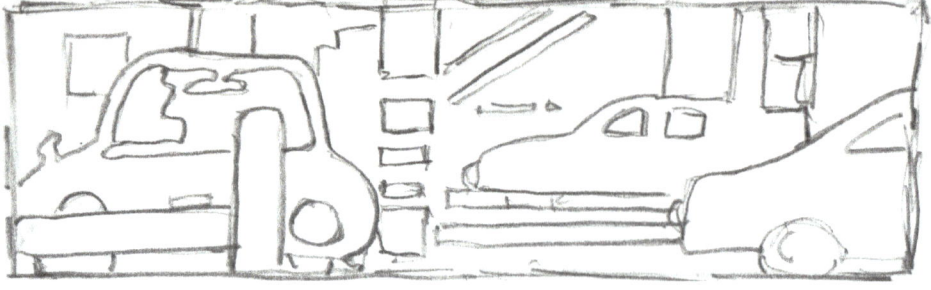

One for Three   *watercolor*   *11 x 14*

Look at these simple puzzle pieces. Find them in the painting?

Simplifying objects can make a stronger painting. Seeing puzzle pieces will make them easy to draw.

CHAPTER THREE

ACQUIRING REAL CONFIDENCE IN DRAWING
SEVEN EXERCISES TO BOOST YOUR DRAWING SKILL

FEATURING FIGURE PAINTINGS AND MISC. DRAWINGS

It is now time to explore some drawing ideas both old and new. What ever we learn it is usually by studying what others have discovered before us, but we put out own stamp on those lessons with use. In this chapter I want to share exercises that help me. There may be one idea that speaks more to you than the others, and that might point to a personal learning style. If so, you'll want to pay particular attention to it, but every assignment will prove beneficial. At this point, I want you to *think* of each exercise as a valuable *thinking* tool for your intangible tool box. At least one of them will be a *power tool* for you.

The Beginning Of Drawing Is Seeing.
The Beginning Of Seeing Is Drawing.

It sounds like *"Which came first, the chicken or the egg?"* This whole scenario goes round and round. You may have heard the expression: *"Seeing with the eye of an artist."* I believe that when you draw a lot, you actually *do* see things differently from those who do not draw. You also come to realize how extraordinary the most ordinary things are. It's simply magical. I believe children should be taught basic drawing in elementary school, not to turn them into little artists, or even because it develops better eye-hand coordination. Drawing awakens an awareness of this awesome planet, our visual surroundings, and life itself. Wouldn't that be a good thing? I believe it would.

LOOKING FOR SHAPES

This first assignment is aimed at helping you stop thinking of subject matter as bird, nose, chair, etc. and force you instead to think purely of simplified shapes. Seeing shapes of things *or parts* of things is the goal. Once you see them, you can draw them.

The little watercolor of the children and their ice cream after the baseball game illustrates how simplified shapes can be exciting. The three figures were actually taken from three different photographs of the same child eating ice cream and sitting on a park bench in Jackson Hole, WY. The background was from yet another photo and changed greatly for my design impulses. Taking a little artistic license is always fun. The more you draw, the better your skills so the more you can and will make things up.

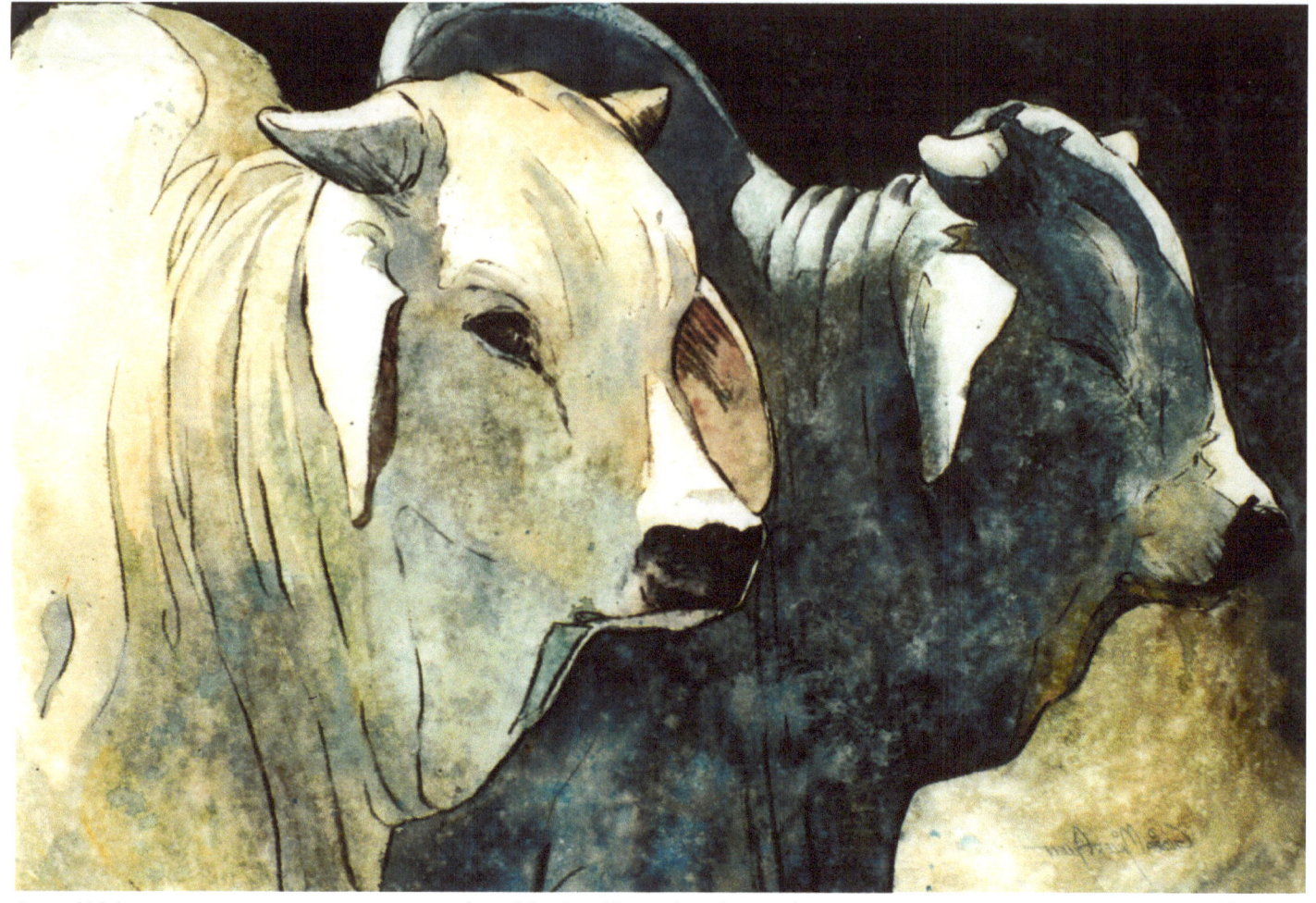

Day and Night   charcoal drawing with gouache and watercolor   22 x 30

LIKE SOME
DRENCHING DELUGE
LIKE MOONSHINE
SOUSED IN
LINE AND COLOR

I NEARLY DROWNED

EVEN NOW
I WALLOW

AGAIN I HOLD
EMPTY PAPER
PREGNANT WITH
ANTICIPATION

AWAITING
THOUGHTS
SHAPING GOALS

GIVING ME BIRTH

VERSE AWAITS
AUTHOR
CANVAS AWAITS
COLOR
SOUL AWAITS
DIRECTION

THE MUSE
IS PRESENT

POWER
ABUNDANT AND
AVAILABLE

PATIENTLY WAITING
READY AND ABLE
AND UNLEASHED

COME
THIS IS
THINE HOUR

2003

DRAWING FROM
THREE REFERENCE SOURCES

Right about now, I can hear a few rumblings about drawing from photos. I will take this opportunity to make a few points.

There are those who frown on the use of photos in any way, shape or form. I am not one of them. I've several friends who are totally dedicated to plein air (drawing/painting on location). These same artists paint still life using fresh flowers and real teapots.

The cry of "purist" is compelling, there is validity to their view, and I love a good plein air painting. However, I submit there are a great many valuable uses for photographic references. We will be using them in many ways throughout the book. I'd also like to recognize those artists who just as passionately use only their own imagination as their reference

material. This would include fantasy paintings, cartooning or non-objective abstracts to name a few.

When I think about drawing, I want to use all three:

- ♦ *Drawing from life*
- ♦ *Drawing from photos*
- ♦ *Drawing from pure imagination*

The reason I am starting with photographs is simple. First of all, it is easier to draw from photos. Why? Because the image is already in two dimensions. When drawing from nature, you are presented with a three-dimensional image but trying to represent it on a one-dimensional sheet of flat paper. Obviously, that's a huge leap.

Our goal is to eventually draw as comfortably from life or from our pure imagination as we do from photos. But we start here.

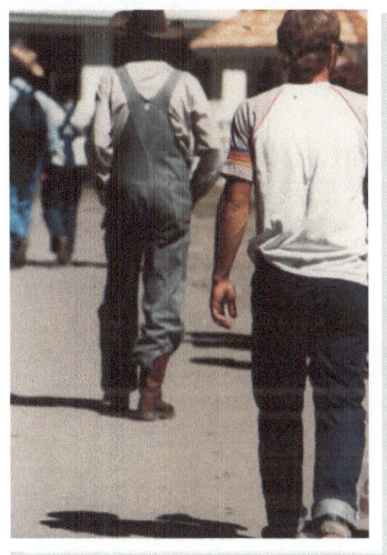

Photo from Idaho State Fair grounds

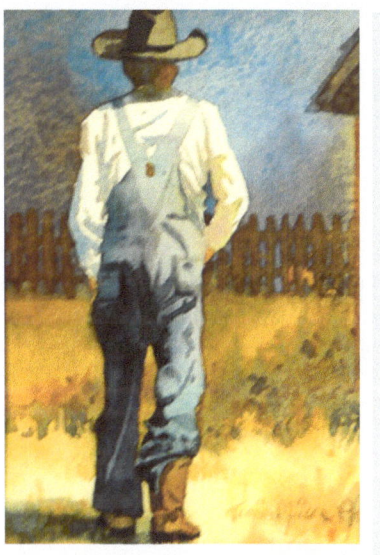

Idaho Spud   *watercolor demo*   *7 x 5*

53

To Copy Or Not To Copy?
That Is The Question.

Drawing from your own photos is acceptable, of course, but it comes with potential problems built in that need warning. First, it is *never* acceptable to use photographic images, drawings or paintings by professionals. Yes, copying the images of the masters has been done through the ages, and although it holds no appeal to me, many people claim they learn a great deal from doing it. As always, learning is a worthy goal; however, it should be done *only* for study purposes. Otherwise, leave the masters to history. I cannot understand why this is even an issue, but it comes into play often in local and even national art shows and competitions. Don't start down that road. If you do, even for some academic reason, I believe it can be hard to break away. Besides, it's unnecessary because developing your own style and designing your own work is so deeply satisfying. It's as simple as this:

"If your goal is to be an artist,
don't copy other people's work."

The other potential problem using photos (even your own) is a tendency to copy verbatim. Again, this holds no appeal to me because I love designing, but I definitely *do* use photos in my process.

Use them as a starting place—a jump-off place—an idea place. Unless your goal is to copy the photo exactly (why?), then sooner rather than later you need to ditch the photo image and take the idea and run with it. Now, let's get started.

PAPER

FROM OUT THE PAST
SOME BARTERED TIME
I CHOOSE TO GIVE AWAY,
SEALED IN COLORS
AND WORDS THAT HOLD
PORTIONS OF A DAY.

POWERFUL LIGHT
WILL COME AND CAST
MY SHADOW ON THE PAGE,
BLACK AND WHITE
COLORS BRIGHT
SOUVENIRS OF THE AGE.

FOLDED PAPER
AIRPLANE NOTES
FLOWN ACROSS THE SKY,
GIVING WINGS TO YESTERDAYS
JUST BEFORE THEY FLY…

JUST BEFORE THEY FLY.

1983

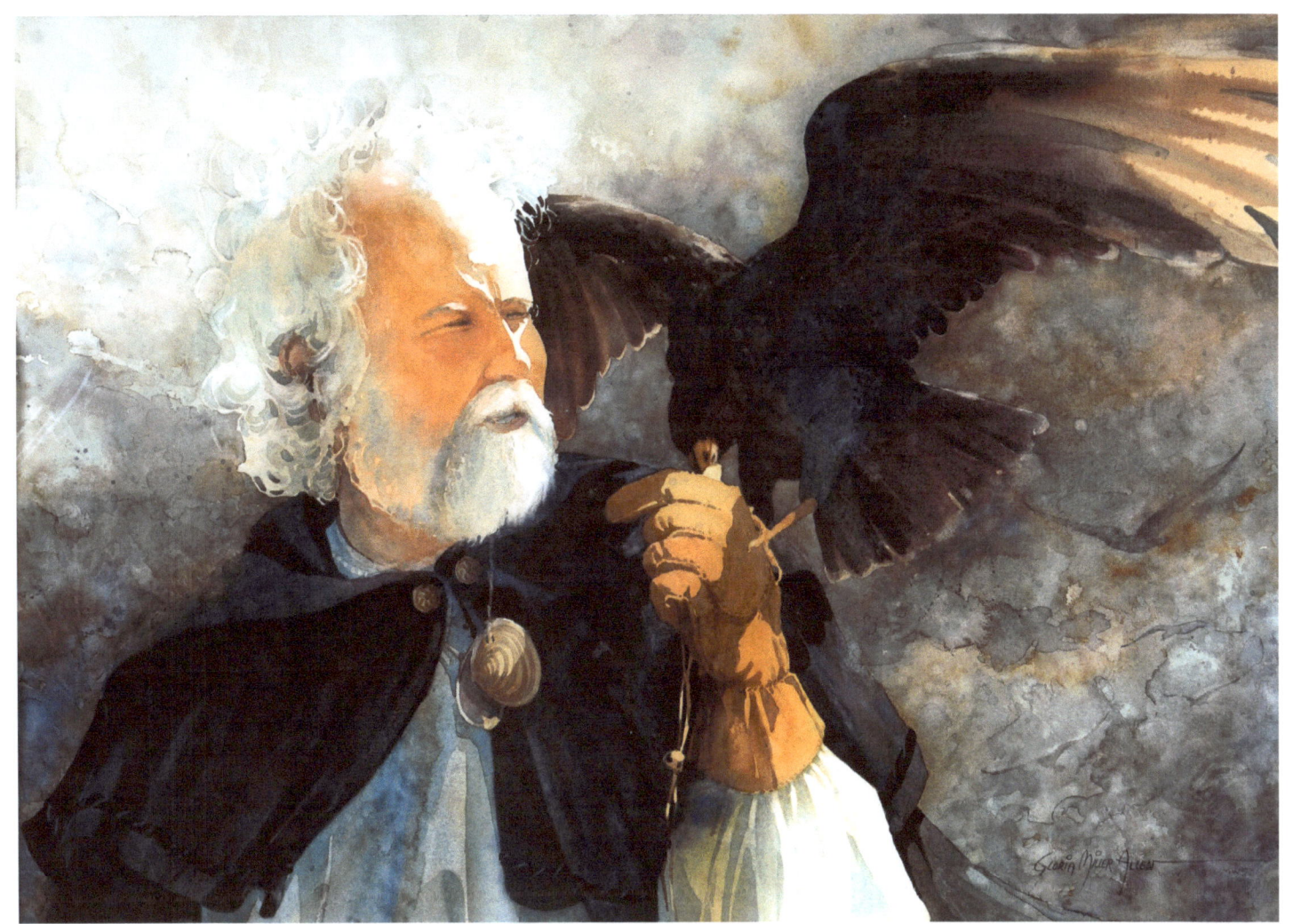

A Message From John   *watercolor*   *22 x 30*

EXERCISE ONE

FINDING AND DRAWING PUZZLE-PIECES

I have chosen this photo for this exercise. We will not redesign it, because that is another lesson. Choose a simple photo like this. The goal is to look for simple shapes. A photo with thousands of flowers and leaves may look great but would not be a good one for this particular assignment. At this time we will pay no attention to details like facial feature or folds in the fabric. (However, they would be handled exactly the same way.) Using tracing paper, find individual puzzle pieces. Cut them apart. Piece them back together. You may certainly take some artistic initiative with design if you choose. After doing this enough times, you begin to *see* the puzzle pieces without disconnecting them.

Concentrating on puzzle piece shapes that make this image, I separated the parts to prove to myself how simple they are. Then I put them back together *thinking* how they relate to the whole. I try *not* to identify items like hair or dress. I'm seeing only simple shapes.

Study this example, and then choose a photo of your own and do the assignment yourself. Do not even imagine you can look at what I've done and get the benefit. Like riding a bike, watching someone else do it doesn't really teach you how to ride. It lets you know it can be done, but you have to get on the bike and ride. This exercise is no different. You have to do the *thinking* process yourself. Looking at my thinking will not do. Find your own photo, do your own work and gain your own skill.

"The beginning of all drawing is seeing."

TO DEMONSTRATE

I took this 2007 photo in Salem, MA, inside the old court house where several young thespians re-enacted an historically correct version of the witch trial of Goodie Bishop. The young woman in this photo played the part of Goodie in shackles, and played it very well.

I choose this photo for it's well defined shapes, and because the window behind her can help us zero in on the spaces around the figure, thereby helping us draw the figure itself.

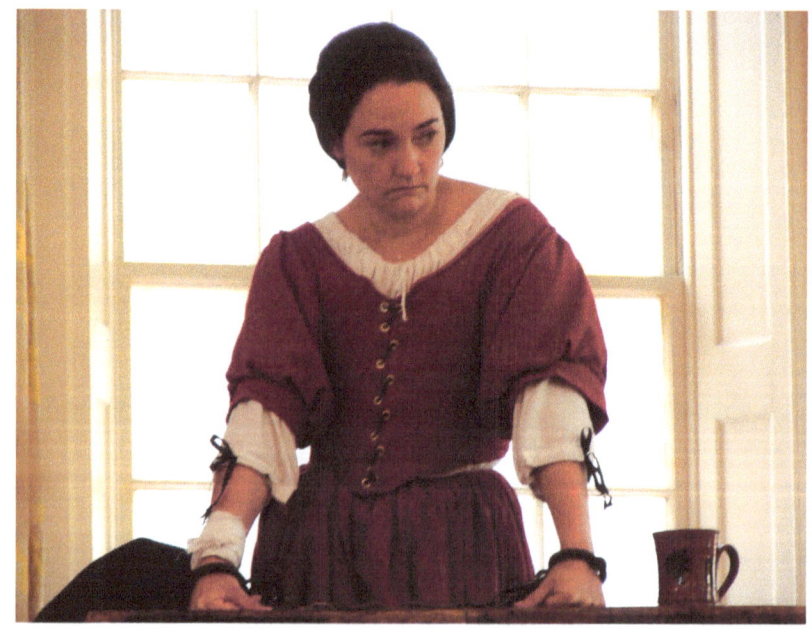

PUZZLE PIECES APART

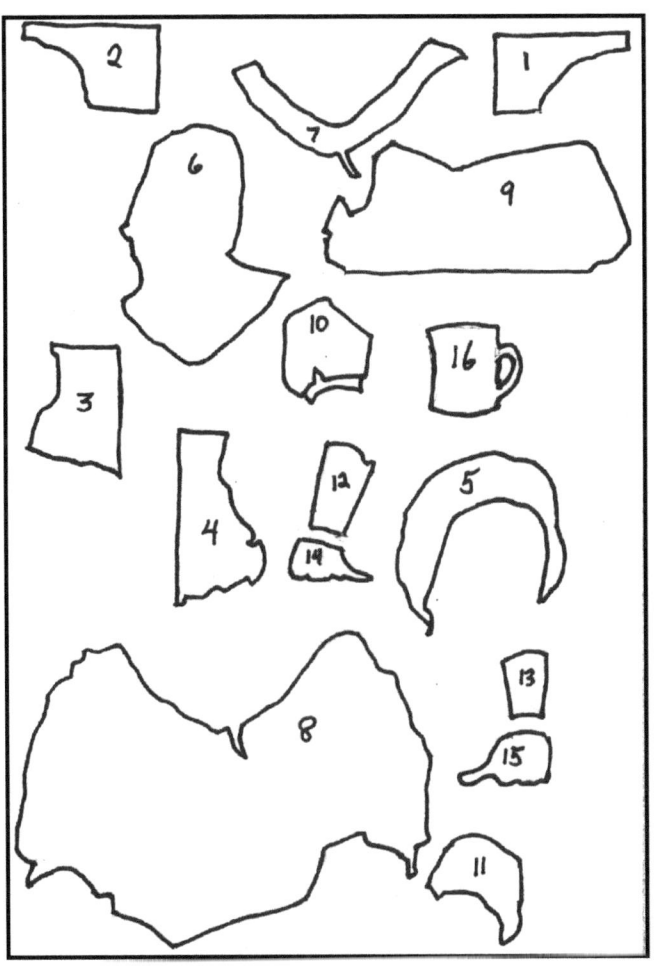

PUZZLE PIECES TOGETHER AGAIN

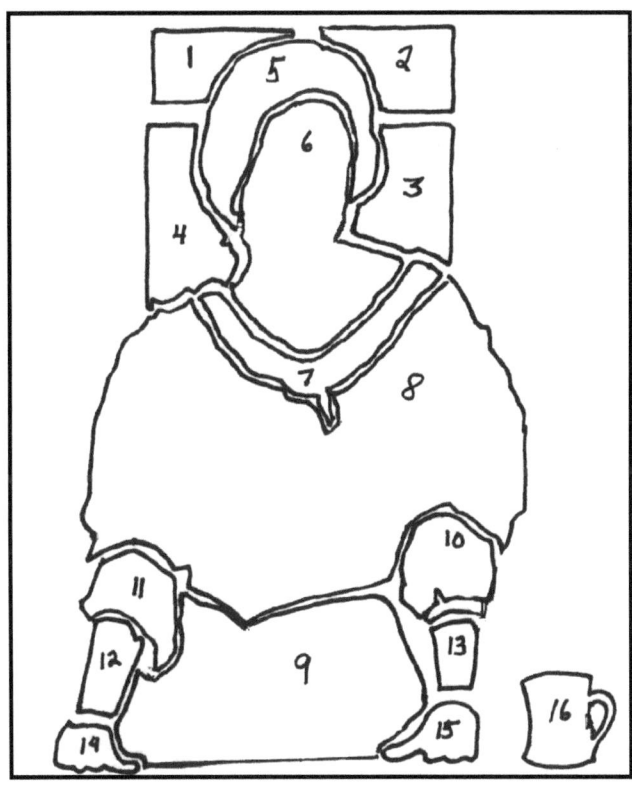

I drew these shapes freehand. Graduate as soon as possible to drawing shapes without tracing paper, and do not worry overly about perfect correctness. Play with the concept without getting hung up on "stuff." Your only goal right now is to see shapes. That's it. Keep it simple.

Learning to see shapes is a skill that grows. This exercise helps you simplify your thinking about shapes—they are simply shapes, nothing more and nothing less. In the above example the puzzle shape #8 is actually the only shape that is difficult to reproduce. Of course, you could simplify it further by making the sleeves and each half of the bodice into separate shapes. Think in terms of big simple shapes first, then when those are defined, go into more detailed shapes within the big shapes exactly the same way...puzzle pieces that can be taken apart, seen, and put back together again. Give it several tries before moving on to the next exercise.

EXERCISE TWO

FINDING COMPARATIVE
REFERENCE POINTS AND ANGLES

This is an entirely different way of looking and seeing the subject. The idea here is to put dots or reference points in obvious or prominent places on the subject you're drawing. Then connect the dots with lines forming angles. As before, it is easier using a photo, but remember, the goal is being able to use the same *thought* process drawing from life. I suggest you start this exercise with tracing paper. It is the best way I know to get started. Over time, you'll find yourself looking for obvious "dot places" and imagining lines between them.

Seeing the angles reveal relationships within the subject. This is just another way of training your eyes to see relative shapes. If you find yourself attached to tracing paper, that is not good. Again, your goal is to gain confidence in drawing...not tracing. This is a beginning step toward that goal. Like a child learning to draw the alphabet first by tracing over the letters, so we begin here with tracing. Eventually you can incorporate this *thinking process* into your everyday habits of drawing, just as you learned to make your alphabet letters routinely with your everyday writing. It becomes a good habit.

Think of the stereotype of artists holding up a pencil toward their subject, closing one eye, and making a mental note. That is what we're working toward. That's how you start being able to relate this little exercise to drawing three-dimensional subjects.

Keep this in mind while doing the assignments. Eventually you won't need to locate the dots, draw the lines, or hold up the pencil. You will just *see* it.

As the title of this book indicates, I believe much of painting and drawing is *thinking*. One or more of the drawing skills in this chapter may turn on a light bulb in your head. Prepare for that as an exciting happening, but also prepare for a bit of frustration along the way. New processes take time. Give yourself the courtesy of time.

For this exercise I will use a photo I took somewhere along the Oregon beach a few years ago. I did not know these children and took the shot from quite a distance as I was walking along the shoreline.

Thanks to digital cameras I was able to crop out much of the foreground, a row of beach houses, all other people and zoom in on the charming kids in their yellow shirts and their beach bucket. That's what interested me, and it should work well for this assignment. I don't want the rock wall or the green vines; I just want the kids.

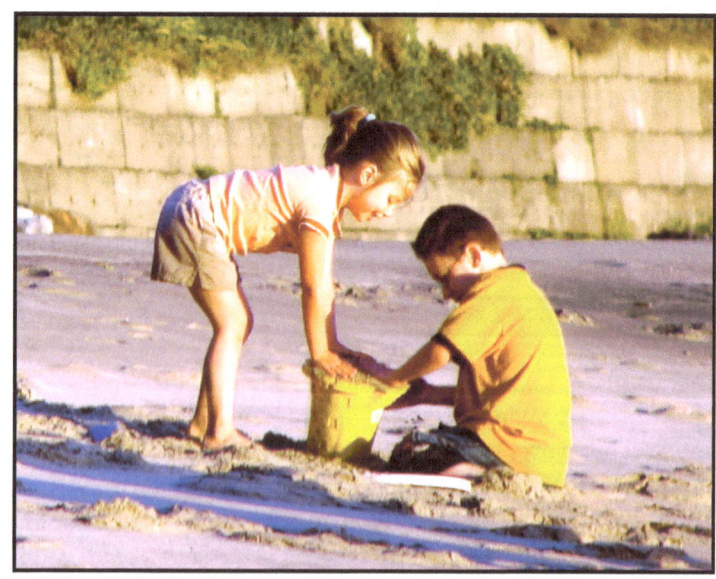

First, with tracing paper over the photo, I'll put a dot on several spots that might be good reference points. Next, I will draw lines between some of them...any of them that seem likely. This is not rocket science. There is no *right* or *wrong* place to put the dots or to draw the subsequent lines. Isn't that a sweet deal? Simply pick out one point and then another and then another. The possibilities are numerous so no worrying about getting it right or wrong. Play with the concept. The key word here is *play*. Make it fun.

Use the tracing paper to place the dots and draw the lines. Then remove the photo from under the tracing paper and draw the image freehand. Use the angles, lines and spaces between the lines. Note how it becomes easy to know where to put things. For instance, his ear goes right into that upper right hand corner of the triangle. There is no guessing where to put it. This process, of course, is a *thinking* process and it will show you much if you will take the time to do it. Your assignment then, is to practice this several times using several different photographs of your own.

A LITTLE SELF-TALK

While working on this homework, talk to yourself like this:

"Let's see, the edge of the bucket is directly below her forehead, in fact, so is his forehead. And look, her nose crosses the line right here. I can see the angles of the arms and legs, I bet I can draw those. What if I drew a few dots and lines around the boy's shirt? I think that would make it easy to draw.

And look how his shirt bulges out behind the line between the dots on his neck and bottom, that's a simple shape." *And so on.*

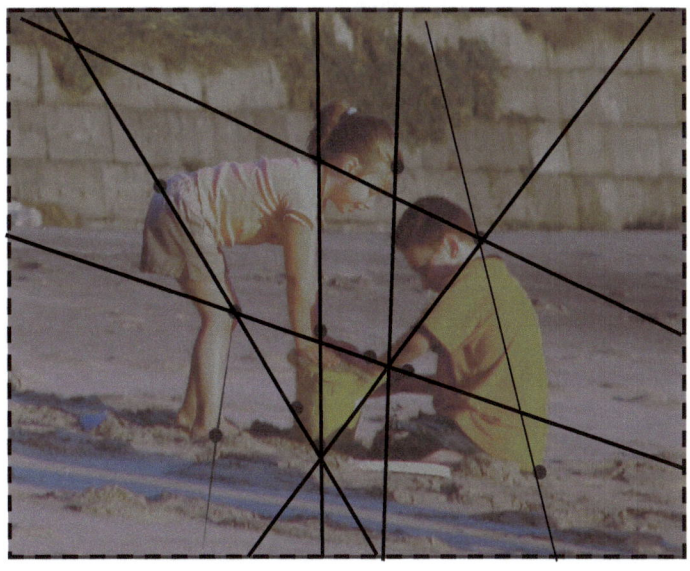

ONE POSSIBILITY FOR REFERENCE POINTS AND ANGLES

(Remember—the dots can go literally anywhere)

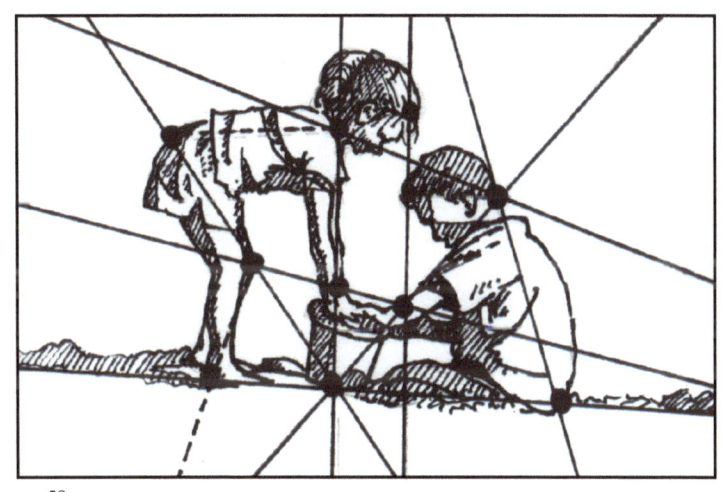

59

Don't get confused thinking these angle lines have to do with composition. They do not. These lines are simply to help you see shape relationships. They help you notice placement, angles formed, relative sizes, and many other relationships within the subject. You will find it surprisingly easy to draw within the triangles and spaces between the lines. While doing so, you can ignore everything else and concentrate on shapes within the angles. The lines tell you where to put everything. Next, choose a larger photo.

This is truly a new frame of mind. Watch yourself and notice while doing Exercise 2 you are somewhere else. The day and the time on your watch seem to be nonexistent and uniquely irrelevant. Also, you might accidentally find yourself seeing puzzle pieces like we looked for in the last assignment. If so, you are skill building. Perfect.

BLANK PAGES

EVERY TURN
HUMBLY TAKEN
WITH BLANK PAPERS
BREATHES LIFE
INTO THEM
AND INTO ME.

SO BE IT.

NOT ONLY WITH ME
BUT WITH ALL WHO WILL
MAKE TINY TRICKS
WITH TIME
NOT ONLY TO PRESERVE IT
BUT TO CREATE IT.

SO BE IT.

CHOOSING COLORS
PICKING PHRASES
TO PAINT OURSELVES
TO AUTHOR OUR LIVES—
HUMBLY ON BLANK PAGES
BREATHING LIFE.

SO BE IT.   *1996*

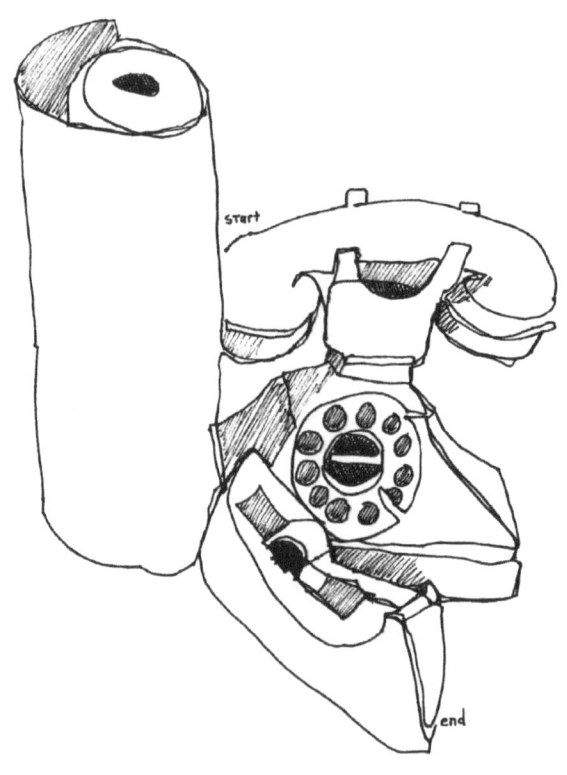

This is a regular contour drawing (not a blind contour drawing) of objects on my desk. The shading, the little circles on the telephone and towels were added later. Otherwise, it is one continuous line. This kind of drawing creates interesting distortions from reality that you might find fun to work with.

EXERCISE THREE

CONTOUR DRAWING

When people first begin *thinking* about drawing, they usually start with a simple contour drawing. That is drawing around the outlines of things. It is a perfectly logical place to start, but it is also a perfectly logical place to delve a bit deeper. We will start with *blind* contour drawings. There is no finer way to train your eyes, hand, pencil or pen. It's the foundation for looking and seeing.

For this assignment you will need no photo, but you will need some inanimate objects. For the first few drawings, use only one object. Kitchen utensils, a piece of folded or crumpled paper, a toy, a pair of eye glasses or anything at hand. It doesn't matter. Place your paper comfortably in front of you and push the object you are going to draw out about two feet in front of your paper. Place your pencil on an appropriate place on the paper then focus your eyes on a place (any place) on the outside of the object. Do not take your eyes off the object, and do not lift the pencil off the paper. One continuous line is the goal. Move your eyes *slowly and precisely* along the edge of the object as you move the pencil *slowly and precisely* along the paper creating the same edge. Slowly, very slowly define *every* little bump, every dip, every tiny change in direction. Move the pencil but do *not* look at either the pencil or the drawing. Keep your eyes on the edge of the object. Your eyes and the pencil move in sync. I repeat, do it *slowly and precisely* without peeking at your paper. That's *Blind* Contour.

Don't concern yourself with the outcome of the drawing. It will be distorted, and when you arrive back at the beginning point, the ends will not meet. If they do, you peeked. In this exercise the drawing itself is not what we're striving for. We're gaining skill at seeing. These drawings are distorted, but often they have a peculiar beauty to them, and I dare not guess why.

Take your time. Everyone has a tendency to rush this. I know I do. Create ten or twenty of these drawings using different objects or the same object from a different angle. Trace slowly all around the contours. It should take you 10 minutes to do a simple contour. Slow. Slow. Slow.

Next try following inside edges as well as outside edges all connected together. Again, do not lift the pencil because you would have to look at the drawing to get the pencil back at the end of the line drawn. It will get distorted. The secret is to force yourself to go slowly. Fast simply will not do. You are looking to record every single change in direction. Spend some real time with this. Fill up several pages in your workbook. Look carefully. See everything. It's called *blind* contour because you never look at the drawing…only at the object before you.

Working truly *blind* for numerous drawings will bring real elation later when you're doing some regular contour drawing. That alone is reason to do many drawings using this process. Practice. Practice.

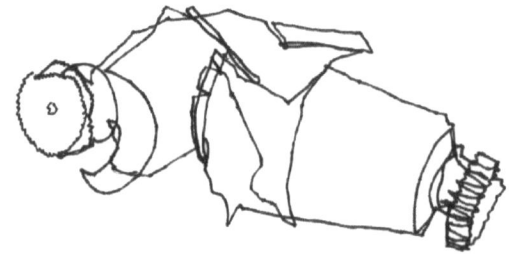
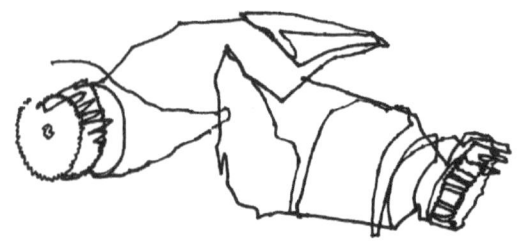

The next part of this contour drawing section is to complicate the drawing with several objects overlapping. Really get into this. Still keep it as blind. No peeking. I believe I can promise the more of these you do, and the slower you do them, the greater will be the learning experience.

ANOTHER STEP INTO CONTOUR DRAWING

The final part of this section is *not* totally blind. Here you permit an occasional glance at your drawing for placement, etc. Still do as much as you comfortably can looking only at the object and not at the paper.

This will be a real joy after the more difficult completely *blind contours*. Continue to imagine your pencil tracing over every single edge. Start again with one object and draw just the outer edges. Gradually advance to two or more overlapping objects and eventually getting into all the little fine edges on the interior of some very complicated subject. Try drawing folds in fabric, your shoe, your fingers. Notice every minute detail. It doesn't matter if you never plan to paint with detail or not. Right now you just want to train yourself to see, draw and be conscious of the detail. After you are confident in your drawing, you will choose how much detail you want in your work. Take your time, do not be judgmental,

have fun, make a whole collection of contour drawings in your workbook. Do many. These are fun.

After you've exhausted your patience with this, at least for today, take a little time *thinking* about combining these contour drawings with the *puzzle-piece* drawings and the *point-angle* reference drawings. Notice if there is one method that speaks louder to you than the others. Can you begin to call on any one of these approaches mixed with any other one, or even two? Can you begin to relate one method to another? The goal is to have them all at your fingertip, in your tool box and at your beck and call.

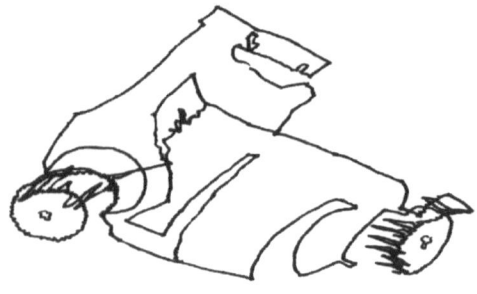

On this page I've drawn the same two paint tubes three different times. Try several objects in subsequent drawings, getting more complicated.

FROM BLIND CONTOUR
TO CONTOUR
AND FINALLY TO
SIMPLY DRAWING

The next step in drawing then is to continually glance back and forth between the paper and the subject. You notice where every line intersects with every other line. You notice more and more details about how eyeglasses and noses, bumblebees and flower petals, trees and lakes relate to each other.

You probably won't always have the goal to create the image with one continuous line, but then again, you might. Contour drawing for me is one of the truly delightful drawing exercises, but each of them once ingrained is a power tool for your tool box.

See what magic you can do in your workbook. Fill many pages

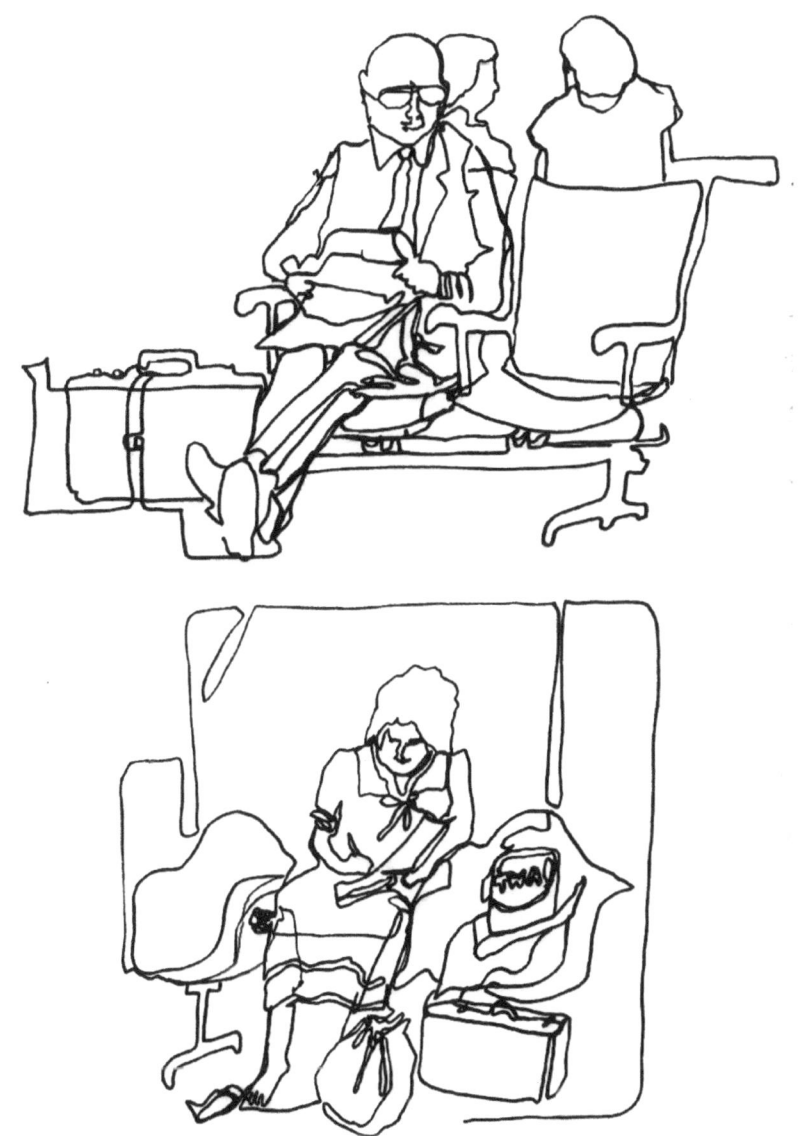

Waiting for a Flight is a contour drawing that was done in an airport. Doing work like this while waiting for something else to happen is a great use of an artist's time. I wish I would remember that every time I wait. It's certainly worth remembering.

63

EXERCISE FOUR

GESTURE DRAWING

Dealing with the human or animal figure is something we all want to feel confident about. Some of us will be very drawn to figurative work while others may only occasionally want to place little figures in a painting. Either way, we do not want to be skittish about it. So, let us *think* specifically about the figure in this section. We want to capture quickly the essence of a body, its movement, its posture and its ultimate bulk form. Absolutely, it is useful to study anatomy, and some of you will, but that is another book. Here, we will look at some practical practices of tried-and-true methods aimed at helping you get over figure frustrations so you may easily incorporate them.

As with most of the exercises we've discussed, photos are easier to utilize. However, the ultimate goal will be using these techniques in life drawing and sketching. My best advice is to join a figure drawing class or group and use the time to practice. I don't think there is any better gift you can give yourself than that. It doesn't matter if the figures are nude, draped or heavily costumed, your drawing skill will grow. When drawing a live figure you must *look* and *see* correctly. There can be no fudging. In figure drawing groups, it is quiet work time and visiting has no proper place.

ANOTHER NOTE ABOUT PHOTOS.

Years ago, I found that in a crowd, say the state fair, a parade or a ball game, I could get photos of many figures all at once and nobody seemed to worry about a camera pointing at them. One photo can yield many gestures. Dads with kids on their shoulders, moms with kids on their hips, elders, youngsters, side pro-

files, backs, walkers, standers, runners and often a wonderful surprise I didn't even know I was getting. Photos like this have been a real boon to me. When I want a figure in a painting, I look through my *people-photos* and usually find just what I need. Give this idea a try and file the photos in your studio.

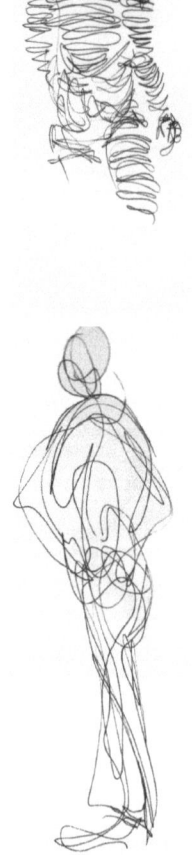

SPAGHETTI GESTURES.

For this kind of gesture drawing, put your pencil or pen to the paper and move it rapidly making one continuous scribble line that defines the form. Drawing figures in this brisk manner seems somehow less intimidating. Try starting in the center and rapidly put meat on the bones of the drawing. Give it several tries. Relax, loosen up and have fun. You are looking for bulk and weight distribution. Which foot holds the weight? Where's the center of gravity? Drawing quickly allows the capture of surprisingly subtle nuances in the gesture, stance or pose of the figure. In drawing from a live model, you can capture gestures in seconds. Subtle differences within the figure rapidly captured make such a difference in the story the figure is telling. Practicing quick spaghetti drawings like this is not only fun, but helps you *think* differently about figures than contour drawings alone do. With spaghetti gestures you are looking for bulk, for suggestion of weight and/or movement. Again, I use the word *awareness*.

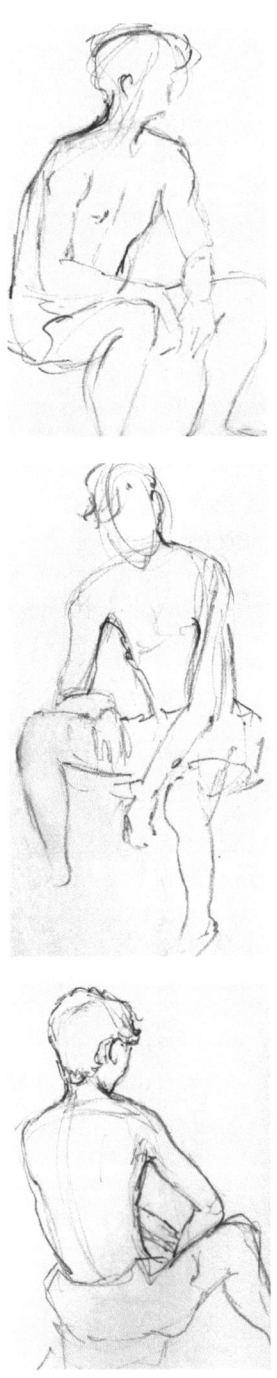

On the left are three one minute gesture drawings. These are not *spaghetti,* but they are fast and simple gestures. They certainly do convey the pose of the young man in a convincing way. Fill pages in your book with these quick simple exercises and it will teach you much. Get a model, a timer and go to work.

On the right is a sample of a twenty minute drawing done on the same day. In compiling this drawing I used three techniques we discussed previously in my *thinking.* Visualizing dots and angles helped with placement. Puzzle pieces helped relate parts to the whole, and it is a simple contour drawing. Being able to combine several of the exercises in this way is helpful.

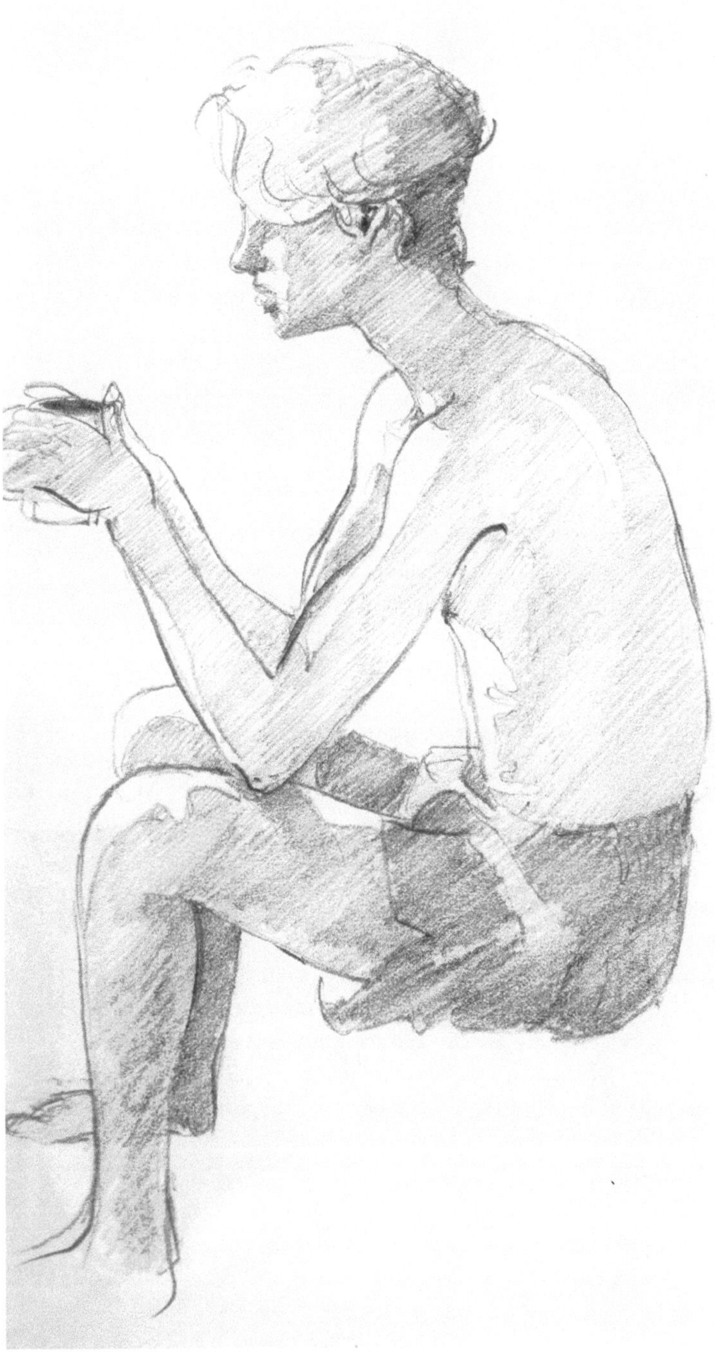

65

Exercise Five
The Art Of Sketching

The next exercise we will work on is the art of sketching. There is nothing quite like going outside in the back yard or driving to some remote spot, getting out your sketch book and losing yourself in sketching. This is something that periodically we all need to do. I find I do it less and less with years. As I write this, I am reminded of the great desirability of doing it more often. There's a sign in my studio that reads, *"Remember, Constant Renewal."* Sketching is an exercise that I need to think constantly of renewing. I find sketching not only pleasurable, but if I go back to the studio and paint using my sketch as the reference material rather than photos or plein air, I get a painting slightly removed from reality, and I enjoy that. Every once in a while, I have to re-up my ante and go sketching.

Exactly What Is Sketching?

Sketching can be done any number of ways. It can be strictly about contour. It can show lights and darks (values). It can be detailed, or not. It might have notes written all over it to remind you of things or ideas that caught your eye in the first place. Basically, sketching is a way to take visual notes. An artist's sketch book is as individual as his or her paintings. Use the art of sketching not only to help you see, but also to record *what* you see. You can bring it back to the studio for painting, or simply have the sketch and the sketch book be an end in

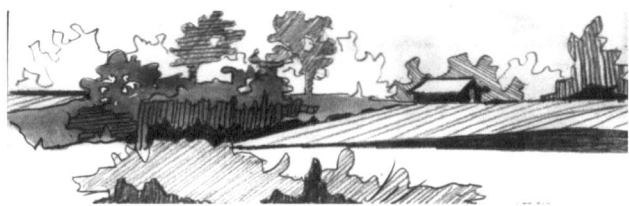

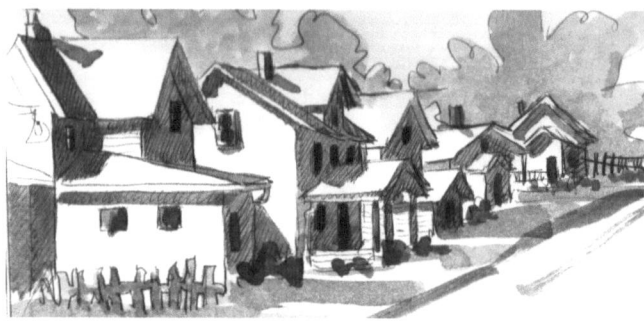

itself. Many an artist loves filling little blank books full of sketches- quick, extremely detailed or in between.

Sketching can be a diary of short trips, of overseas travel or even a diary of your life. It can certainly be a beautiful kind of history. Carry a sketch book in your car, back pack or purse. Get yourself a nice one and enjoy the heck out of it.

An interesting thing about sketching: it is like plein air painting because you remember the smells, the sounds, the weather and the whole experience better than when you simply snap photo after photo. It is true you can bring home a greater number of images in your camera, but with sketching, the treasure is not the image alone. It is a greater depth of experience. It is drawing practice and perhaps real preparation for future painting. It can be a quiet meditative lesson in awareness. It might be fellowship with artist friends and a picnic lunch. Sketching *will always* create a memorable time. That alone is worth a great deal.

We will not be going out sketching together, but hopefully this little discussion will tempt you to go out on your own. Sketching can be done in the studio drawing from your imagination alone for designing work. Sketches can be used to combine images from multiple photographs. Remember, sketches are

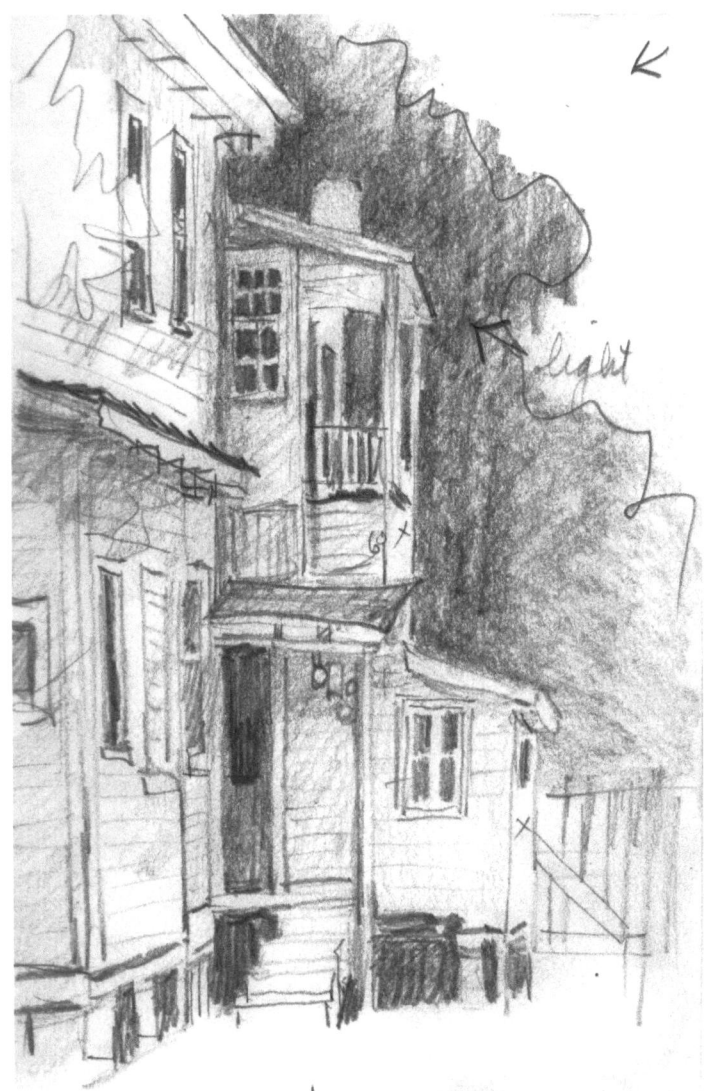

COMBINING TRICKS

While sketching, think about the puzzle pieces, the reference points and angles and contour drawing. Try to incorporate them all and remember those words written by my young son,

"Practice is boring, but soon you'll be scoring."

Here are some of my sketches using a variety of approaches. Some are with pencil concentrating on line. Quick watercolor has been added to a few. Some show emphasis on contour drawing, Others block out value patterns connecting hunks of light and dark together to simplify shapes. Learn to use sketching as a tool for obtaining information and notes. Resolve to go out sketching more often.

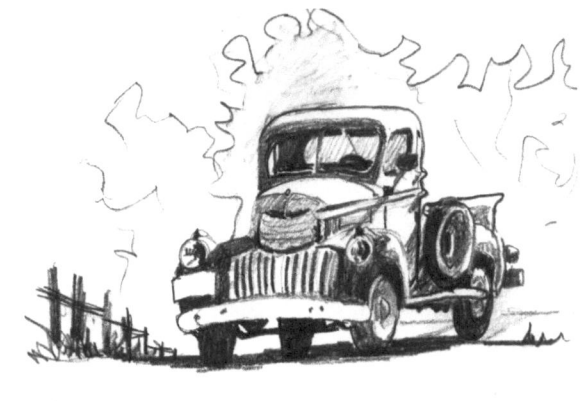

for *your* use alone. Put down whatever it is *you* want to capture. It creates a tangible item to bring home or turns imaginative thought into a concrete image. Plus it will develop drawing skills.

What's not to like?

I have painted from this little sketch of an old truck many times including in the painting *Young Mechanic* found on page 28

Think about creating books of sketches for your own pleasure. They'll become treasures while you're not looking.

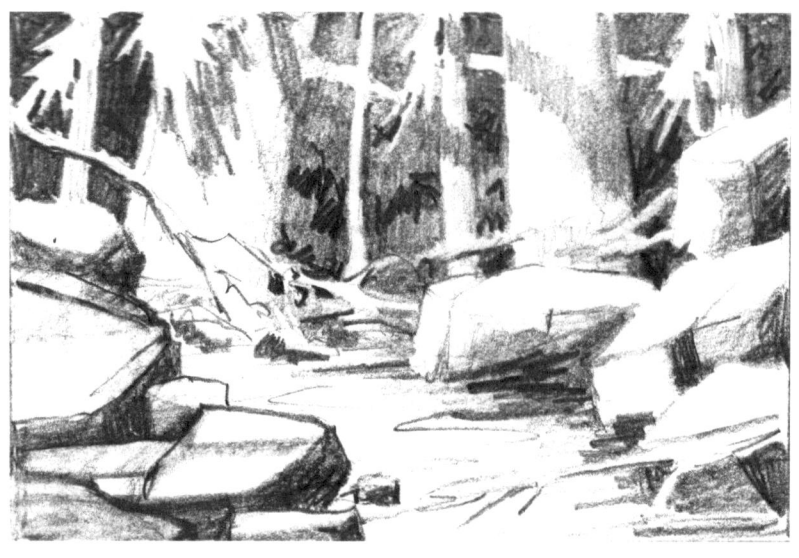

Two little pencil sketches out of my sketch book. One with an emphasis on value patterns (the light and dark), and one with an emphasis on line.

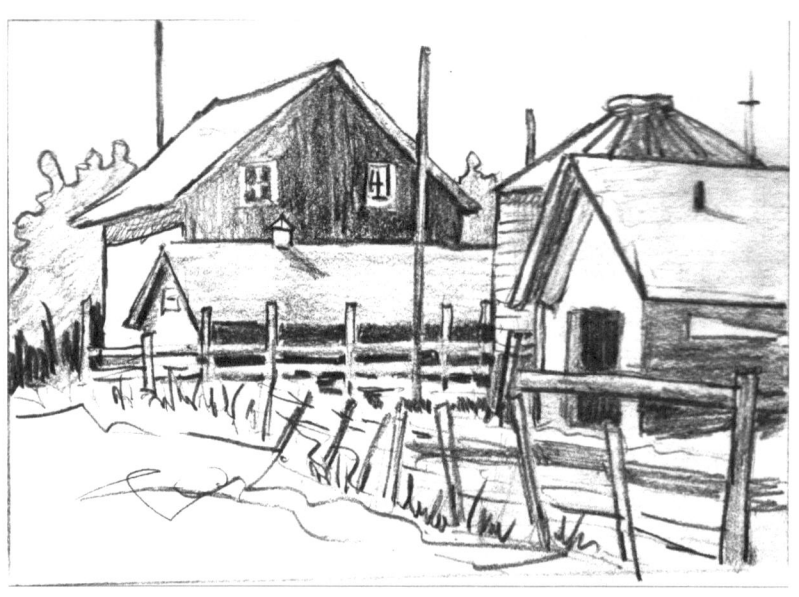

FIRST ONE MARK
THEN ANOTHER
LIKE BREATHS ALL
STRUNG TOGETHER

WITHOUT EFFORT
FEAR OR LABOR
SIMPLE GESTURES
NOW ON PAPER

NOTHING MORE
NOTHING LESS
PLAYFUL MARKS
OF AWESOMENESS

PENCILS WAITING
EVERYWHERE
AND PAPER READY
TAKE THE DARE

2012

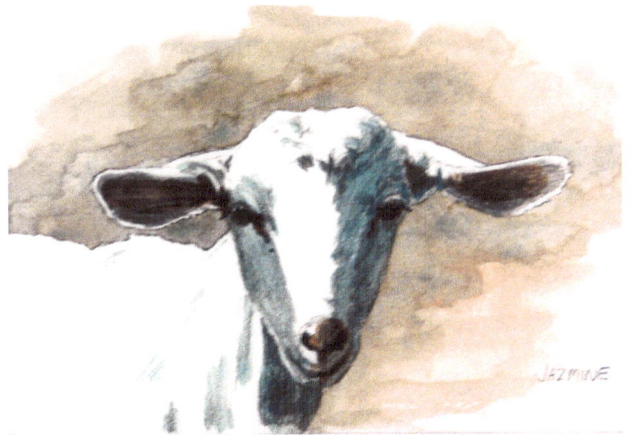

Jasmine   *pencil and watercolor*

In A Garden
Or On A Plane
To Paper And Pencil
It's All The Same

Sketching can be done with pencil, ink or with a combination of either but the addition of a few watercolor washes can add a quick easy coverage for larger areas. Sometime the results are pure and fresh little paintings. Also, there is something rich about quick little studies done with paint alone.

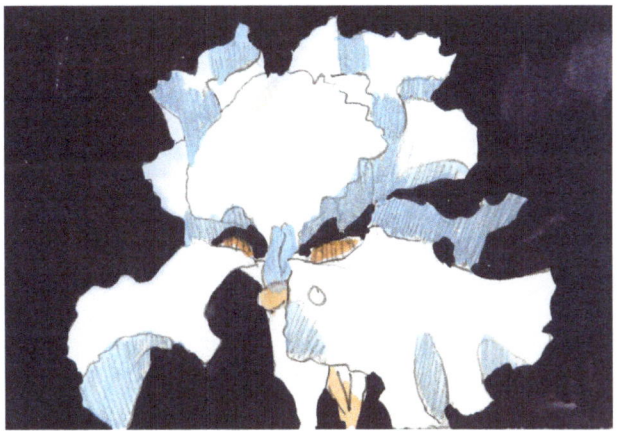

Iris   *pencil and gouache*

Glass Porch   *pencil and watercolor*

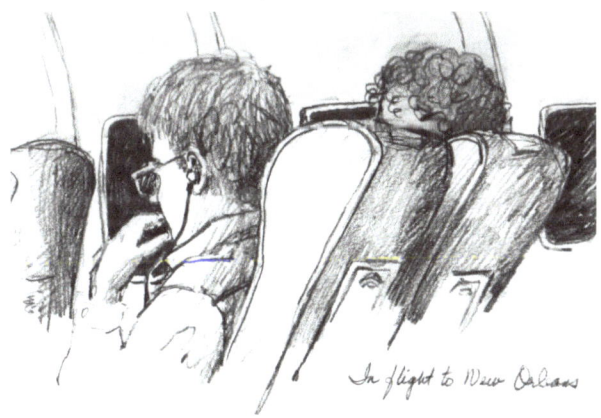

In Flight to New Orleans   *pencil*

69

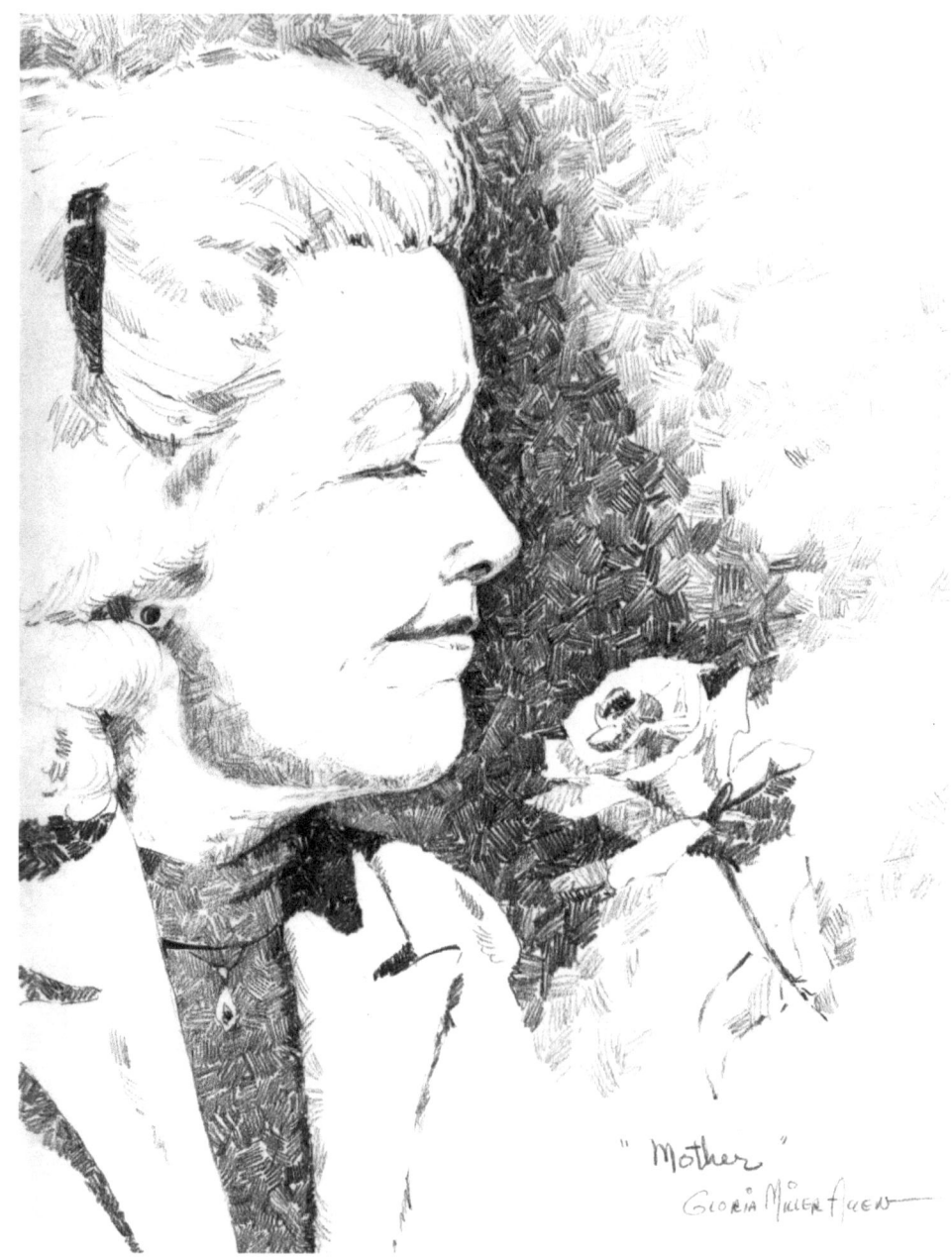

This is a drawing of my mother, Blanche Miller , who always smells the roses.

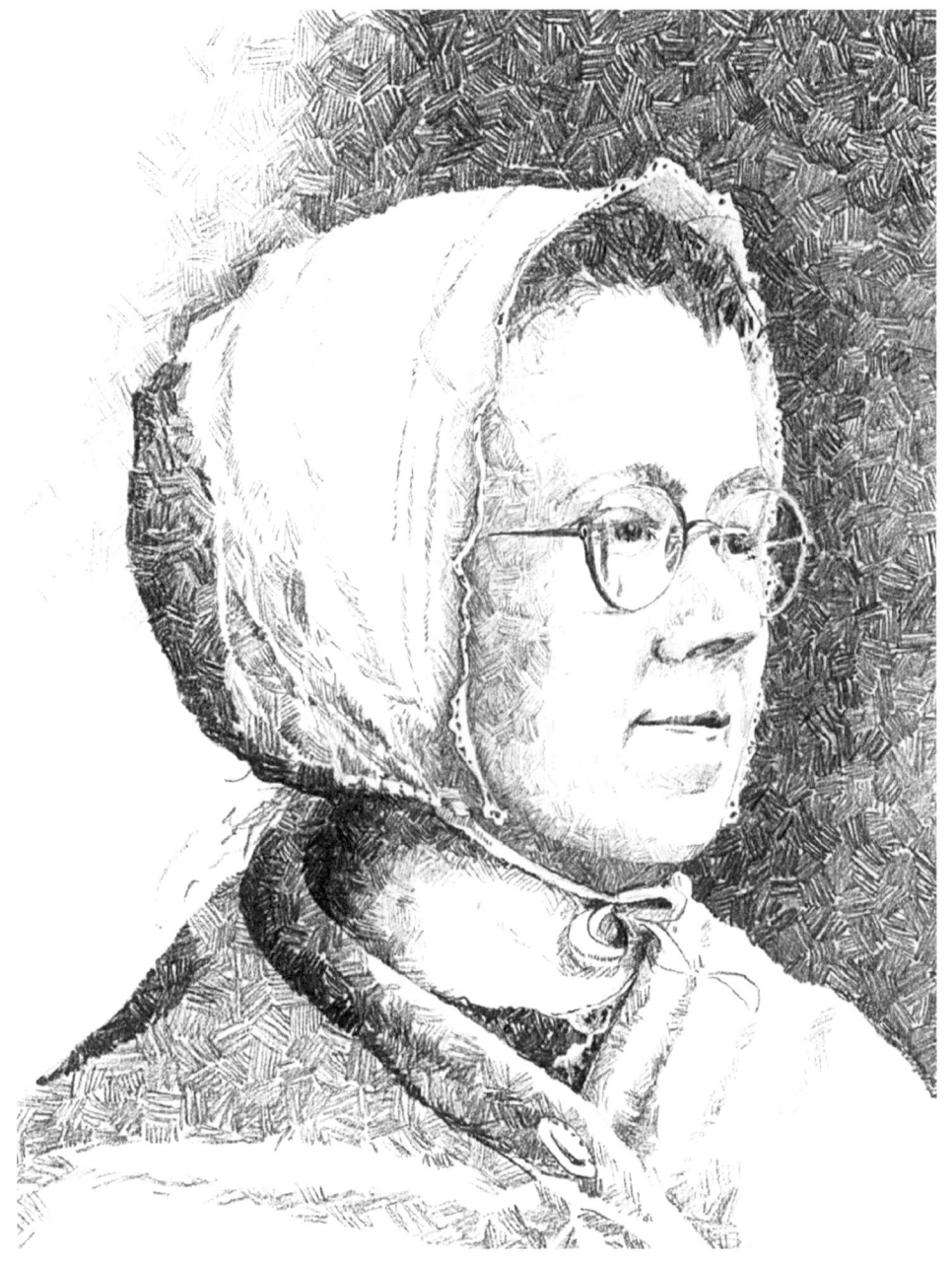

DRAWING
DRAWING
LET IT BEGIN
I WANT TO SEE
WHAT LIES WITHIN

DIGGING
DIGGING
AS WITH GRASS
SOON GROWN OVER
AS TIMES PASS

EXPOSING
EVERY ROOT
BELOW
JUST HOW DEEP
WILL I GO?

2012

Pencil drawing from photo of a woman at a Pioneer Festival in Iowa.

71

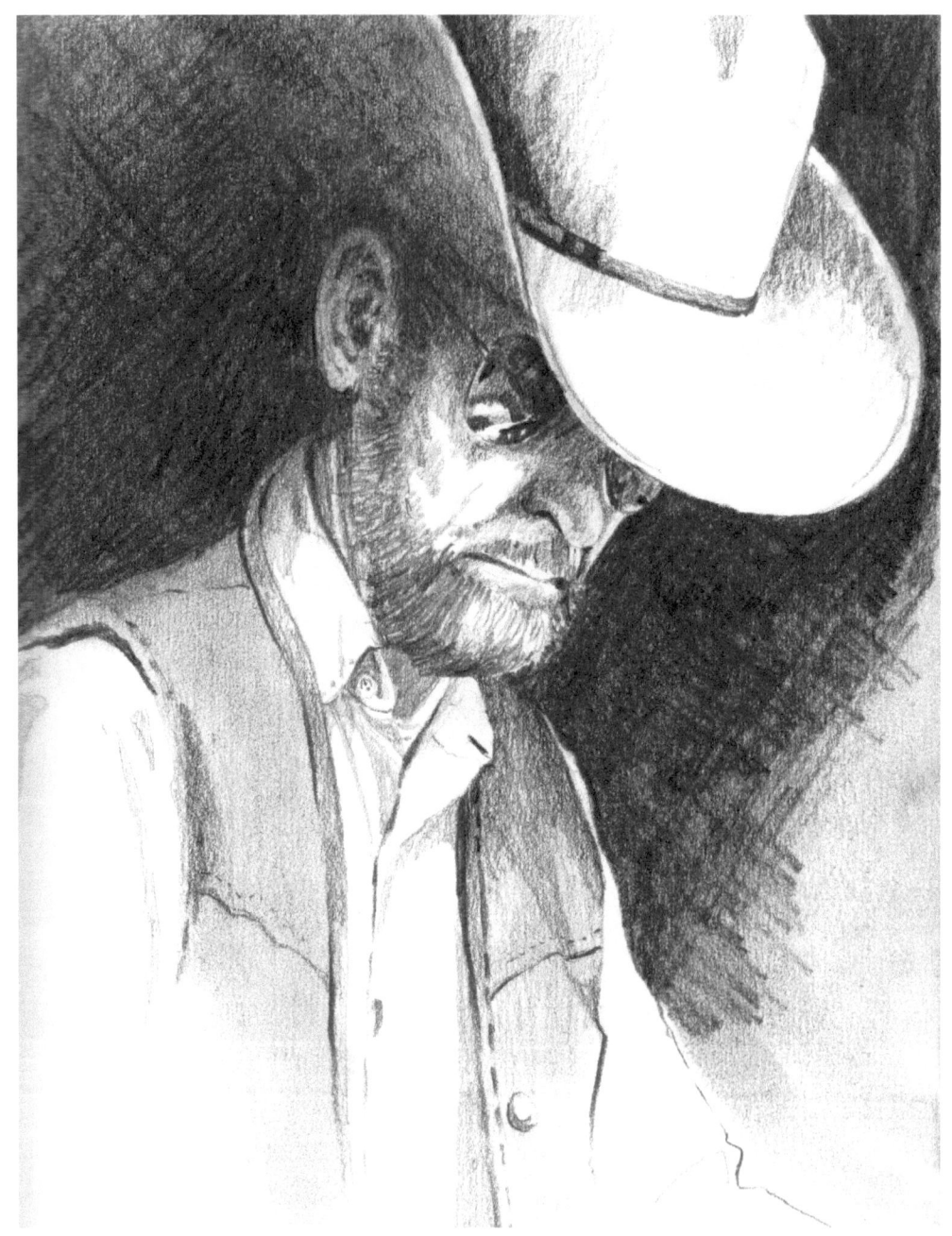

Cross hatching with a soft leaded pencil is a great way to go. Give it a try.

ASSIGNMENTS

TO PLAY WITH:

♦ Set dates with yourself to go out
  into the world and sketch. Put it
  on your calendar. Could be one
  hour, a week or a day. Just priori-
  tize the time for yourself.

♦ No one is watching. Draw with
  self abandonment and ease.

♦ Mix and match the exercises.
  Come up with some of your own.
  Be *conscious and think* about
  which methods you're using.

♦ Be aware.

♦ Sketch with ink, or paint without
  pencil first.

♦ Try my idea of sketching from a
  photograph. This is great when
  you actually cannot go outside.
  No excuses for not sketching.

♦ Enjoy the work experience. Salary
  is paid in confidence and skill and
  a full sketch-book. In other
  words -
  "Paid in full."

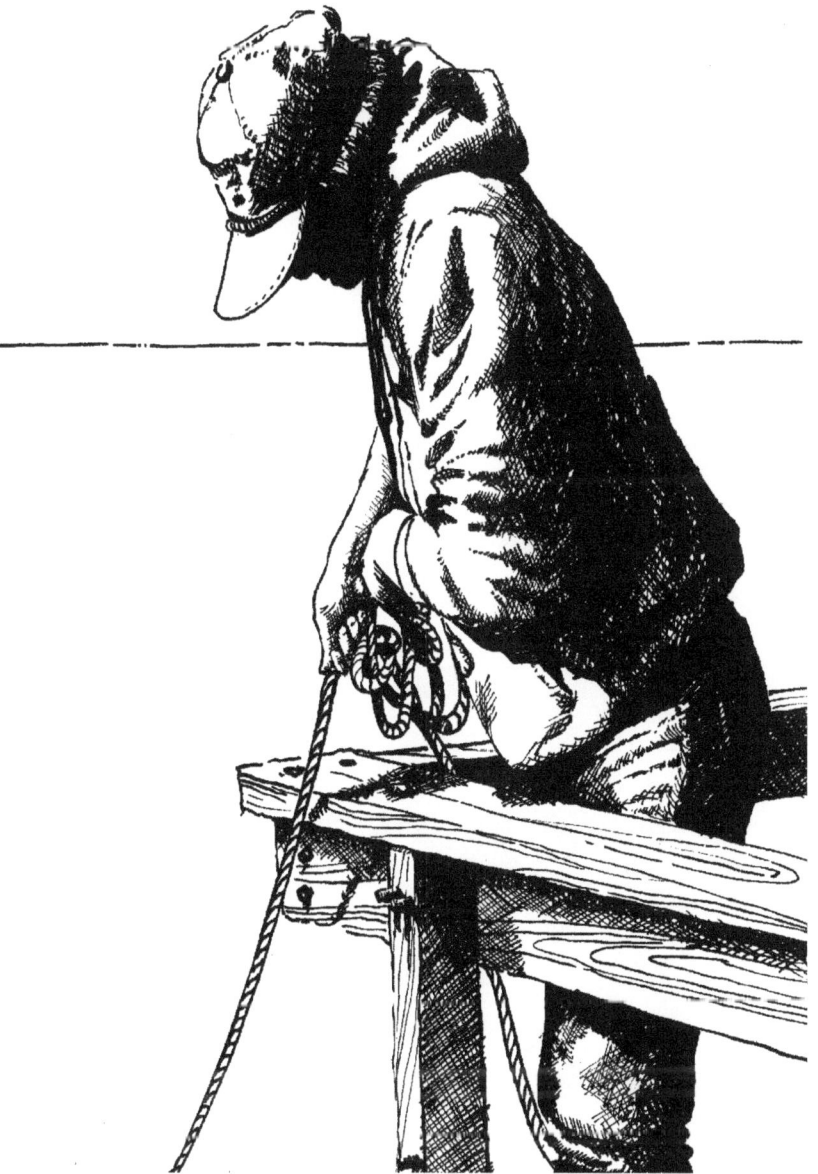

Mullet Fisherman in Pensacola, FL   *Ink crosshatching*

73

EXERCISE SIX
DRAWING WITH A BRUSH

Start with a pencil drawing and then with a brush dipped in ink or paint, block in shapes of light and dark. See puzzle pieces here. It's always amazing how little detail is actually needed to tell the story. This is a wonderful exercise and one of my favorites.

Next, try going directly to the ink or paint with no preliminary pencil drawing. Try doing this exercise in watercolor. It is excellent for honing brush skills. Also it's a perfect step from drawing into painting. With white paper, gray mid-tone and black you realize how simply paint can be used for drama. Give this a try in your book

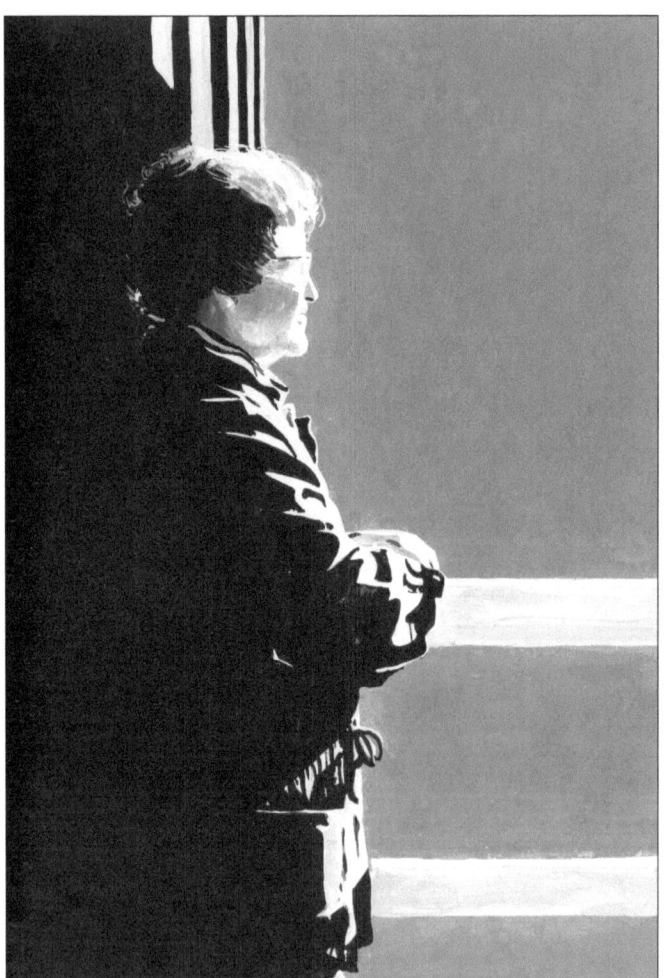 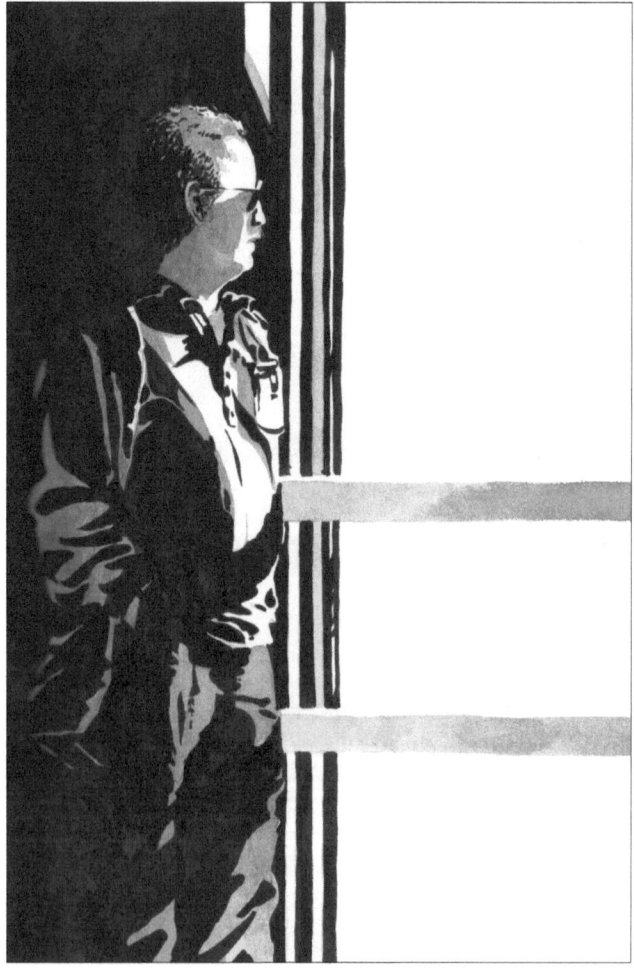

Here are two brush drawings done the same day from two photos of my husband and myself standing at a large window.

There are so many ways to draw. It is fun to think up ways to express yourself, or represent the awesome images we see around us every day. There simply is no limit. *Veterans Day* was done with a fine -tip marker. Working with ink makes you decisive. Drawing lightly with a pencil first may help the finished product. The watercolor sketch of *April* was done during a figure drawing session. These quick watercolor sketches are not meant to be finished paintings, however I find that in some cases, the fresh and spontaneous work is pleasing enough that I wish it was on nicer paper than is more commonly found in my sketchbooks.

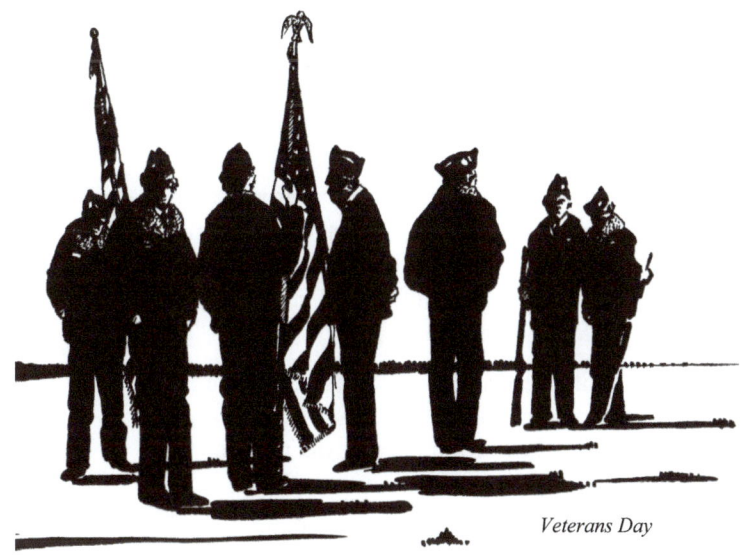

Veterans Day

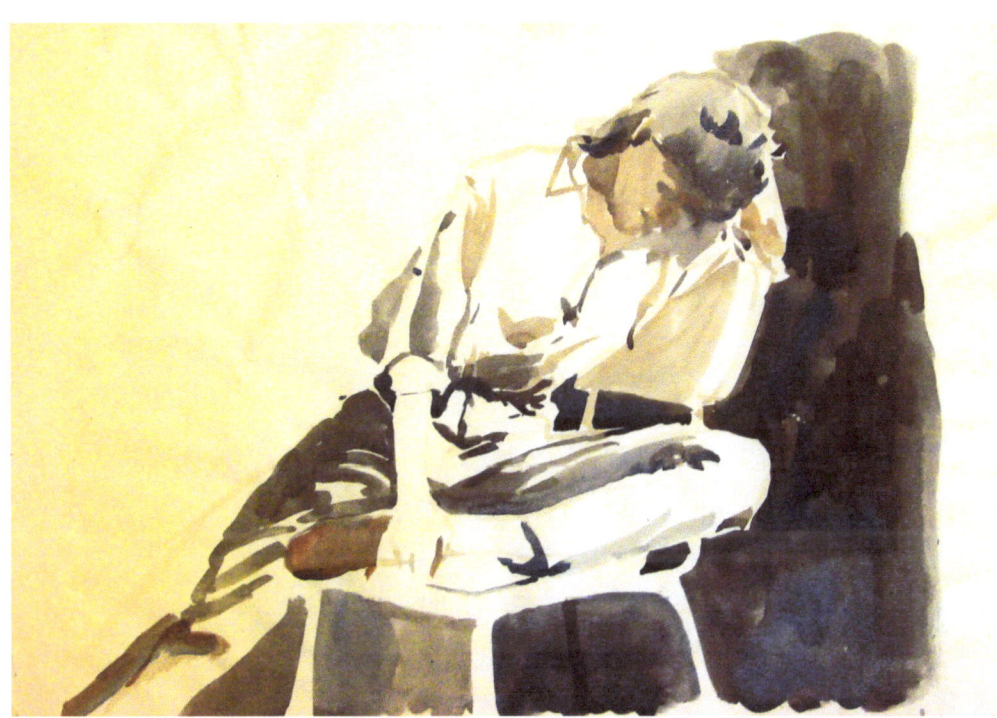

April   *direct watercolor sketch working from model*   *12 x 16*

More Assignments

♦ Find a small container like those restaurants give you with salad dressing. Put a small dab of one color in it. Try Payne's Gray or Burnt Umber. Grab a few brushes, your workbook and go out into the world to sketch directly with the brush. Again, these are exercises, not to be fussed over as a finished painting. Just let it flow off the brush.

♦ Go out a second time and this time take colors. Note which sketches you find more enjoyable...the color ones or the monochromatic. Pay attention to your preferences.

♦ Using a pen, do some contour drawings or even some blind contour drawings outside.

♦ Back in the studio, do a little painting with full color and then, with a pen, *doodle* over it creating internal patterns or simply outlining the contours of the shapes. This can be rather magical. See the African Women on the next page as an example of this *doodling*.

♦ Again in the studio, choose a photograph and try sketching directly from it. Redesign it. Play with it. Turn it into a value sketch for a future painting. Paint it in large hunks of light and dark with your brush. Drawing is satisfying in itself, but most of us want to go into painting. There's no substitute for spending many hours drawing. These exercises slip you easily into the painting process.

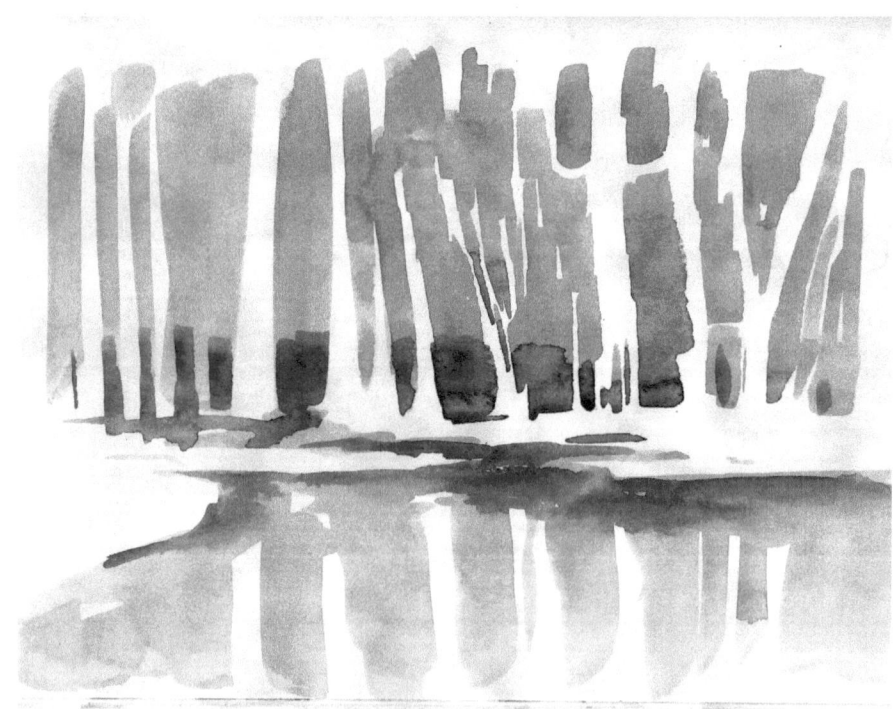

A fast watercolor brush drawing using negative spaces and simple values

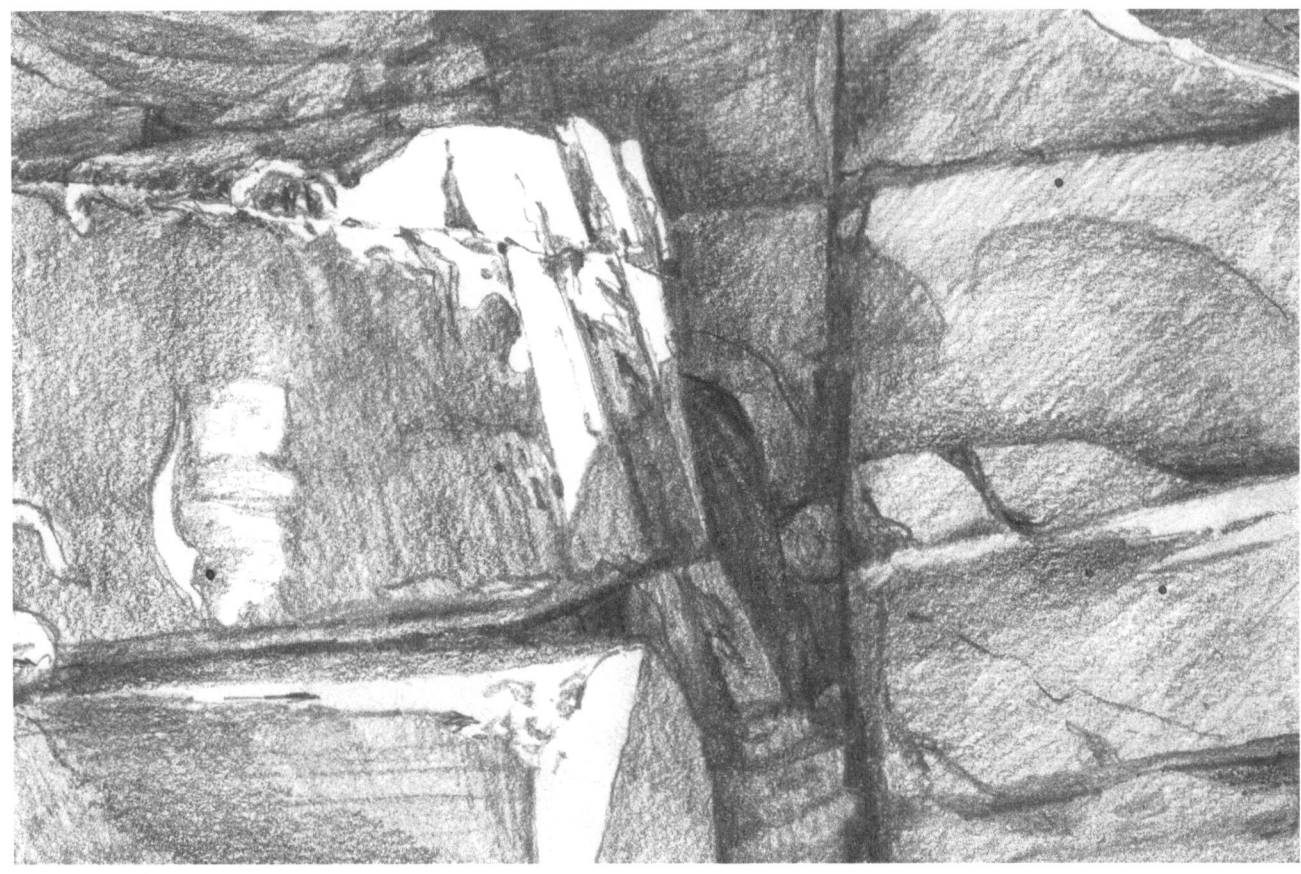

This is a redesigned sketch from a snapshot of rock surfaces.

USING PHOTOGRAPHS FOR SKETCHING?

REALLY?

Have you ever thought about sketching from a photo? The thought may seem strange, but I've found it to be a wonderful tool. It gives you the chance to redesign the image, but more importantly, when painting from the sketch you work just a little removed from reality. Personally, I love this approach and use it often. I use one or more photos, draw it in my sketchbook, then lose the photo and paint from the sketch alone. One of my little sketchbooks has any number of these redesigned photos. When I travel around teaching workshops and it's demo time, I get that book, choose a sketch and get going on the demo. Colors and details are not there, of course, so each painting is different even though I may have used the sketch before. If you have not done this exercise, I encourage you to give it a try. It frees you up far more than photo references alone, and it taps far more into your imagination which results in paintings that are not photo realistic and truly yours. That is desirable to me personally. How about you?

EXERCISE SEVEN
CONCENTRATING ON THE NEGATIVE SPACES

I have been talking a bit here and there about negative spaces without a real definition of what they are. So, let's spend a little time *thinking* about them and how they cannot only help you see shapes while drawing, but also how they are vital to the process of painting. Indeed, working with them is magnificent preparation for painting. This is particularly true with watercolor, my personal favorite, but it's very valuable to have a real grasp of this in your tool box no matter what medium you are using to draw or paint. When you can start *thinking* and seeing in terms of negative spaces, you automatically take a giant step along your own artistic journey. Each of the previous six exercises has its own role to play in building your skills and growing your confidence, but perhaps none more so than the

negative shapes.

In my paintings, I use negative spaces constantly by glazing over layers of color leaving negative shapes from previous layers.

OK. What are negative spaces anyway? They can be defined one of two ways. They can be the shapes around an object, or they can be the part you don't paint at any one step of the process. Note the little brush drawing of trees and water on the previous page (76). I painted the spaces around the trees, not the trees, but by doing so, the trees magically appear. It doesn't matter wheather you think of the brush marks as the negative space, or the tree as the negative space. Either way, you are seeing in a new way.

Being able to utilize negative shapes literally doubles the possibilities for you when you're drawing or painting.

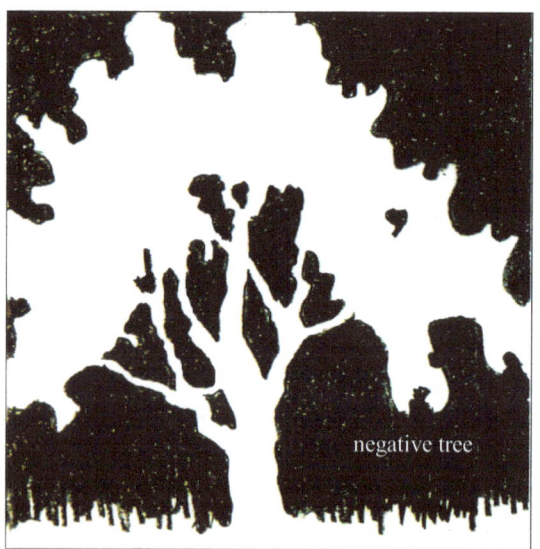

positive tree

negative tree

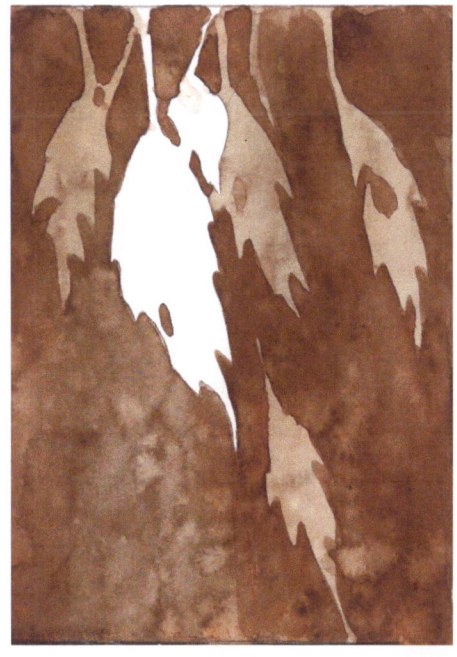

Step One: Paint around one or two shapes that will remain white (or as a negative shape).

Step Two: Paint around three or four more shapes leaving them as new negative spaces and also painting around the first two shapes (that were left white).

Step Three: Now create another layer of negative shapes by painting around the first two layers of shapes (leaves) and at the same time, create several more new negative shapes.
This is called glazing.

Step One   *Step Two*

ASSIGNMENTS USING NEGATIVE SPACES

1. Practice going around looking for negative spaces between things. Look for the holes between. Take a handful of pencils and pile them on a piece of typing paper so that they protrude off the edges. Draw the spaces between them and don't draw the pencils at all. Do it again, with leaves or blades of grass.

2. Try first one, then two and finally three layers of paint creating negative spaces on each layer with your brush. Study the examples of leaves on this page and do some similar exercises. Keep it fast and easy with no concern for a finished painting. This is an exercise, but nothing I could say about this exercise would do it justice when it comes to graduating into painting. Nothing. Work with this concept on several pages in your workbook and I think you will begin to see what I mean. *This is a golden tool*.

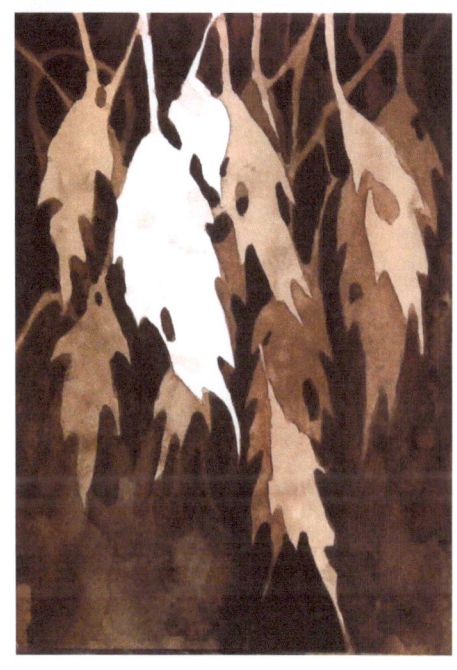

Step Three

TRAVELERS ON THE PLANET
SAILORS ON THE SEA
FOR RICH OR FOR POOR
WE'LL ALWAYS BE
    DRAWING OUR TIME
    WRITING OUR RHYME
CREATING THE LIFE WE SEE

WE OURSELVES
STAND AT THE HELM
OURS IS THE SHIP
OURS IS THE REALM
    WE CHART THE COURSE
    WE OWN THE FORCE
BLUNDERS TO OVERWHELM

WE LEARN
NEGLIGENCE DENYS US
AND STEADFAST RUDDERS
GUIDE US
    THOUGH NOT EVERY ATTEMPT
    IS FAILURE EXEMPT
WE LEARN STEERING IS EVER INSIDE US

EACH MOMENT GIVEN
EACH MOMENT WE SPEND
AWAKE OR UNCONSCIOUS
OUR LIVES WILL DEPEND
    HOW WE DREW THE TIME
    HOW WE WROTE THE RHYME
BEFORE OUR DAYS GO WITH THE WIND

2012

CREATIVE DIALOGUE

USE PHOTO ~ BUT CREATE ART

Unless you can divorce yourself from the photo you will never experience the joy that comes from creating something the likes of which the world has never seen.

You can completely redesign the information in the photo. You can choose parts and leave out other parts. You can change colors, proportions, center of interests, shapes, sizes or anything else that speaks to you - the artist. This is part of what I like to call *Creative Dialogue*.

Creative dialogue is when the paper and the paint speak ideas to you. The trick is to listen. Oh, I know this sounds ridiculous to some of you, but it does happen. Have you ever heard yourself say anything like this? *"I shouldn't have put that bush in the corner,"* or *"I wish I had made the sky a lighter gray."* That's what I'm talking about. Let the image speak. It will speak differently to you than it would to me, and that is the beauty and the magic of it all.

Here is a painting from my trip to Africa and the reference snapshot I took from the car window as we passed these people going about their daily lives. Actually, only two of the women were carrying babies. I gave one to the third woman because I

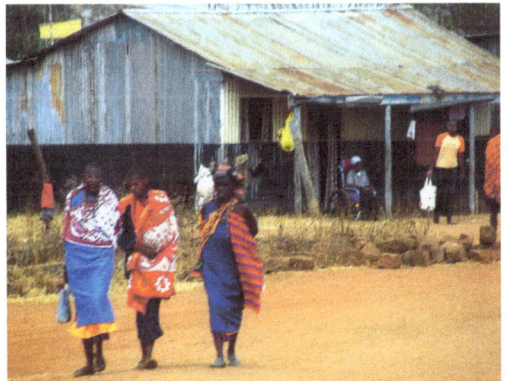

This image is here not only to convince you that photos are wonderful tools and never tyrants for copying, but also because the ink drawings on top of the painting had little to do with the actual images in the photo, or even the painting. They are simply doodles.

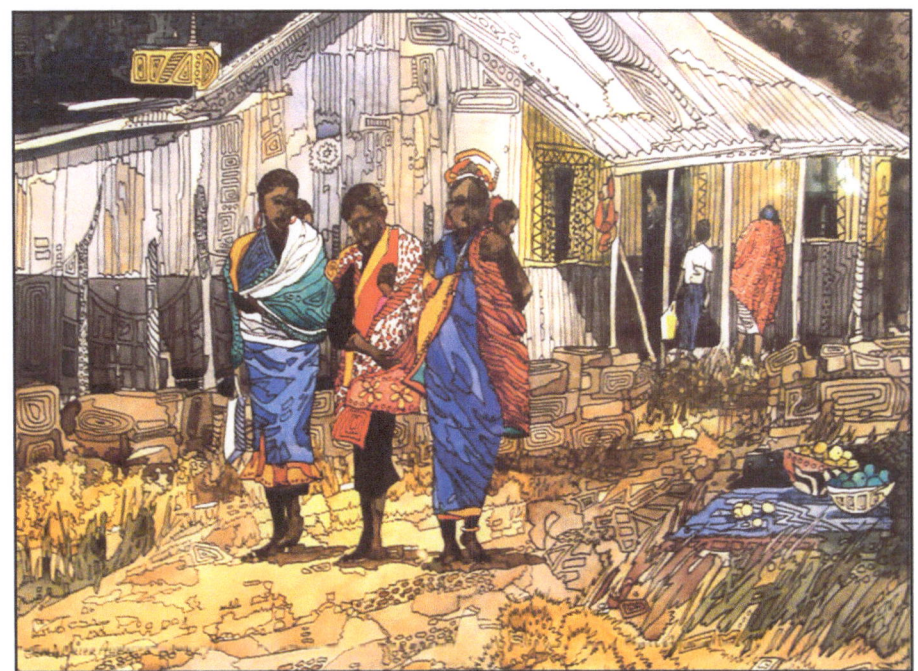

African Mothers   watercolor   *10 x 14*

wanted the title to be *African Mothers*. This is creative dialogue in action even in choosing a title. Of course, I used suggestions the photo gave me, but then I went off in directions the painting and I wanted to go together.

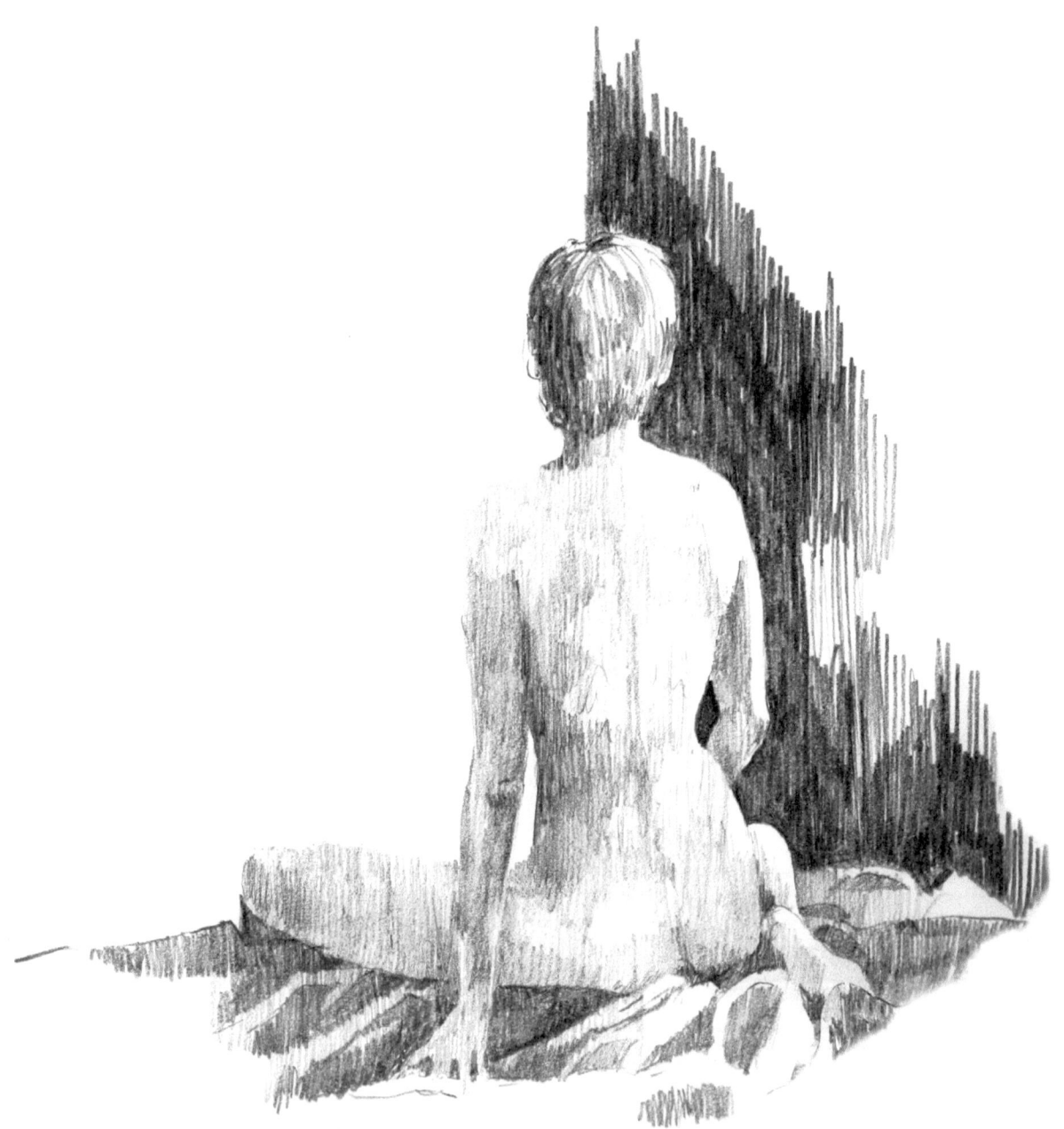

Pencil drawing of model where I blocked in forms of light, mid-tones and darks with straight lines.   *7 x 9*

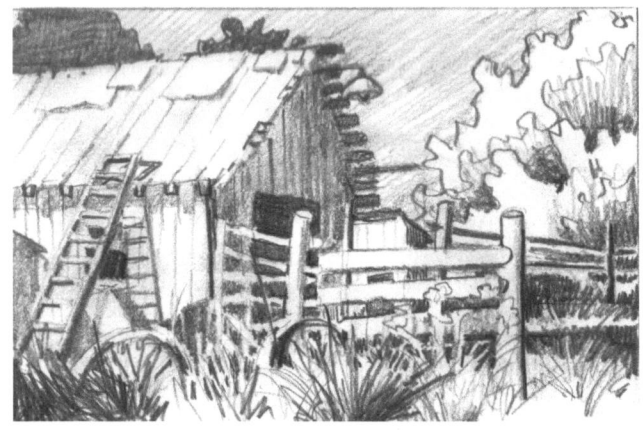

Pencil Sketch - Leroy's Barn

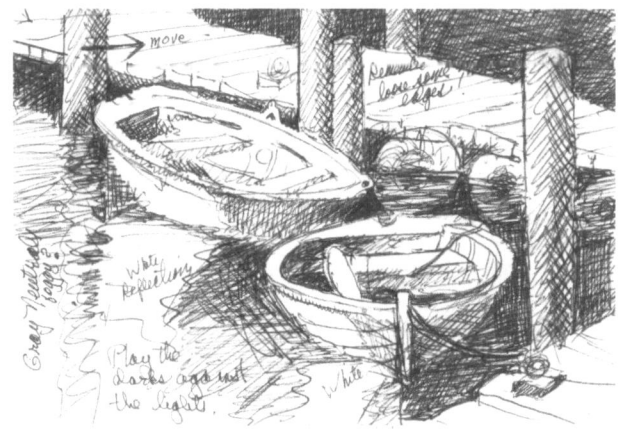

Ballpoint Pen Sketch

A FINAL NOTE ON DRAWING ~ IN OTHER WORDS, AN EXCUSE TO REPEAT MYSELF

Here's an important bit of *thinking* to put into your head.   Keep these exercises on your "to-do" list—not just while studying this book, but always. For instance, doing blind contour drawings every once in a while is an excellent use of time. It sharpens your senses and your skills. Just because you've done it once, doesn't mean you need not ever do it again. On the contrary, *because* you now know how, you'll be able to continue doing it repeatedly in the future. I'm talking to myself here as much as to you. With *every* exercise presented here the frequency of repetition is directly related to the speed of development of that skill. Whether it is drawing, playing the flute or practicing yoga, the time spent reaps the reward.

As I mentioned earlier, there is no free lunch. Developing the habit of drawing pays off big time in all your future art work. Even those persons working in abstract images benefit from drawing. The only way to hone skills is to use them. That's a fact we all know. Imprint it. There are many approaches to drawing and many books on that subject alone. I have tried to present a few general yet diverse types of drawing that with use become habits in seeing.

Michelangelo is credited with saying something like this: *"An artist draws with his eyes, not with his hands."*

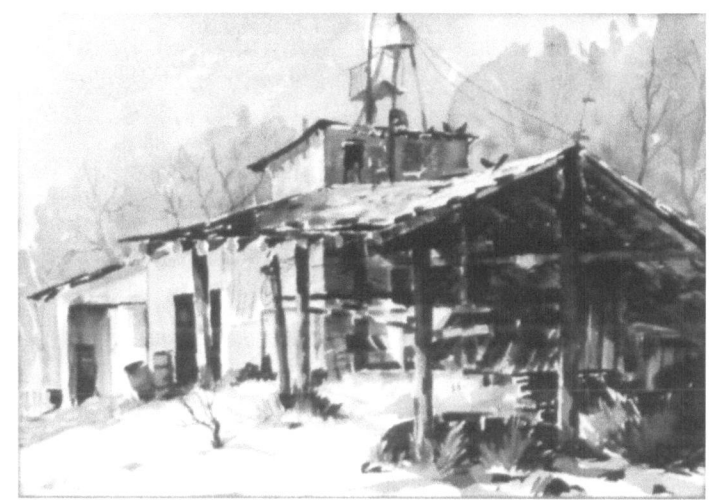

Watercolor Sketch painted in my car   *12 x 16*

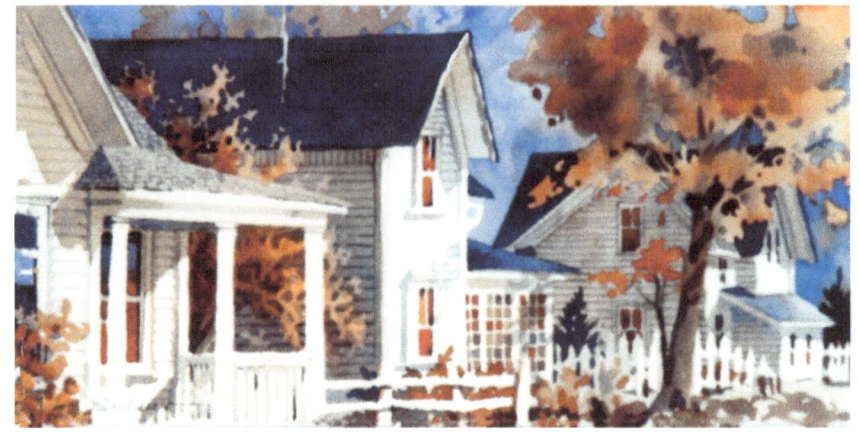

Americana   *watercolor*   *6 x 14*

COME PERSPECTIVE COME

LIKE QUIET DOVE DESCEND

COME SPREAD YOUR WINGS

COME SPREAD YOUR PEACE

THAT I MIGHT FLY AGAIN.

1982

*O*f course this tiny poem is not referring to perspective in the drawing sense, but rather to perspective on living life. So very often I can't help but notice with awe and wonderment how the very words we use to describe the making of art relate so easily to the very same words we use in philosophical terms about our lives.

Personally, I don't think it is coincidental.

84

CHAPTER FOUR

THE WIZARDRY OF PERSPECTIVE AND THE TRICKS IT PLAYS

FEATURING PAINTINGS AND PERSPECTIVE DRAWINGS

About 15 years ago I took a workshop on perspective from a friend, Richard Bird, who, at the time, was head of the art department at Ricks College in Idaho and a very fine artist indeed. It was just a one-day class comprised of professionals who wanted a deeper knowledge about perspective, and Richard certainly delivered. We drew corners of rooms with furniture and mirrors on the wall reflecting the perspective of the room and its contents in reverse. It was great fun, a wonderful day, and it all made perfect sense to me...at the time.

For the most part though, a simple lay person's description is sufficient. If one of your intangible tools is an extremely analytical mind, the whole technical approach could actually be fun and exhilarating instead of terrifying. In that case, you will find a book or teacher who plunges you deeper. It's all good stuff especially after you've been drawing a while. But for most of us it's probably *not* the best place to start. Right now thinking about perspective in its most challenging intricate details is not my goal.

In this chapter I will present a few basic principles and thought processes that when fully in your consciousness will take you a long way without much frustration. I use these lessons in my workshops and have been thanked for them. Hopefully, these little tricks will take some of the bafflement out of perspective for you.

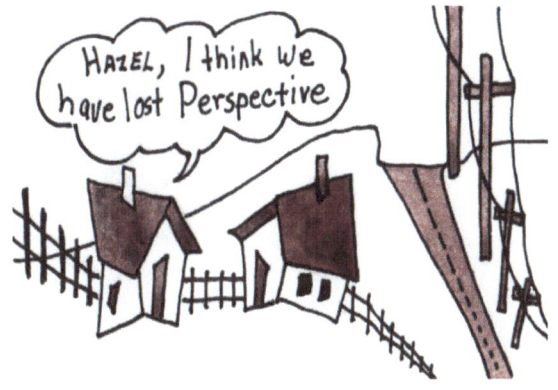

Perspective really is *wizardry*, and a basic understanding of it is essential for anyone trying to draw things in this three dimensional world in which we live, walk, draw and paint.

WHAT IS PERSPECTIVE ~ REALLY?

When you stop and think about it, perspective is all about *optical illusions*. It's all about tricking your viewer into believing or seeing depth and dimensions on a piece of paper or canvas that is flat. Isn't that really what we are trying to do...trick people's eyes? We want to create the illusion of depth when there cannot actually be depth. We want to play games with the viewer's head, to pull off a little magic pure and simple. That is the purpose, the goal, the effect, the use and the true wizardry of good perspective know how.

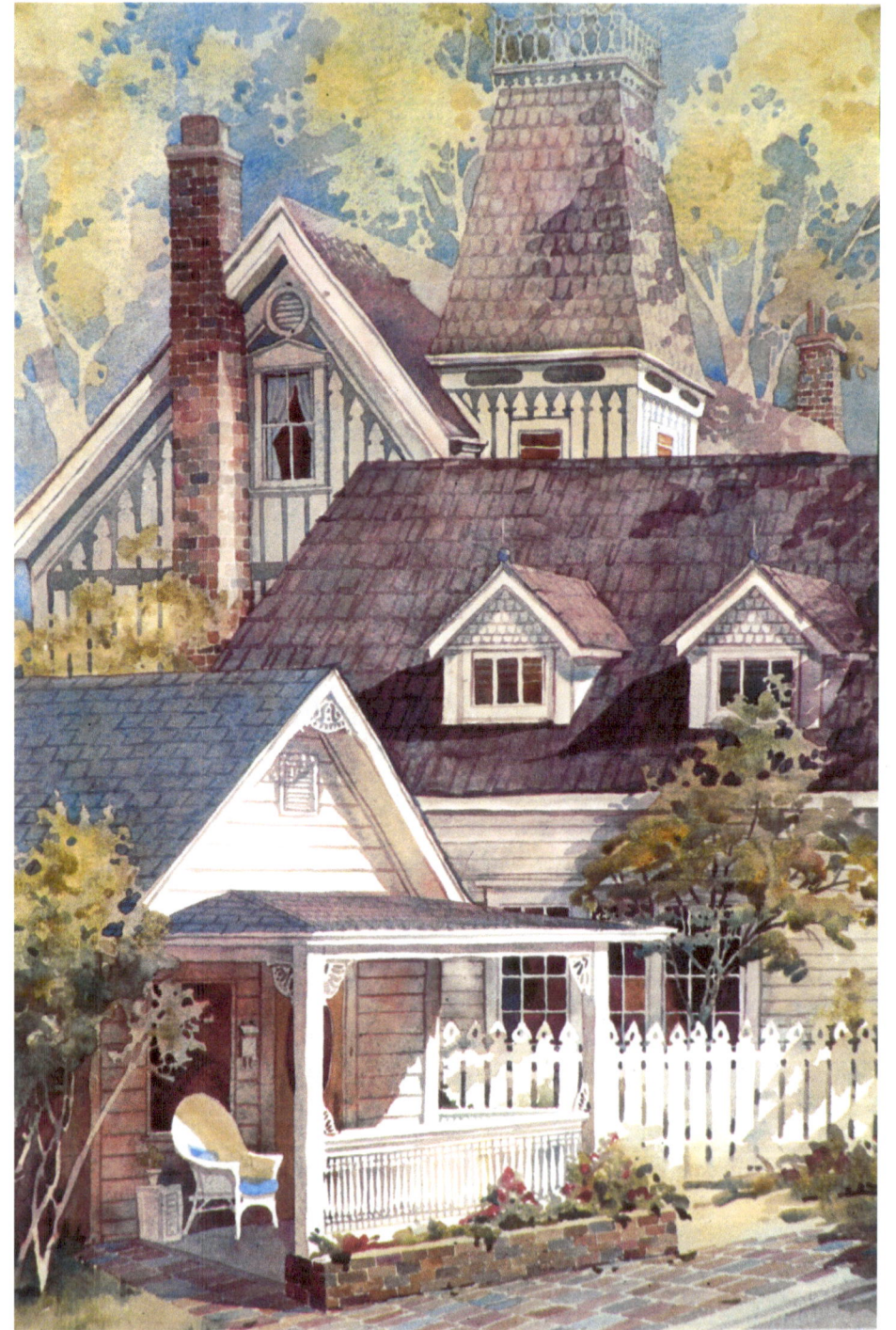

Village USA ~ Eureka Springs   *watercolor*   *15 x 10*

SIX SPECIAL EFFECTS ~ TO TRICK THE EYE

We want perspective know how at our drawing boards. Every one of us has drawn buildings and other objects that somehow just didn't sit right on the page. So let's spend time *thinking* about and gaining better skill and understanding in the perspective department.

Having discussed what perspective actually is, an optical illusion, it's now time to learn about six simple tricks that help accomplish that. We'll get to one- and two-point perspective later, but we'll start at what I believe is the beginning of understanding the perspective challenge...I simply call it:

SPECIAL EFFECTS
1. Horizon Line
2. Size
3. Overlapping
4. Climbing the picture plane
5. Shading
6. Ellipticals

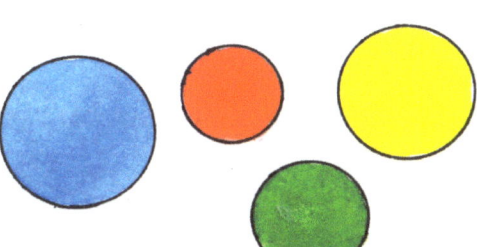

The use of *relative size* seems like a no-brainer at first, but as we spend a little time *thinking* about *size,* we discover its ramifications, its limitations and its sneakiness. If I paint four balls of differing sizes on a piece of paper, we are very limited in what we can deduce about their *relative size* or

their *perceived* distance from us. They appear to be floating and so could be close or far away. We simply do not know. Let's play around with this simple illustration using the same four balls and see what the first four *special effects* can do.

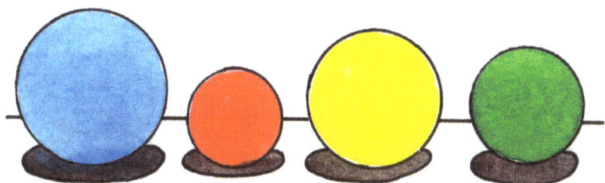

By lining up the balls and drawing a simple line—a table top, or a *horizon line*, the balls suddenly relate to something...the line. The addition of the line (*horizon*) begins to show some depth. If I place the base of each ball in a straight row they *appear* to be the same distance from us. Now we know for certain they are four different sizes.

When I incorporate *overlapping*, it leaves no doubt which ball is closer and which is farther, but here I've also incorporated the third special effect— *climbing the picture plane*. Now they appear to recede convincingly. Note the base of the red ball is significantly higher on the page than the blue.

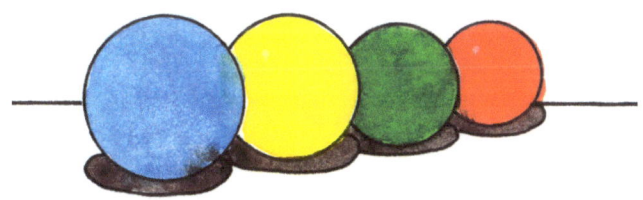

When we arrange the same balls according to size, starting with the largest, they *appear* to recede. In this illustration, I've lined up the centers of the balls which automatically makes the bases of each of the balls *climb the picture plane*.

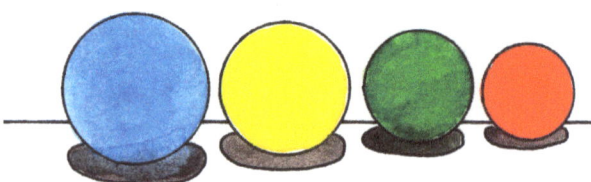

What happens when we exaggerate *climbing the picture plane* just a little, and use *overlapping*? We can tell exactly which ball is in front, and which is behind and they now begin to read as if they could be close in size simply because the closer one is largest and the farthest one is smallest. However, notice it's the position of their bases higher or lower on the page (the picture plane) that really tells the story. Their *relative size* by its self cannot describe this scene satisfactorily.

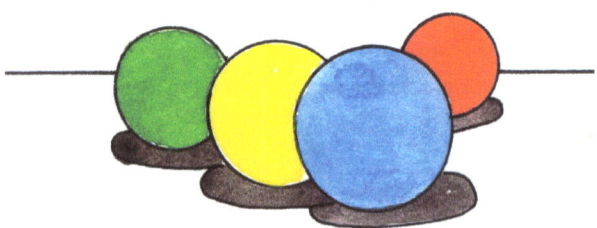

What do I mean by the picture plane? Simply that when objects are drawn higher on the paper, they appear to be farther away. Their placement (up or down) is critical. Perhaps you never thought about it before in quite this manner, and probably would not

have considered it part of perspective, but I believe it is the basic understanding that leads us naturally into vanishing points and linear perspective. In fact, *climbing the picture plane* is where the magic begins.

Normally, the largest ball would seem closer. Let's see if I can make it appear to be the farthest away. Climbing the picture plane will trump relative size all together every time. Note the base of each ball.

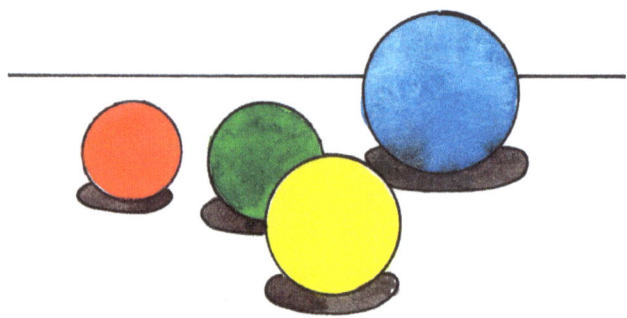

YOUR ASSIGNMENT

USING THE FIRST FOUR SPECIAL EFFECTS

In your workbook spend an hour discovering what you can do with a *horizon line, relative size, overlapping and climbing the picture plane*. First, draw four similar balls and make the little red ball appear closest. You'll see how *relative size* is *relative* no longer. After bouncing these balls around, try drawing bottles, pumpkins, boxes, or whatever you like. See how far you can push the first four special effects. Get these concepts solidly in your tool box. As in previous chapters, simply looking at what I've done will not be worth much. You should *do* it.

In the painting ***Extravaganza*** the small rocks are *not* farthest away, though the closer ones *are* the largest. With this vertical format, it's easy to see how the use of *overlapping* and *climbing the picture plane* are the special effects that tell the story. Here again, r*elative size* of individual rocks is *irrelevant.* However, where the *base* of each rock is drawn in relationship to the picture plane *is absolutely* relevant. Notice how the perceived horizon is very *high* on the paper in this painting. In fact, where is it? Keep reading.

When we look out at any landscape our eyes are approximately at the horizon line. As objects get closer to our feet, they get lower and lower on our visual plane. That's why this works. Drawing higher or lower on the page creates the *illusion* of depth.

This works perfectly until we start drawing things over head—*above* the horizon—*above* eye-level. Now it is the exact opposite. The placement of the horizon line affects the placement of everything else. So let's shift our *thinking* and see how this trick relates to things *above* the perceived horizon line. It's the same rule actually, but up-side-down.

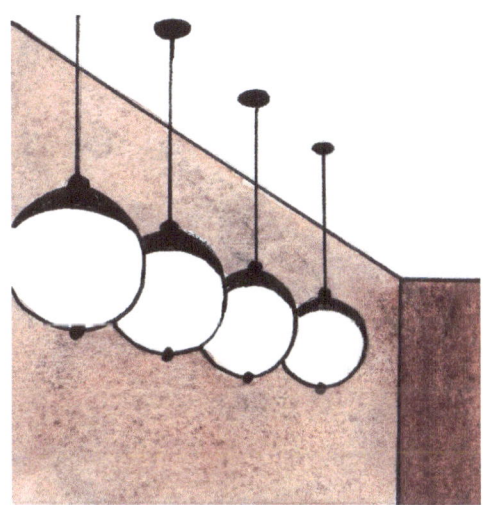

Perceived Horizon Line

We must reverse the rules when draw-ing objects over-head or *above* eye-level. You've used this principle in the past but perhaps without consciously understanding its role in *perspective*.

Using it *consciously* adds believability, confidence and clarity to your work.

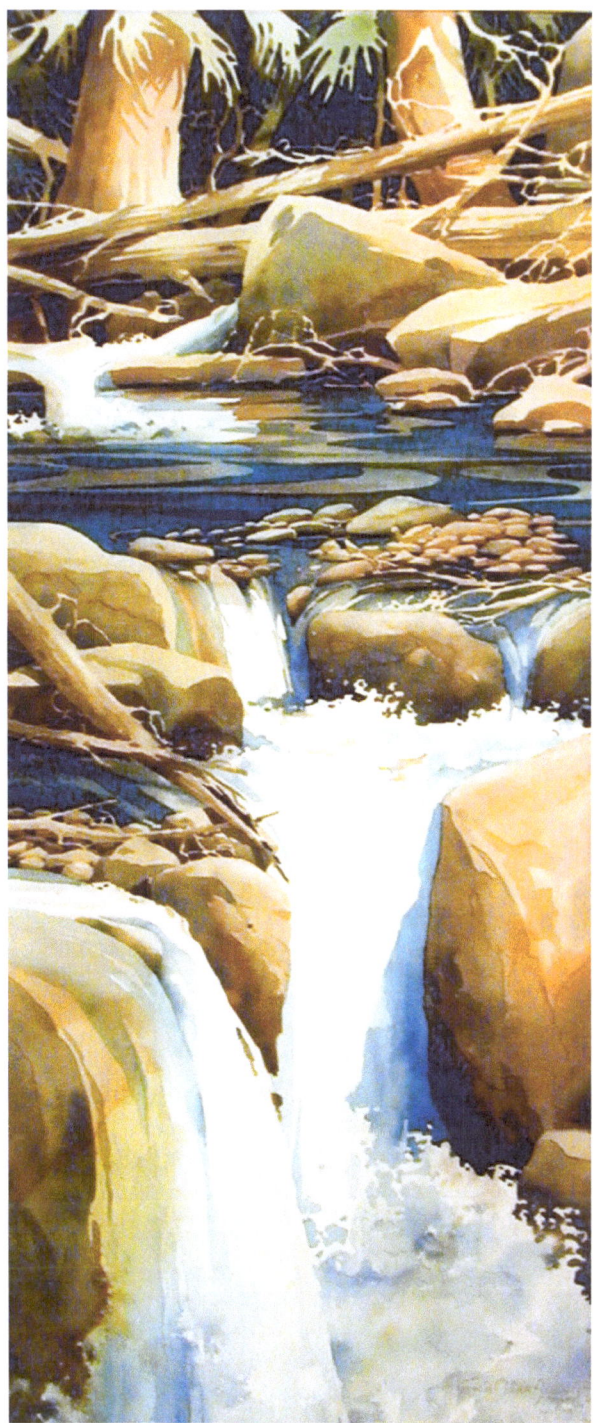

Extravaganza   *oversized watercolor*   *40 x 25*

I'll repeat: "Our eyes are approximately at the horizon line." Whenever we draw objects overhead or *above* eye level, such as lights hanging from a ceiling, the rule switches around. In this scenario, as objects *descend* the page, they *appear* to be farther away. You see how this leads us into one- and two-point perspective? If not, keep reading.

The horizon line is where everything shifts. Above it, objects slant the opposite way they do below it. This is necessary knowledge.

THE FIFTH EFFECT ~ SHADING

I remember the exact day in St. Louis, MO, in third grade when an older girl showed me how shading made objects look round. I spent weeks shading everything in my coloring books. Funny how well I can remember that day and what an impressive discovery it was to my youthful self. At the time, it seemed enormous, and although most of my friends simply were not impressed, I was hooked. Shading had magic. As an adult, I spent years perfecting the technique of graded washes with watercolors. Making things appear round like apples, faces and flowers, I grew skilled at making a smooth gradual change from light to dark. Interesting to note that later in life I became intrigued with flat washes that go from light to dark abruptly without shading. For many years there's been little shading in my work. A personal preference will emerge.

~

Still, I fervently believe you need a grasp on shading and what it can do before you can either use it effectively or abandon it altogether.

The *thought process* your brain goes through *thinking* about shading is what makes or breaks the believability of round objects, and yes, I do consider this part of perspective. You must pursue learning about light and the shadows that create shading.

Spend some valuable time practicing and *thinking* about how shading can trick and coax depth and 3-D qualities onto flat paper. Here are some simple shapes for you to look at, but then your assignment is to shine a lamp on some objects on your table with all other lights out. Talk about magic! The core shadows, shading and cast shadows are exquisite.

Learn the beauty captured by light and shadow.

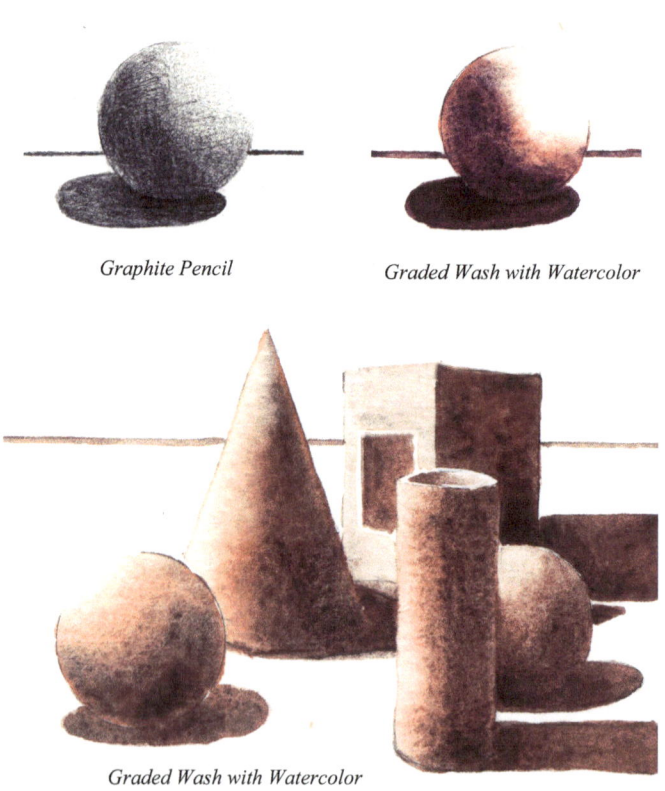

Graphite Pencil   *Graded Wash with Watercolor*

Graded Wash with Watercolor

6TH SPECIAL EFFECT ~ THINKING ABOUT THE ELLIPTICAL

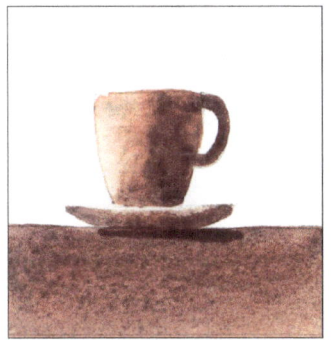 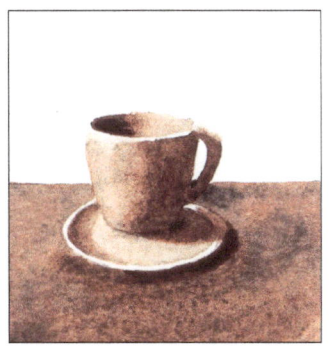 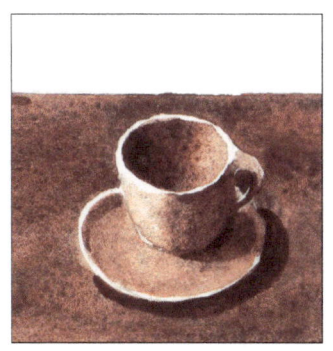 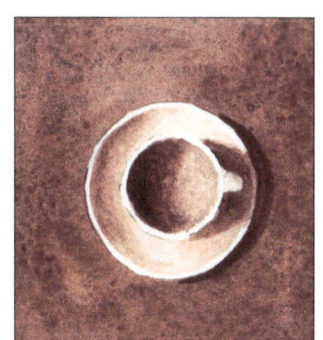

Understanding how an *elliptical* creates form, depth or the *illusion* of 3-dimensions is essential to drawing convincing trees, flowers, faces, cups and thousands of other objects. The placement of and curvature of an *elliptical* changes dramatically as the table top (or horizon) moves up or down on the picture plane. Notice the progressive changes in the illustrations above. As the table edge climbs the picture plane, the elliptical opening in the cup must also change.

Place a glass on a table and lower your face till your eyes are nearly even with the edge of the table closest to you until you cannot see any elliptical opening in the glass at all. Now rise up slowly until you are directly over the top of the glass. Observe the elliptical or oval going from a line to a circle. Own that observation.

When drawing, the placement or the *perceived* placement of that horizon affects literally everything else and therefore should be decided first. I say *perceived* horizon because as previously mentioned with many paintings the horizon is completely out of the picture plane. It can be above or below it, but *consciousness* of its location is absolutely critical.

Learn to see every rounded object as if you could see through it to its back side. This is *drawing through*.

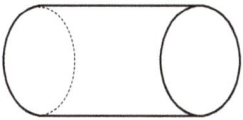

Notice below how the incorrect placement of the table top (horizon) in relationship to the elliptical prevents the cup from settling convincingly on the page. That line is always important to *think* about.

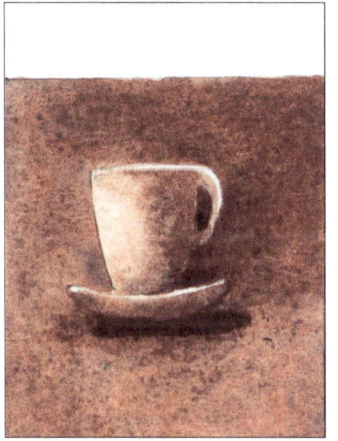 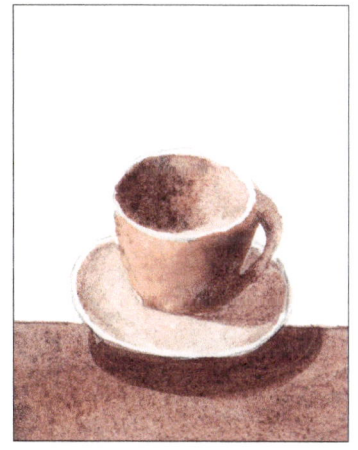

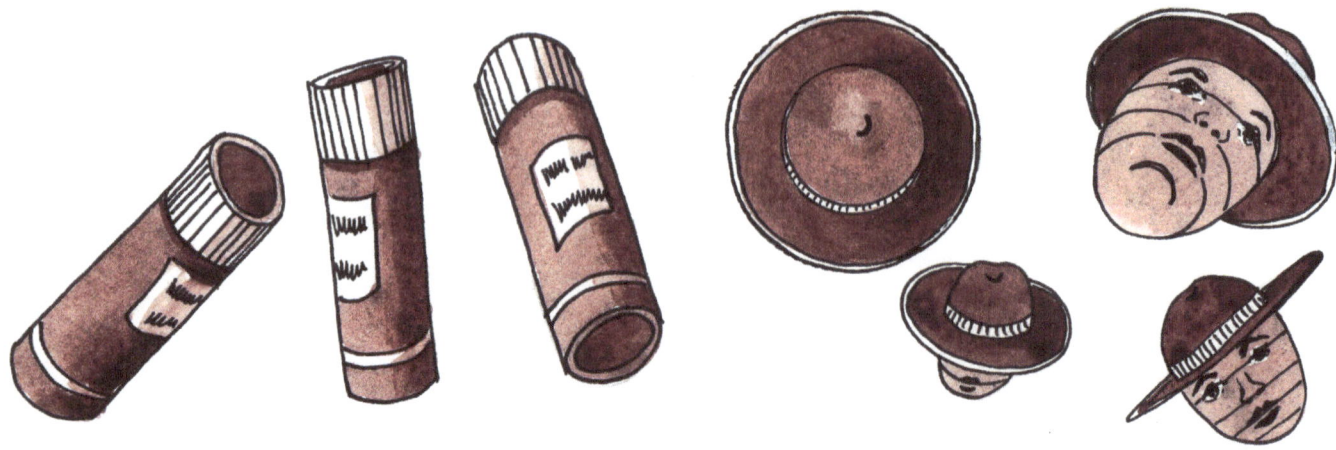

A simple way to remember all this is to think about the closest part of any elliptical as a smile or frown. Put frown marks on a tree trunk and it will *appear* round and *appear* to lean away from you. Smile marks on a tree trunk will make it *appear* round and *appear* to lean toward you. Is this not magic?

Play with this concept in your workbook. Twist and turn objects in the air. Gain command of the six special effects: horizon line, size, overlapping, climbing/descending the picture plane, shading and finally ellipticals. Fill several pages in your workbook. Now we are ready for one- and two-point perspective.

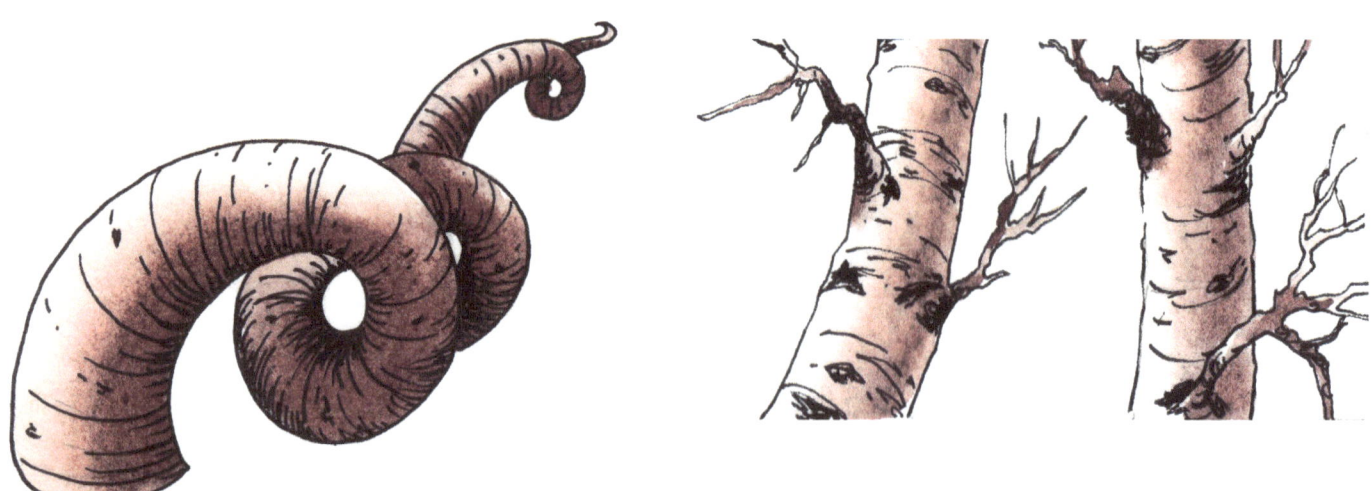

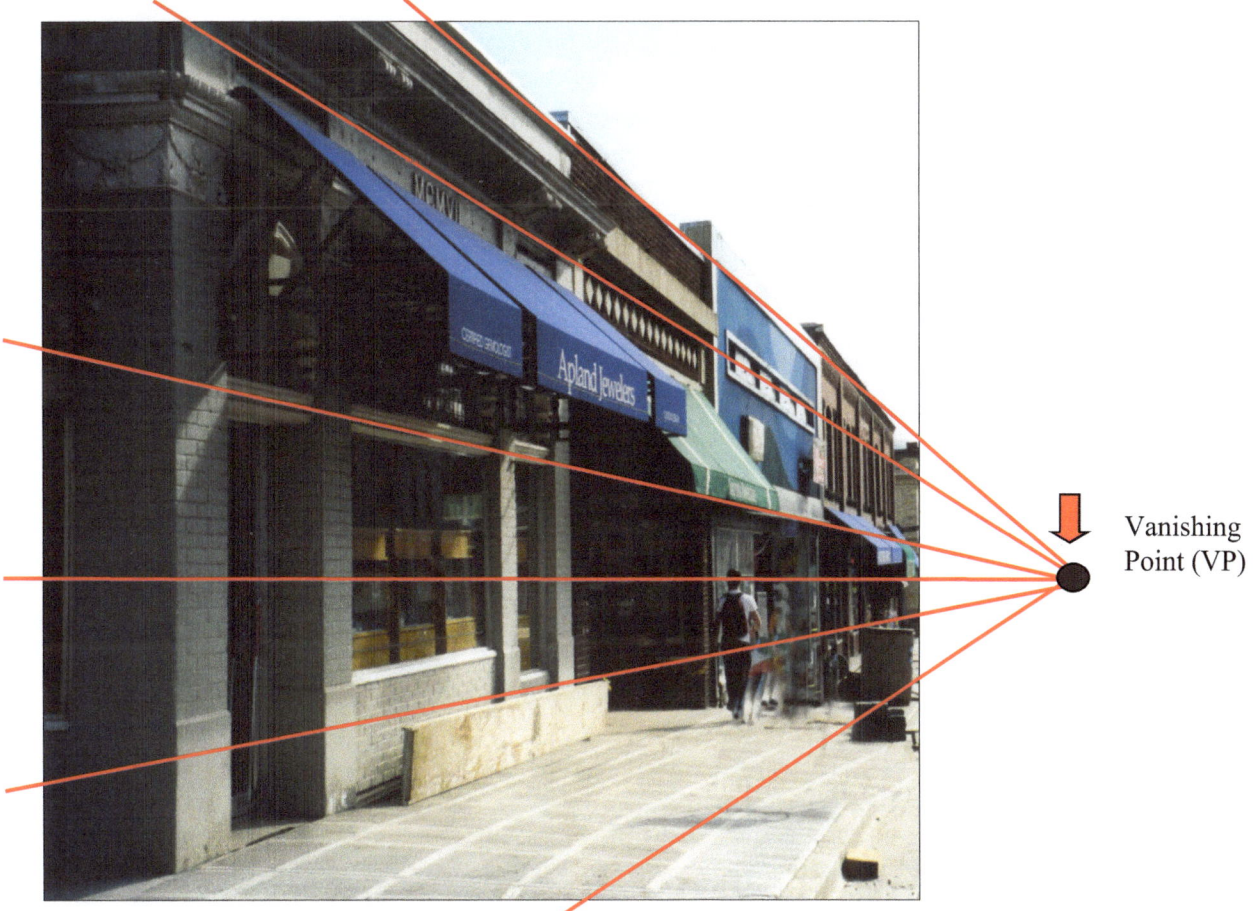

Vanishing
Point (VP)

This little photo shows us so much about the *spokes* radiating from the vanishing point (VP), which is in this case, completely off the picture plane.

The *spokes* affect every surface on the *fronts* of the buildings, but do not involve the *vertical lines*. In this photo, you cannot see the sides of the buildings but they would not relate to these spokes either. Be aware, however, that those two planes have vanishing points of their own ~ but again, I'm getting ahead of myself.

Let's dig into this with some more illustrations and drawings that will help us solve the perspective

dilemmas involved in reproducing such a scene as this one. Every spoke must go to the same VP.

Before we go further though, can you point to the spoke that would be perceived as the horizon line? We can not see a horizon line, but we can perceive it. If you don't know, read on. After you've read the next part about *One- and Two-Point Perspective*, you will be able to name it decidedly, so let's keep going.

Notice the painting of the street car on the next page. Study how VP spokes relate to this painting.

ONE- AND TWO-POINT PERSPECTIVE

By the time I was in sixth grade, I was fascinated by drawing and also baffled by it. There were many things I could draw fairly well because I practiced drawing a lot. I remember sitting in Mother's flower garden in Topeka, KS, drawing iris in particular. The more I drew them, the more beautiful they seemed. The marks on my paper were beginning to perform, but not for all subjects— buildings for instance. I was stumped by something that at the time I didn't even have a word for. The word was perspective.

I remember lying on my bed trying to draw the ceiling, the corner of my room and my open door. I could not settle it on the page in any convincing manner and for quite some time I remained stumped. Eventually, I learned to draw those angles simply by observation and stubbornness. Perspective was hard fought for me and remained somewhat intuitive, illusive and intimidating for years. I learned to sight the angles eventually, but it was still somewhat daunting.

When in my 20s and living in New Jersey, the local YMCA asked if I'd teach a class on perspective. Being optimistic, I said, "Yes," and that's when my real knowledge base began. Of course, by then I knew the word, but in high school art classes, words like perspective were a bit tossed to the winds. It was the late 50s, and art was being pushed aggressively toward non objective abstract— or as we called it back then, Modern-Art. There were so many groovy boundaries to break, and we were told over and over, "Just put your feelings on the paper, Baby, and let it all hang out."

Preparing to teach that class, I found a book about perspective in the library. Upon examination, I was not only shocked by what I read about something called a 'vanishing point,' but frankly, I didn't believe a word of it. What on earth were they talking about? I got out some of my old barn paintings, found a piece of string, and proceeded to test the validity of this theory. To my surprise, the angles on my barns followed fairly closely the angles of a vanishing point. I became a believer and drawing buildings began to lose some of its mystery. So, yes, you can learn to use perspective by learning to sight angles, but it is a blessing to learn about vanishing points. For me, it was a great late discovery.

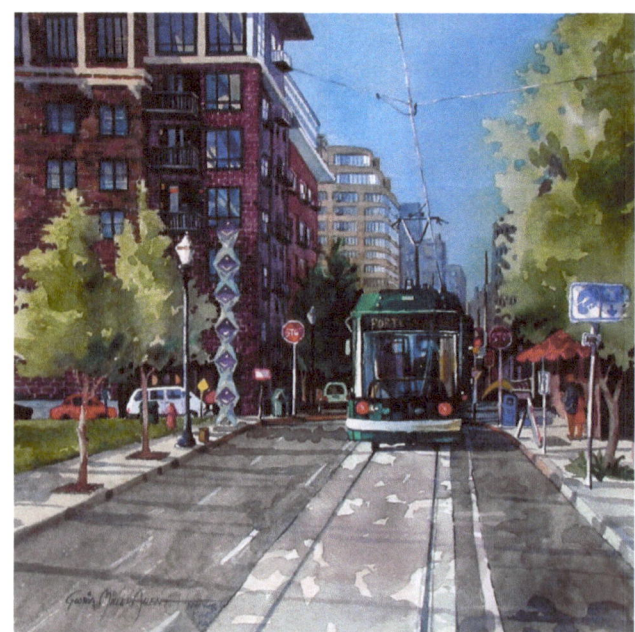

Take the Street Car ~ *Portland, OR Pearl District   watercolor   10 x 10*

ONE-POINT PERSPECTIVE ~ THE HORIZON LINE KEY

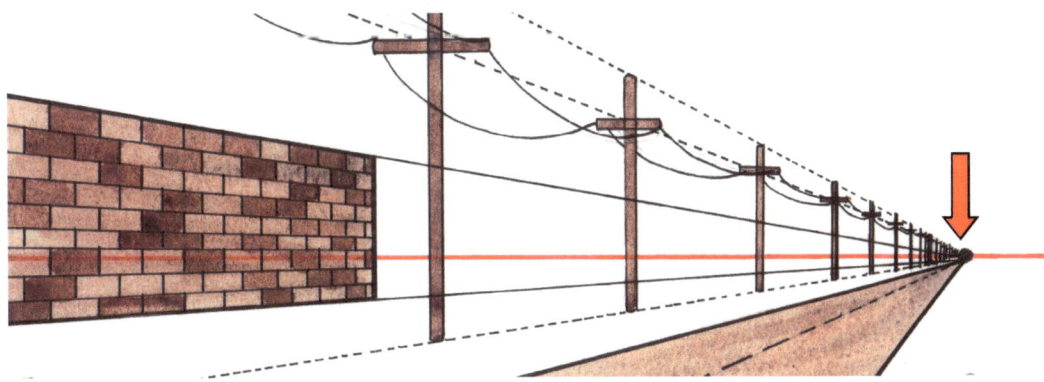

The vanishing point is where the farthest telephone pole and the road vanish *from sight and it's* always *on the horizon or perceived horizon line. In this illustration the red arrow points to the vanishing point and the red line indicates the horizon line. Both items are necessary to understanding perspective.*

While tackling this universal problem in drawing, the fact that eye level is at the perceived horizon line is basic. Repeating that:

"The horizon line is at eye level."

Earlier in this chapter, we started down this line of reasoning by *climbing* and *descending* the picture plane. The next logical step is the *vanishing point* which brings us into one-point perspective.

First, understand that you can place the horizon line anywhere, up or down, on the picture plane. You can even put it completely *off* the picture plane. It can be perceived *above* the top or *below* the bottom of the paper, but it *cannot* be ignored. You must give yourself and your viewer some clues as to its location, or the image will not sit convincingly on the paper. The horizon is the perfect place to begin any drawing. *(Non objective abstract doesn't relate.)*

So, your first decision—where to put the horizon? We know that when looking out upon a landscape,

the objects *appear* to get smaller as they get farther away. We've played with that; so next let's *think* about very tall objects that actually cross over the horizon line, such as telephone poles and buildings. Now the vanishing point becomes all important. Telephone poles seem to be the standard when it comes to showing vanishing points because they are uniform in size...buildings are not. The top of each telephone pole is *above* the horizon line, and the bases are *below*. Remember, the horizon line is at eye level. When cell towers make telephone poles obsolete, whatever will the next generation of artists use to show the vanishing point?

All you have to remember is that *everything* changes at that horizon. That's a simple but oh-so-important realization. Literally, everything relates to that one line. As we discovered earlier, objects drawn above the horizon *descend* as they recede, and objects drawn *below* the horizon *climb* as they recede. This makes perfect sense while we're looking at an illustration like the one above, but when we are out somewhere painting a barn on location, all that stuff we thought we knew while looking at the book abandons us, and we find ourselves stumped again much as I was while trying to draw the corner of my room in sixth grade. Confronting perspective head-on is challenging at any age. Why is that so?

I believe the reason for this befuddlement is because our brains actually fight us on this issue. We've grown accustomed to our brain helping us solve problems so it's hard to ignore what it is telling us. However, when drawing, we must learn to ignore some of what the brain is saying and learn to rely on what the eyes are seeing instead. Let's just call this *"Optical Illusions 101"* and work toward getting the degree.

Here's how I think it works. Our brain *knows* the telephone pole a mile away is actually the same size as the one closest to us—that's a fact, but our eyes *see* the poles shrinking. Our brain *knows* absolutely for certain that the rows of bricks are in straight lines, not slanting ones, and that the bricks are just as big at one end of the wall as at the other...but our eyes *see* the bricks shrinking on an angle as they recede.

Our brain is programed to insert itself into problem solving, that's what we hire it for, but when drawing

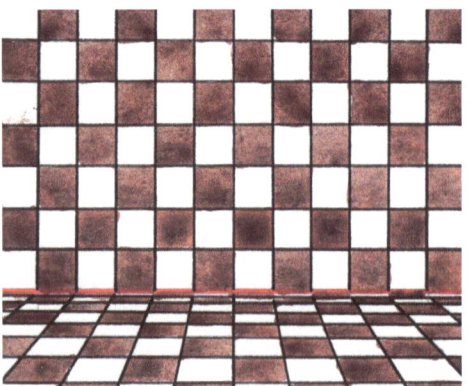

Is it a wall, or the floor? The angles at the bottom give an illusion of directional change. They are simply the spokes from an unseen VP behind the wall and the red line which in this drawing is not the horizon line.

we need our brains first to think it through and then *yield* to our eyes. We've all heard it said that artists see differently than non artists. Perhaps it's because artists do eventually learn to draw with their eyes. Eyes take the command position at the drawing table. It's a difficult shift for everyone, but it will happen. Perspective is a particularly difficult brain shift for us all. I assure you that if you keep working with it, you will understand it and get this very powerful tool.

Here's another mind game. Hold your index finger up close to your eye. You can actually hide an entire person across the room behind that finger. Putting it in words makes it sound absurd. The finger is so tiny and the person is so big.

"How the eyes see isn't the way things are, but it is the way to draw them."

The vanishing point is simply a tool that helps us draw like our eyes see. It is our guide for *how* to climb or descend the picture plane. It's a road map. Whether moving toward or away from us we know that if we follow the VP spokes, it will work.

YOUR ASSIGNMENT

Get a sheet of drawing paper, a piece of string and a thumbtack. Draw a horizon line (anywhere, high, low or dead center) on the paper. Pick a vanishing point on that line (anywhere side to side) and indicate it with a dot. Put the tack into one end of the string and stick it into that dot. Rotate the string up, down and round and round passing above and below the horizon line. The angles made by the string are spokes going into or out of that dot. Draw along the spokes made by the string. Make ten or more spokes. Remove the string and then draw within the spokes.

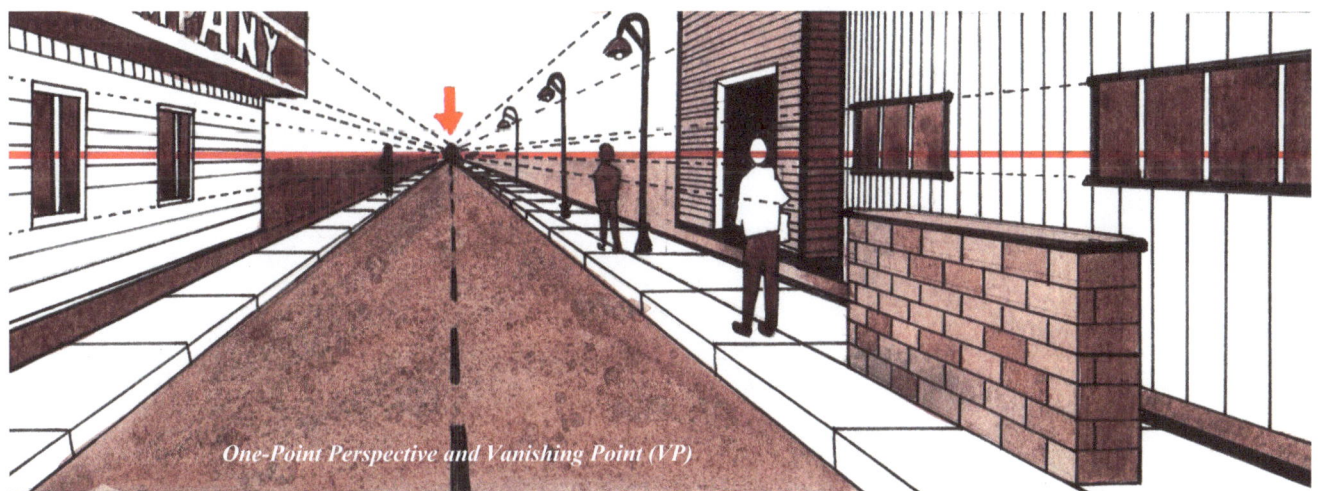
One-Point Perspective and Vanishing Point (VP)

Challenge yourself to do several of these. Copy mine first if that helps, then try other scenes of your own. Do not stress out about this. You'll not use the string and the spokes very much after you internalize them. Doing it several times will set it in your mind, and soon you'll abandon them altogether. In fact, using them renders a severe drawing, more like an architectural drawing. The goal is to understand the vanishing point so completely that you don't need to draw it. This will happen sooner than you think. Have faith and just keep working.

If one day you are outside painting and having a difficult time with the perspective, you'll know you can whip out the string or a straightedge, consider the perceived vanishing point, make the spokes and get on with the drawing. You'll have the tool.

Here are several things I'd bring to your attention about the above illustration of one-point perspective.

- The vanishing point affects ONLY the horizontal lines. Vertical lines do *not* relate to this VP
- The horizontal boards on the building are flat at the horizon line, and then slope up or down toward the VP as discussed.

- The heads of the people are all *approximately* at the horizon line. Why? Because their eyes, like yours, are at eye-level which is at the horizon line. Of course, there are tall and short people, but still, their heads will be near to the horizon, and their feet will climb the picture plane.
- Because this brick wall (unlike the first one) is totally below the horizon line, we can see its top. Remember the cups. If I had drawn it taller than the man, the lines of the bricks would, like the horizontal boards, have started going the opposite direction at the horizon line.. Compare this shorter brick wall to the taller one on the previous page. *Everything relates to that horizon line.*
- I need to mention here that there are mathematical equations that tell you the exact increments where objects like telephone poles, light posts, sidewalk squares, etc., gradually get smaller as they recede. You can get that far into it if you choose, but I find that with the vanishing point spokes guiding me, I can eyeball those distances in close enough to suit me.
- Every window, top and bottom, every brick, every board, and every sign, relates to and changes at the horizon line——everything.

TWO-POINT PERSPECTIVE

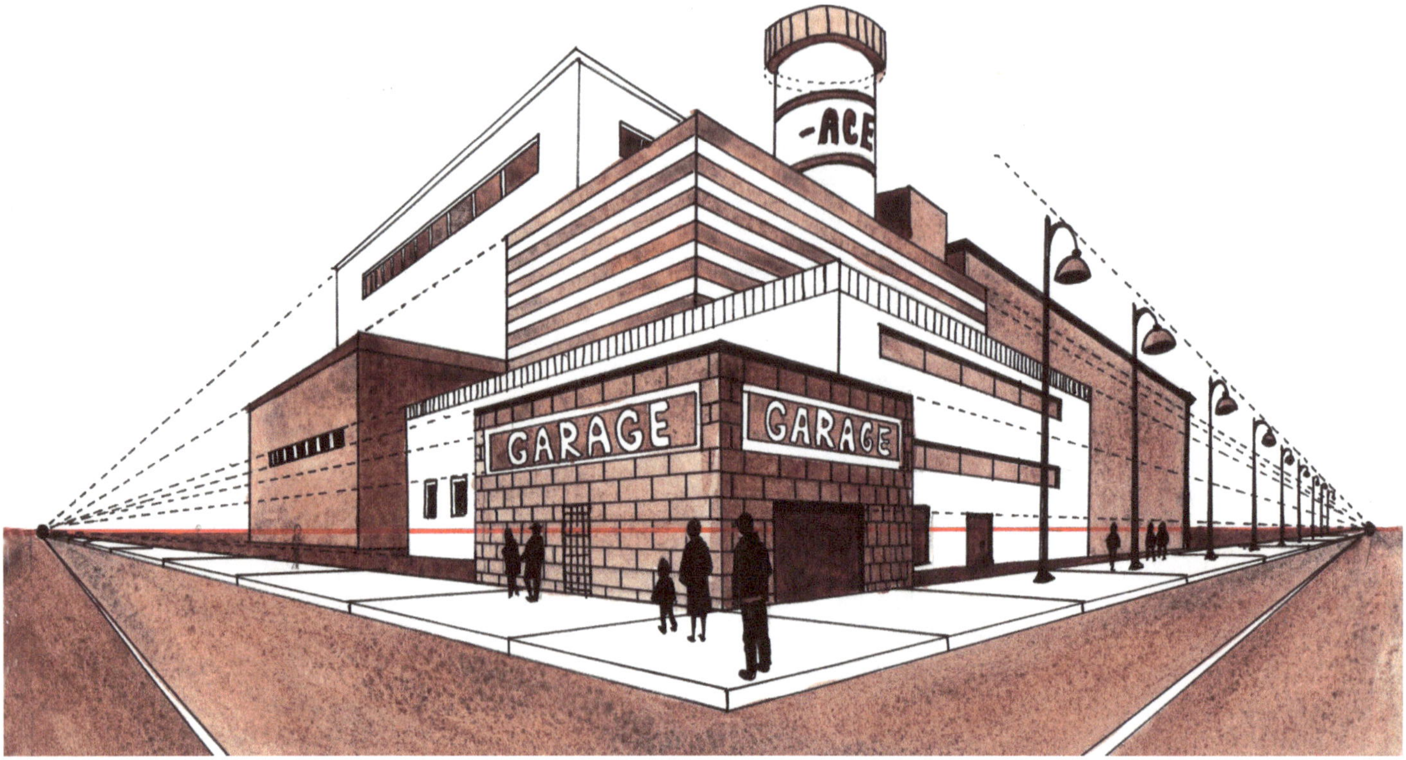

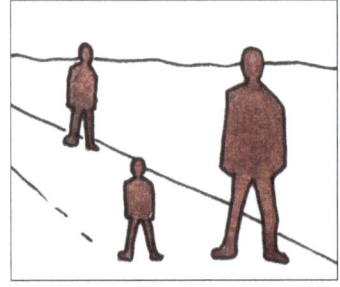

In this drawing, the two little figures are the same height. When/if the heads are at the horizon line, they relate fine to each other. But with their feet lined up, one is perceived tiny. Why is that?

Two-point perspective is the natural expansion of the same principles and illusions that we learned about with one-point. Two-point can describe buildings and other objects somewhere in the middle of the picture plane with vanishing points going away from the closest object on both sides of it. Study the illustration above. Unlike one-point perspective where everything seems to accumulate in the center somewhere on the horizon line, two-point perspective describes how everything slopes away from the center to twin vanishing points on either side. The center subject seems to protrude.

In this drawing the angles are severe, too severe for a pleasing painting, but I did that better to show how it works. Every board, window, brick, building (top to bottom) and even every letter on the sign, follows a spoke from one of the twin vanishing points. You could play with this all day. Get out your workbook, draw a horizon line and two vanishing points, draw the spokes as your guide and create the illusion of buildings where the closest corner *appears* to advance.

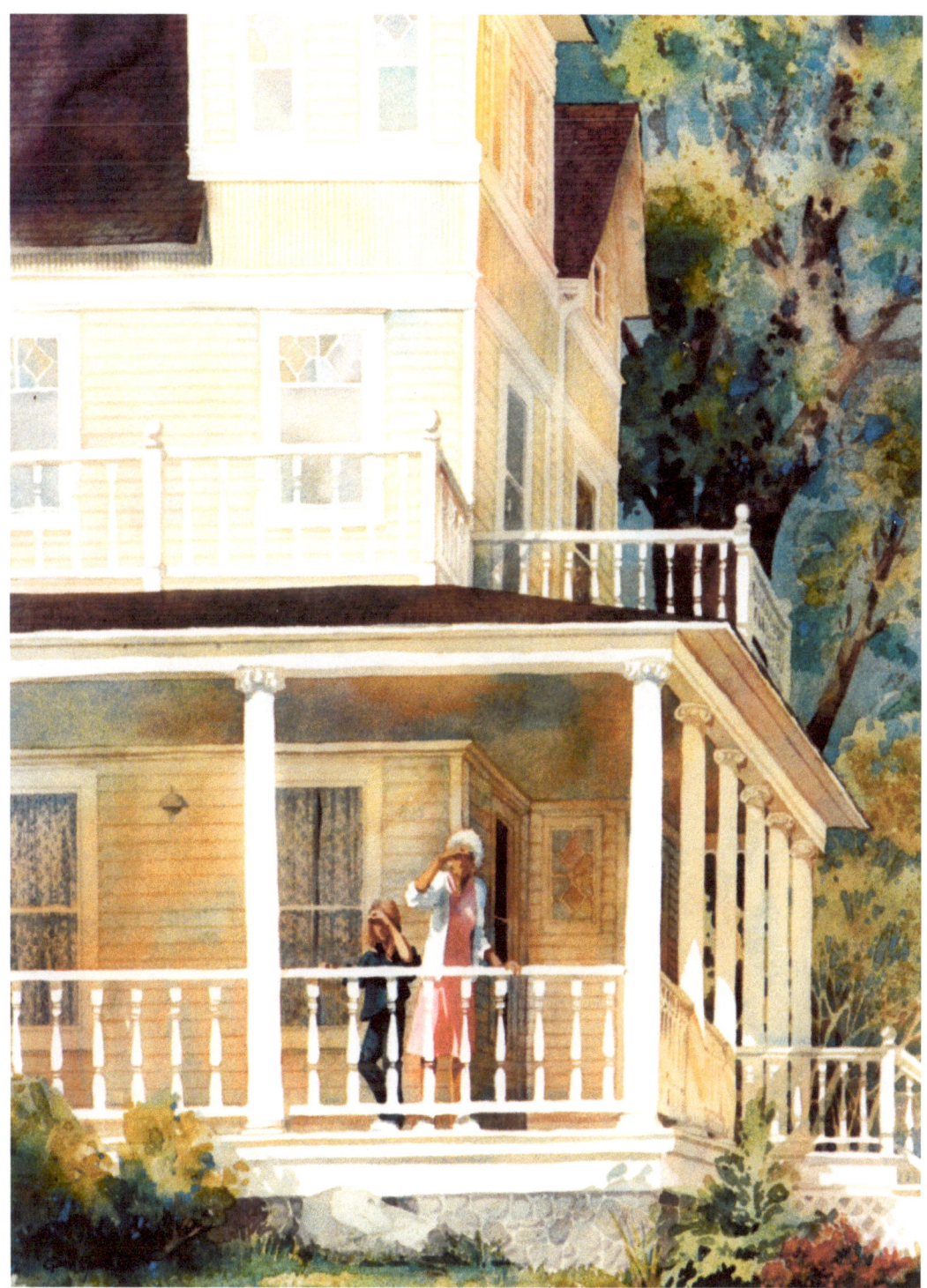

Sparky, Come Home   *watercolor*   *30 x 22*

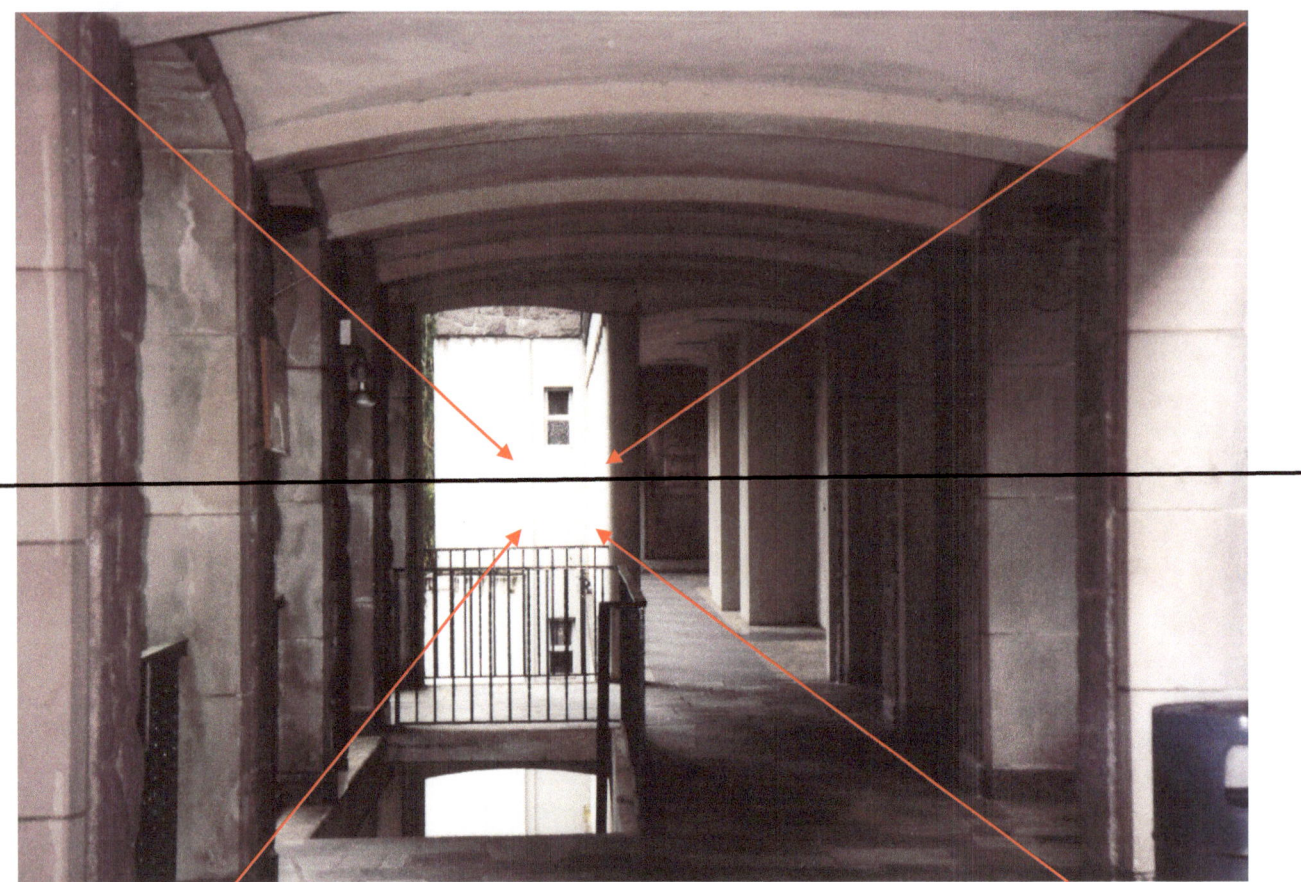

Here are a few images to show with photography (real life) how things like VP and the spokes radiating from them come into play when drawing. We are so thoroughly accustomed to *seeing* everything in perfect perspective every single minute of every day, yet it's a bit daunting to analyze how we actually *do* see with any true understanding. So let's dig deeper into all it.

this head knowledge may desert you. That's somewhat to be expected, so simply refer to this chapter as often as needed. I promise you that with practice, perspective will be no problem, *but you must practice.*

FINDING THAT HORIZON LINE

In order to settle our drawings, particularly of buildings, convincingly on a flat paper surface, our analysis needs to be fairly thorough. Take some time studying both the drawings and the photographs in this whole chapter on *perspective* until you feel you understand it. Later, when you are drawing your own buildings, some of

In the photo above there's no visible horizon line but we can perceive one. How? Search for a place where the angles switch directions. The black line above is where I found it, and yes, it is at the photographer's eye level. I snapped this shot somewhere in Portland. You could draw as many spokes as you want. I drew only four, but they all point to the same spot. That spot, of course, is the VP.

The State Capitol Building in Boise, Idaho is extremely complicated to paint, but I have done it. Note here also the elliptical *frown* and imagine *drawing through* as discussed earlier on page 91 in this chapter.

Notice how the rows of windows get increasingly smaller as they move toward the VP. We know, of course that every window in any given row is actually identical in size, but if you draw them as such, they will not fit.

On the opposite page, we know the columns are all the same height, but they certainly do not *look* the same. When you are an artist, you will often find yourself leaving the realm of reality. Here is one step in that direction.

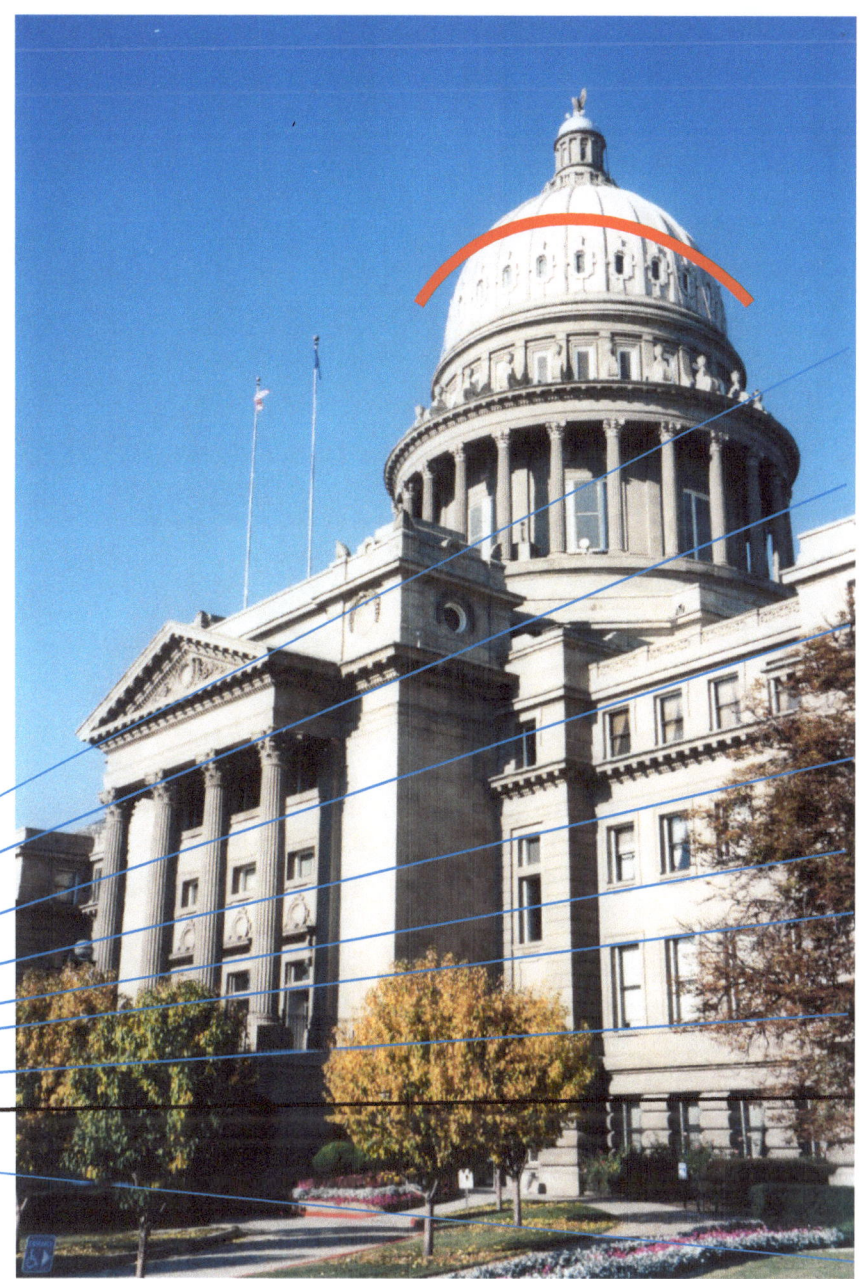

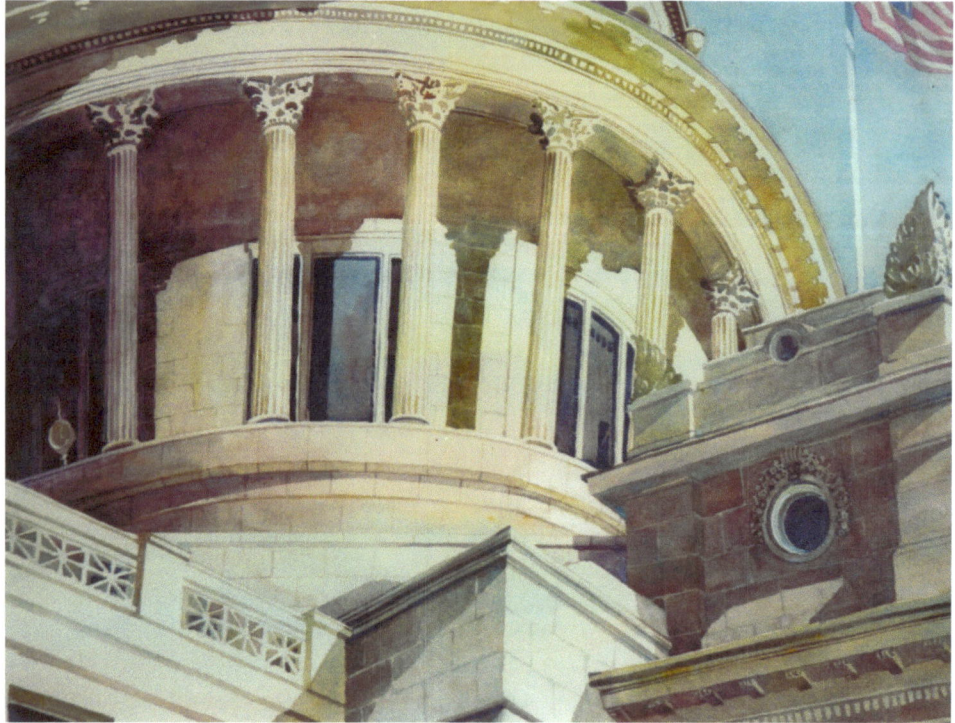

Boise Rotunda   *watercolor*   *22 x 30*

The perspective on *Boise Rotunda* is jauntily off, but it makes the structure look more imposing. You can actually design perspective to suit yourself, but when you know how it all works, you can confidently play with it.

If you have already solved these problems, then you probably skipped this chapter anyway, but for each of us, sometime on our artistic journey we come face to face with wanting a better command of *perspective*. Usually we start *thinking* more about it when drawing buildings, but it truly plays a roll in everything relating to representational drawing and painting.

Perspective is surely one of the more frustrating concepts to grasp. In a way, I was lucky because I'd hammered out much of it before I seriously studied it. For me, that worked, because when I finally read about it, it really clicked into my brain. Perhaps we learn better after a little bit of struggling.

When I was a Girl Scout leader, I remember learning how to teach girls to light fires with one match. The first year I went through all the proper things to do. First, you gather the tinder, the kindling, and the fuel. I explained it all and even demonstrated it. The girls were giggling and not really paying much attention. When it was their turn, they could no more light a fire than they could have flown. So, we tried again and repeated the scene over and over, but they never really gained true skills at fire building.

Next year, with new recruits I took another tack. This time I gave them all the stuff they needed, including a full box of matches, and said, "Go light a fire." Of course they could not do it. I watched them get through the giggling, watched them get more serious and finally watched them get frustrated. My plan was in action. Then, I called the girls back to me and said, "Now, I am going to show you how to light a fire with just one match." I had their attention. It worked exactly as I'd hoped. Struggling a little first definitely did help.

~

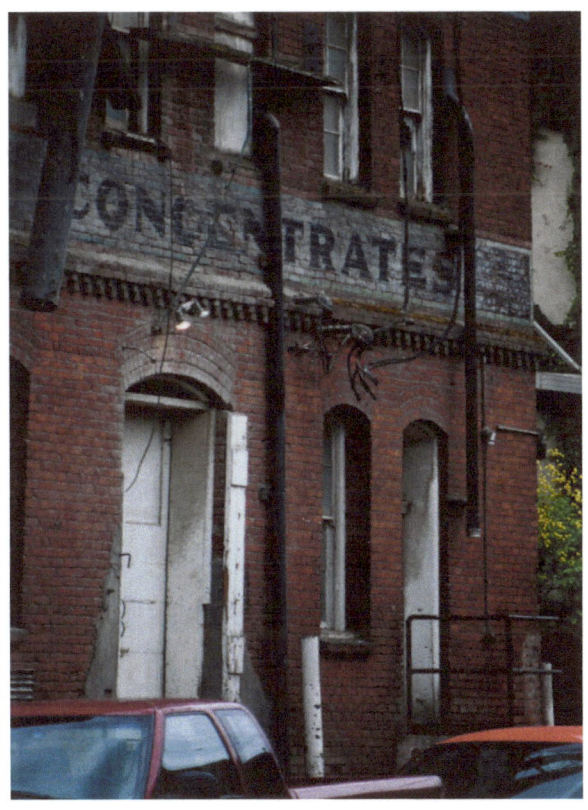

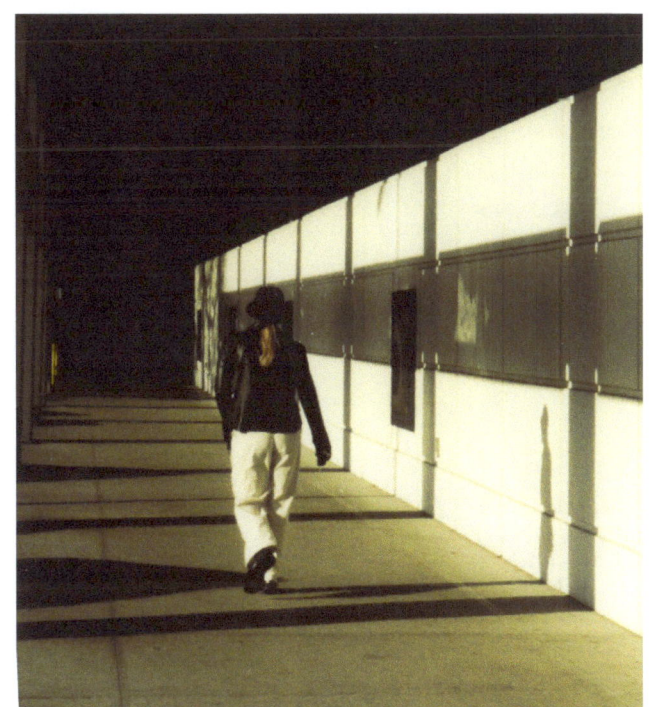

PRACTICE PHOTO PAGE ASSIGNMENTS

♦ Analyze these photos. Are they one– or two-point perspective?

♦ Using tracing paper and a ruler, find the VP's and create some spokes radiating from them.

♦ Next, determine the perceived horizon line. Where is it?

♦ Just for fun, add a few little figures on your tracing paper. Where do their heads and feet fit into the VP spokes?

♦ Find photos of your own, and repeat these tasks.

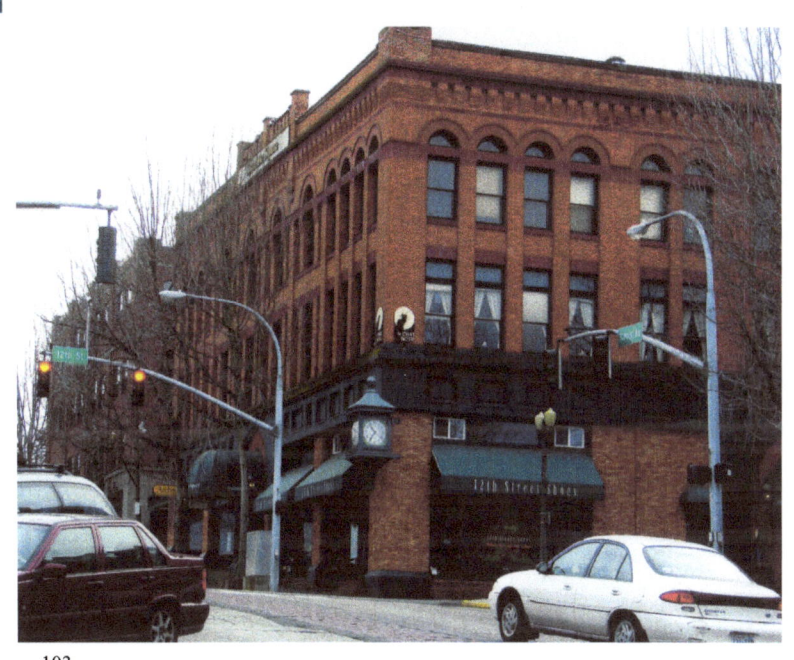

103

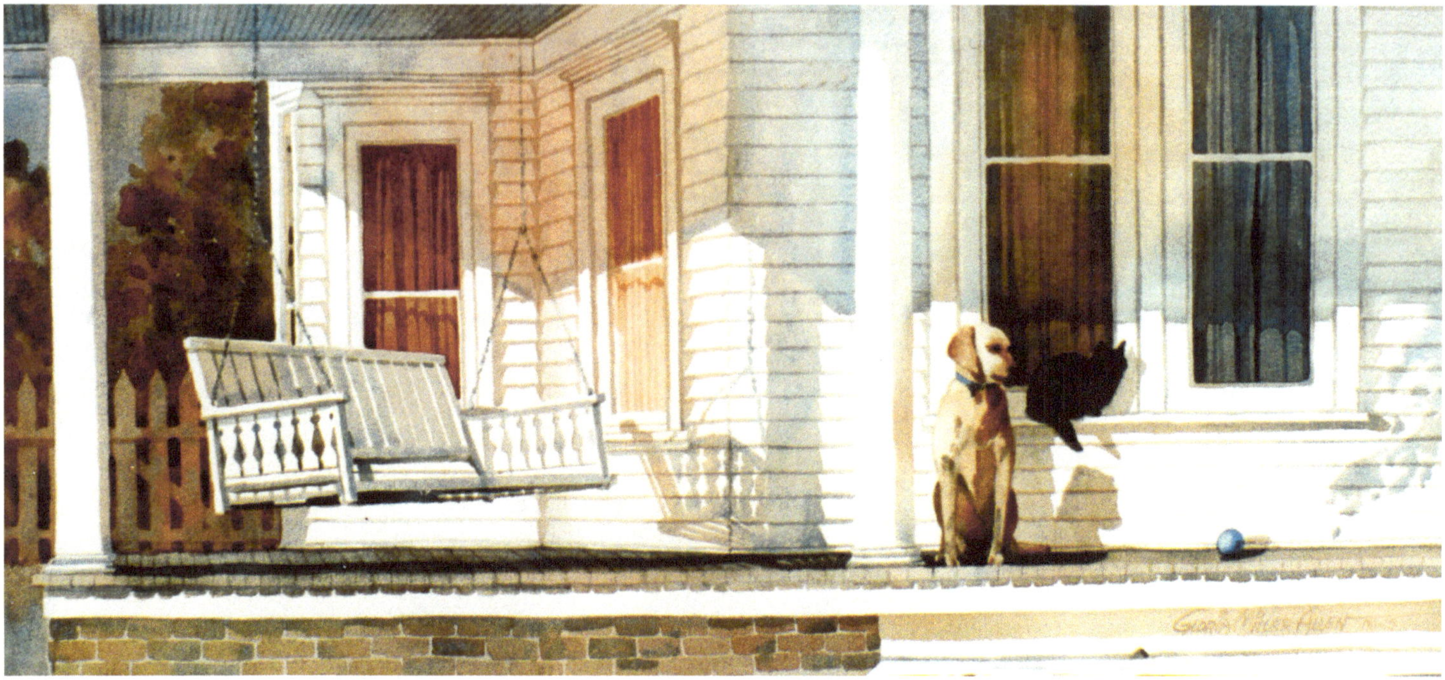

Anybody Want To Play?   *watercolor*   *16 x 32*

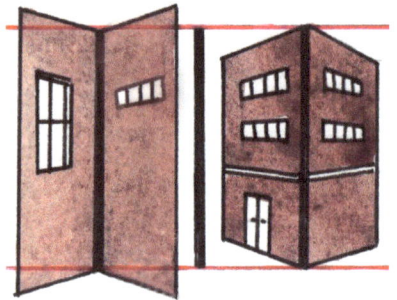

A LITTLE ASSIGNMENT

In your workbook, draw two lines the same size, like the dark ones below. Measure them, they are the same height. With one- and two- point perspective on your mind, create two corners as I've done here. It's an optical illusion, fun to look at, but take the time to actually *do* it in your own workbook and not just look at this image.

Truly, you need to go through the motions yourself.
Yes, I'm a broken record. *Just do it.*

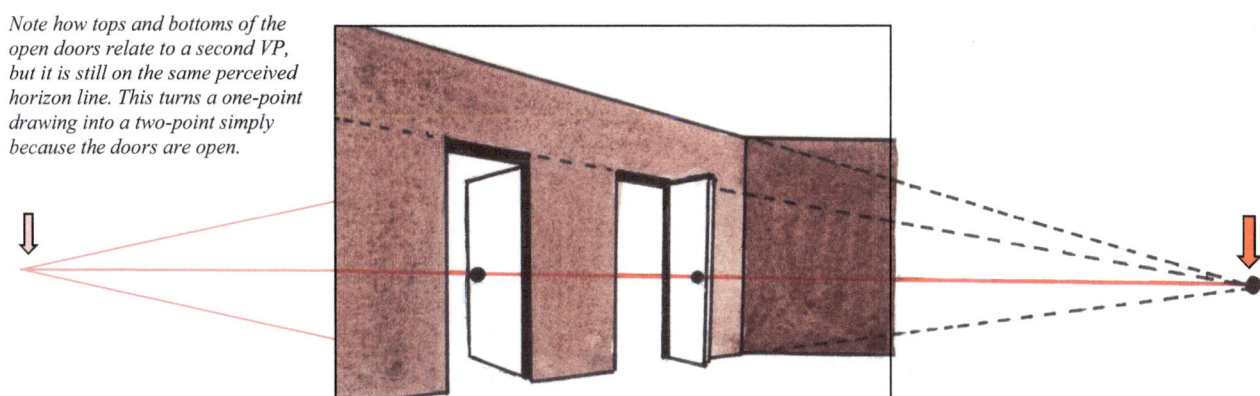

Note how tops and bottoms of the open doors relate to a second VP, but it is still on the same perceived horizon line. This turns a one-point drawing into a two-point simply because the doors are open.

When you are drawing or painting, it's common for the vanishing point to be completely off the picture plane as it is here. The perceived vanishing point is always as important as any drawn on the paper. When you're in the habit of always thinking in terms of vanishing points and the spokes from them, you are able to accomplish this trick quite naturally.

Of course, you could create a scene where the horizon is perceived off the top or off the bottom of the paper or canvas. It's just a view from a different perspective. Think about standing on a tall hill (or flying) with a camera in your hand. Aim first at the horizon then slowly aim it down toward the ground below you. The horizon slips *above* the camera lenses but is still perceived and important. Think of lying down on the grass in a city park. Look through the camera at the base of a tree or a building. Slowly raise the camera lens up the tree trunk or building until all you see is sky. The horizon is perceived *below* the picture plane but it is still important.

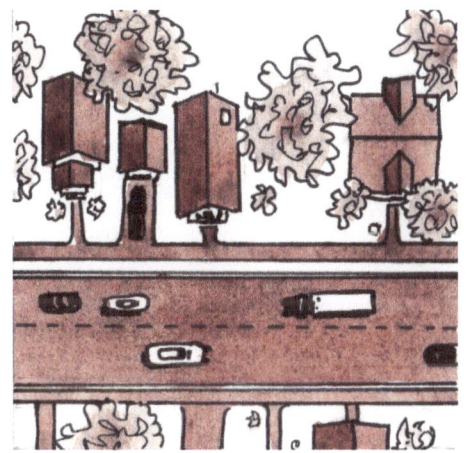

Perceived horizon line is above the picture plane

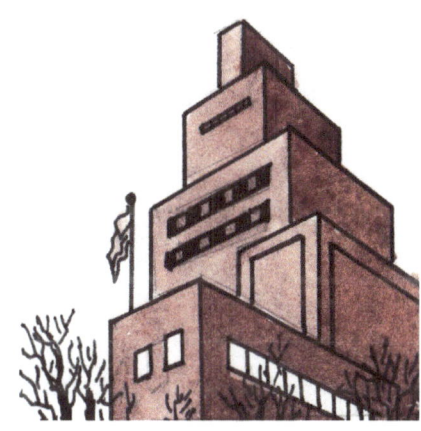

Perceived horizon line is below the picture plane

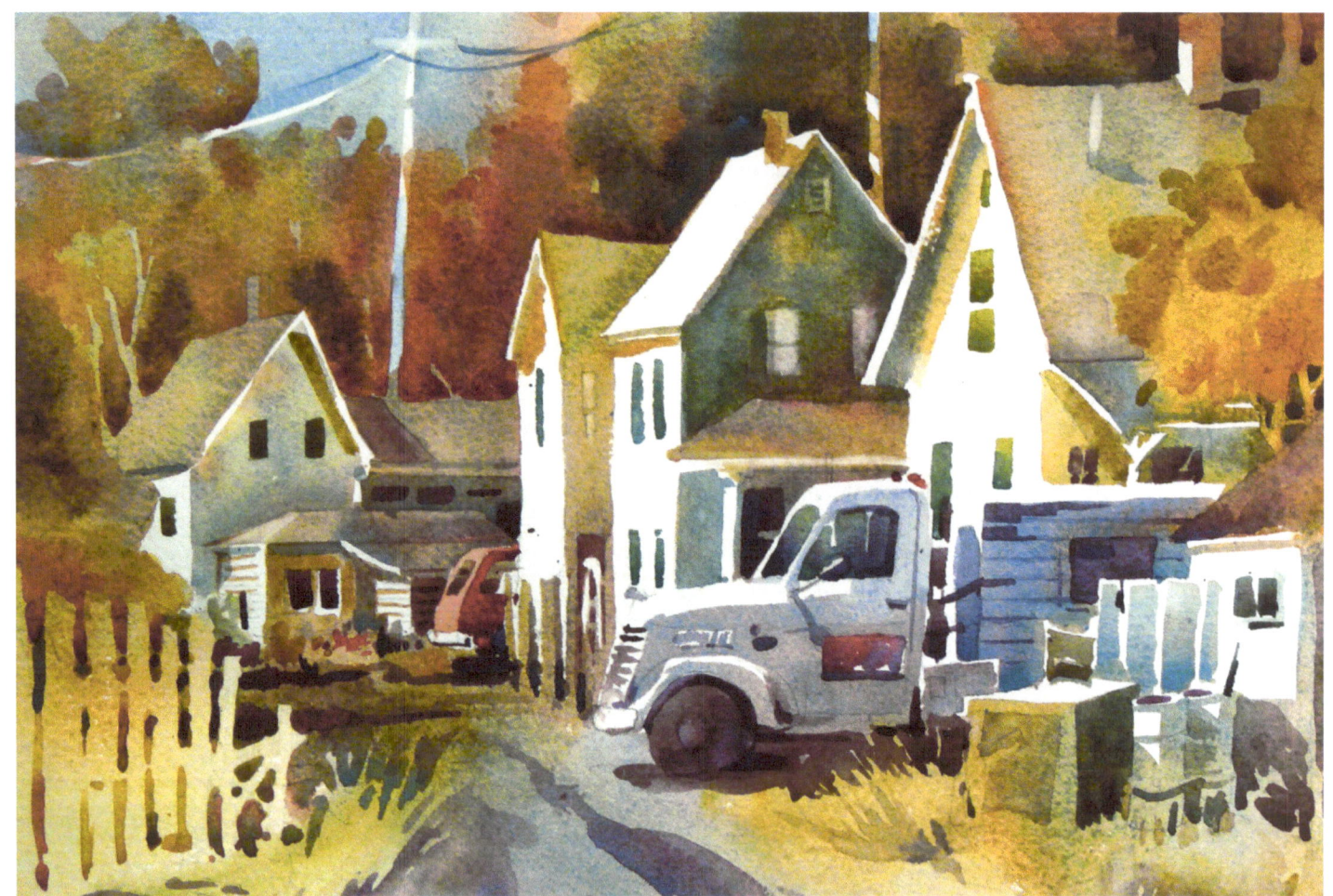

La Crosse   *watercolor*   *11 x 15*

A FEW LAST POINTS ON PERSPECTIVE

♦ When the horizon line is perceived off the top or bottom of the page the little trick of the human heads being on the horizon line won't work, of course. In *most* situations though, it works well.

♦ In the three paintings, *Americana, La Crosse and Union Station, Kansas City* the drawings are not as exact or severe as the illustrations I did showing one- and two-point perspective. In drawing and painting it is perhaps better to be less *correct* and softer. However, having the solid knowledge in your tool box while drawing will settle the images on the page comfortably without actually drawing the VP spokes or the horizon line and it will be in a more *painterly* fashion. I rarely measure boards or VP spokes, but I most certainly do think about and consider them constantly while drawing.

♦ If you want to get deeper into *perspective* you will see that there is also a vanishing point vertically. Study the drawing of tall buildings and you will see what I mean. The vertical lines will emerge above the building at some *perceived* vanishing point in the sky. As I mentioned earlier, there are books about perspective that are very analytical and mathematical and may very well appeal to you if you are an analytical painter. My purpose in this chapter was to give you some simpler laymen type *thinking*.

♦ And finally, I cannot say enough about how much more you will gain from doing these assignments with your own eyes, brains and hands instead of looking at what I have done for you.

ANOTHER ASSIGNMENT CHALLENGE

What would be wrong with taking a whole day drawing perspective spokes and simply playing with these principles? If you do, you will be pleased in future drawing projects and paintings. No short-cut can serve as well.

Think about a child learning to write letters of the alphabet for the first time. Do you imagine for one moment that child would learn to write those letters as well by simply looking at the letters in some book? Or would that same child learn faster and more completely by taking pencil in hand and repeatedly creating the letters on their own paper themselves? *You must do it for yourself.*

FAILURE
UPON FAILURE
BUILDS A MOUND ~
A MOUND UPON WHICH
YOU SHALL
STAND

SUCCESS
AFTER SUCCESS
DECORATES THE MOUND

BUT UNDERNEATH ~
FOUNDATIONS
OF STRUGGLE
AND FAILURE

EVERY EFFORT
SUCCESSFUL OR NOT ~
ADDS A LAYER

SO BUILD

LEAVE COWARDICE
ON FLAT LAND

FAITH IN
EACH STEP TAKEN
EVEN IN FAILURE ~
ALLOWS YOU TO
BUILD

SO BUILD

SUCCESS
STANDS ON TOP
OF SUCH MOUNDS

1982

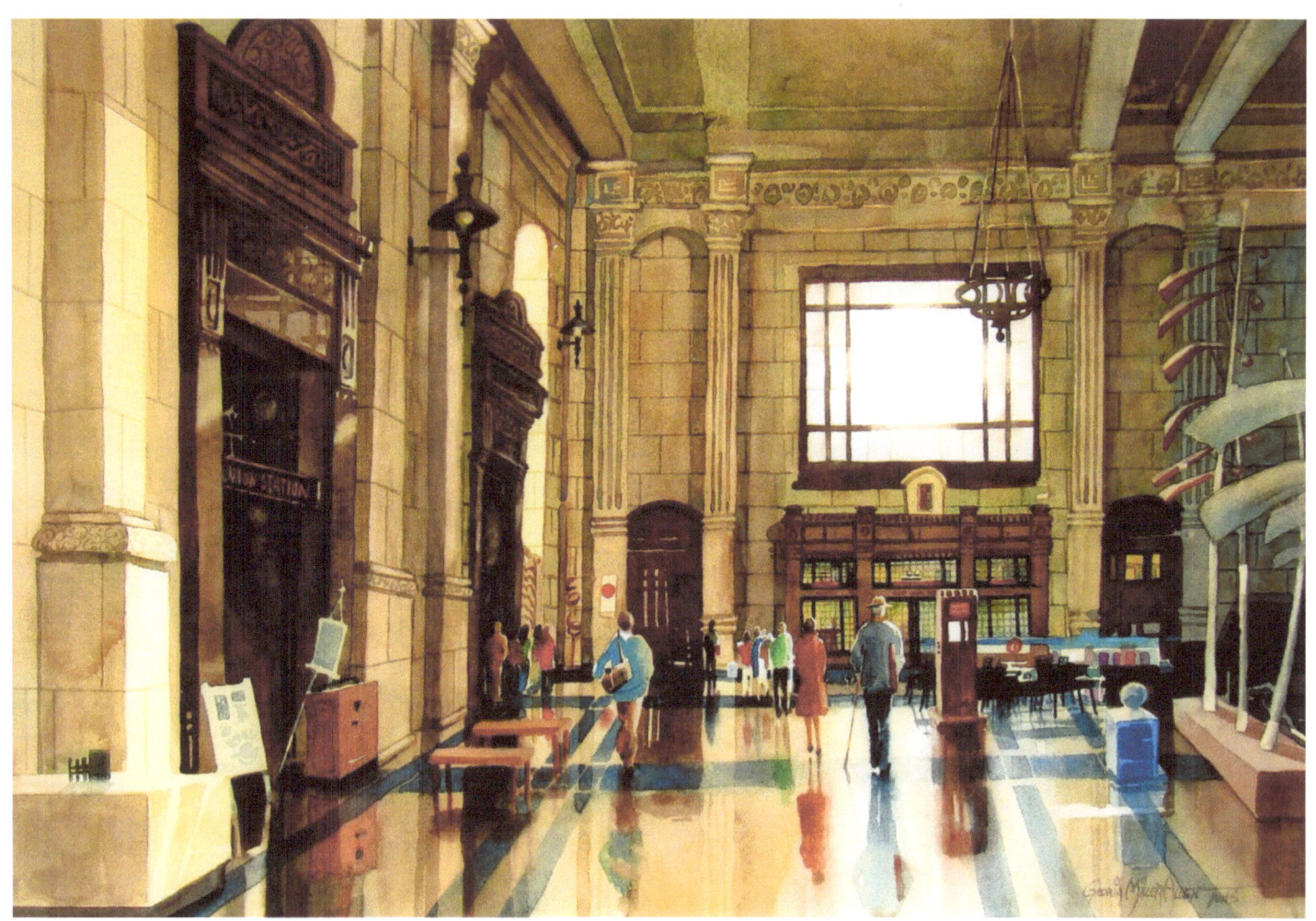

Union Station ~ Kansas City, MO   *watercolor*   *22 x 30*

PART THREE
IN CONCLUSION

THINKING OF GOALS
AS ROAD MAPS

CHAPTER FIVE:
PUTTING YOURSELF IN
THE DRIVER'S SEAT

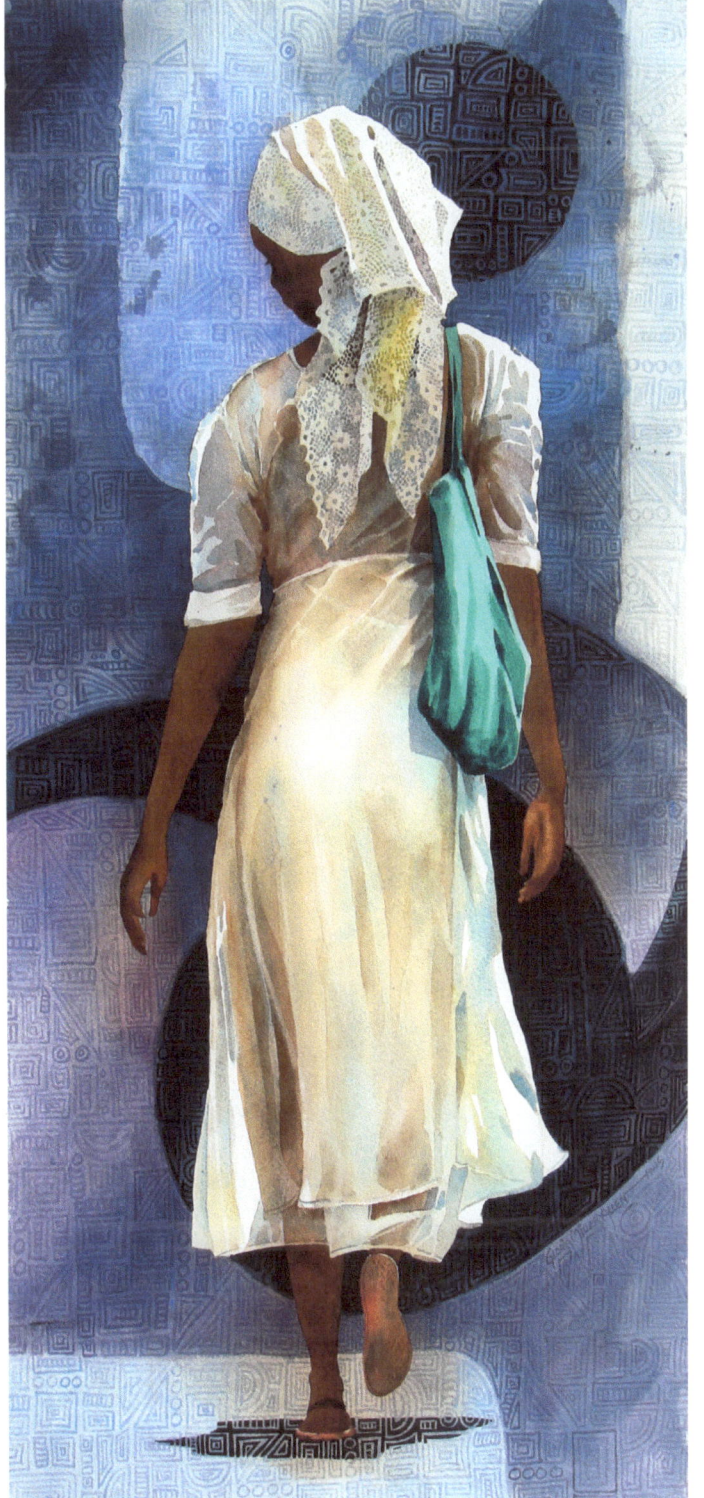

Zimbabwe *~Africa Facing the Future Series   oversized watercolor   38 x 26*

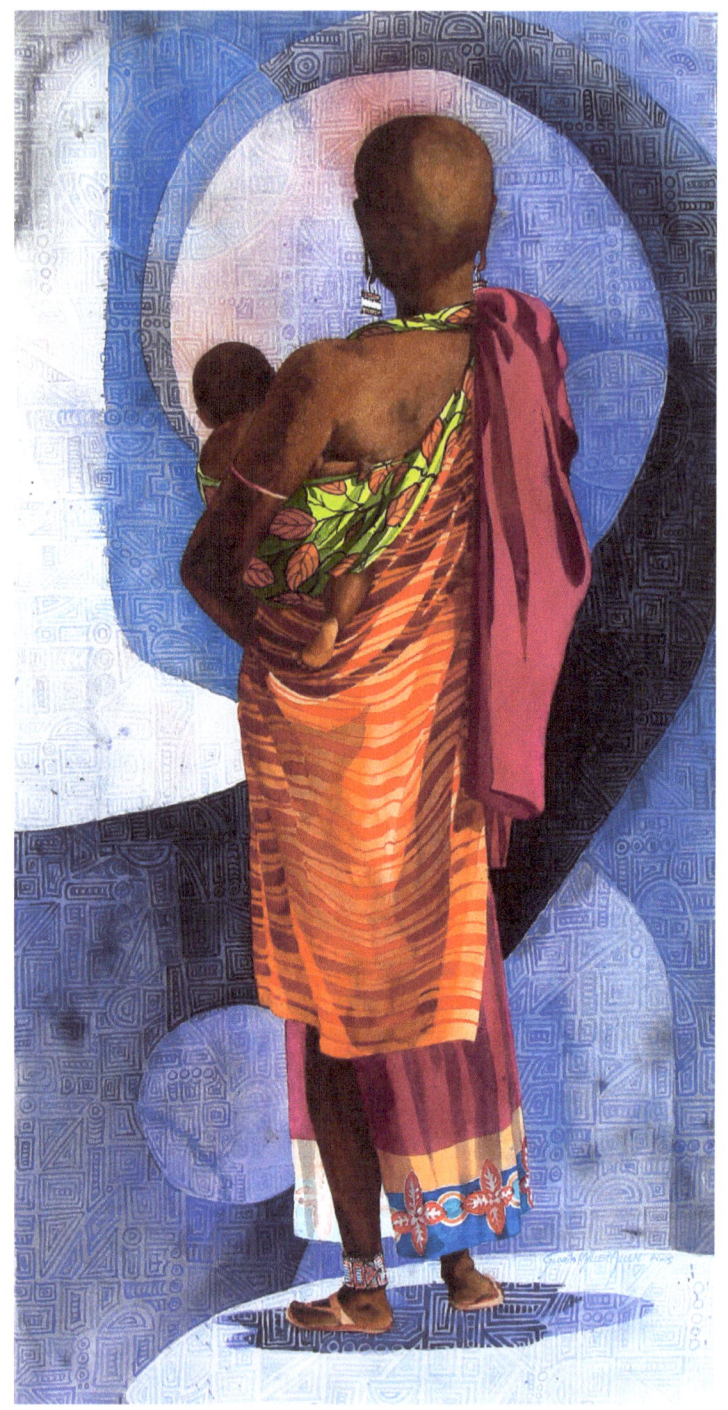

Kenya ~ *Africa Facing the Future Series*   *oversized watercolor*   *38 x 26*

CHAPTER FIVE

PUTTING YOURSELF IN THE DRIVERS SEAT

FEATURING PAINTINGS FROM MY TRIP TO AFRICA

GOALS AS ROAD MAPS

If you have done the assignments and not just skipped around the book looking at the pictures, you are well on your way to a more confident and satisfying relationship between you and papers, pencils and pens and are to be congratulated. This book has dealt only with drawing tools, but for most of us, painting with colors and understanding values and solid composition calls our name rather loudly. That is another book, but I believe the fundamentals of drawing and perspective are too often glossed over with little attention paid to them by people altogether too impatient to get to the painting. Later frustrations will surely cause us to return again to our drawing skills so that we can come confidently to the easel. Perhaps that's what brought you here.

If that's been your story, you were probably ready, willing and able to spend your time doing each of the assignments as given. You know you want to own those skills. Like the story I told earlier about Girl Scouts learning to build a fire better after they had struggled some first, you're more likely to go back and pay attention to the lessons you skipped lightly over in the beginning. Let's face it, it's all good stuff when you are ready. The good news is all this information will certainly wait until you are ready. But why wait? If you are reading this book, you are stepping out on your own artistic journey now, so *now* is the perfect time.

Let's go back to the beginning of the book when you wrote down your dreams and your bug-a-boos. Retrieve them. What do they look like to you right now? Have your ideas changed any? Are they still holding? Do you want to add or subtract any of them. There is serious work to be done with that list. Honesty and sincerity are all that counts. Art will inevitably lead us to know ourselves better. Sometimes, that can bring us to our knees.

GOALS ~ OLD AND NEW
YOUR SECOND CHANCE

_____

_____

_____

_____

_____

_____

_____

_____

_____

_____

BUG-A-BOOS STILL BUGGING

_____

_____

_____

_____

_____

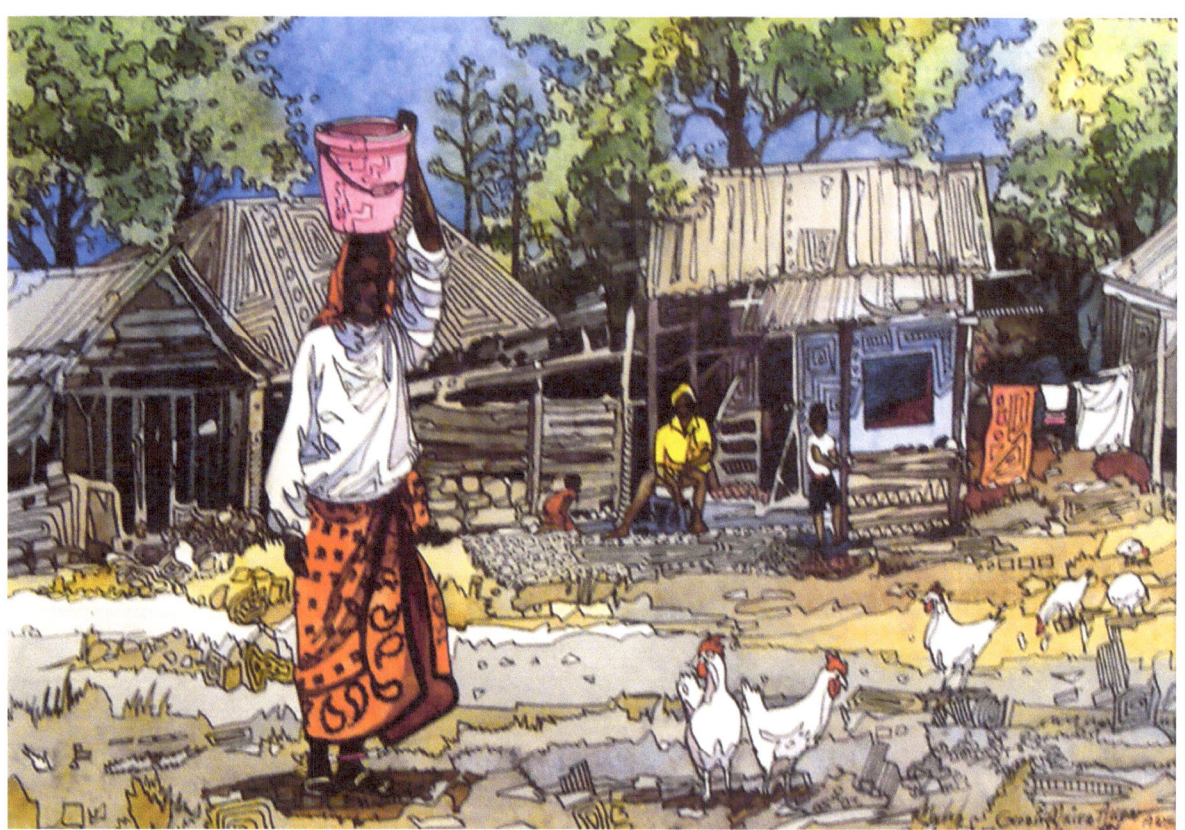

Water Carrier   *watercolor and ink*   *10 x 14*

THINGS THAT HELP MAKE GOALS HAPPEN

- Pick goals that fit where you are right now and write them down. Otherwise, they are thin air. Written down, they start to become something more real in your life.

- Strike a bargain with the universe. Your goals will take time. Decide how much time you are willing to give and then give it.

- Make a promise and keep it. Failure in this one simple statement cannot be allowed. If you can't keep it, don't make it. This takes serious work.

- Think of where you want to be with all this in one year or in ten years, and list what you'll need to do in order to arrive there on time.

- Never underestimate the intangible tool of *getting to know yourself*. Take the raw material that is you ~ recognize it, mold it and work with it. Your strengths, weaknesses, wounds, dreams, history and everything in between.

- "Steady as she goes." "Hold your line." "Keep your eyes on the goal." "Be flexible." All good adages. Keep them in mind, even tack them on your wall with a smile.

- Educate yourself. Join art groups, take workshops, read books, talk with other artists and watch instructional videos. These things all help you stay on your road and are exciting gifts to give yourself. Be generous.

- Experiment, play, try new subjects. Laugh, sing and even dance sometimes along the way. Do whatever you need to do in order to keep it fun. If it is being fun you'll just keep on going.

- Remember you are a human being, and human beings are by nature creative. The muse dwells inside. Never let yourself doubt that and do not let anyone else cause you to doubt that.

- Never allow doubts to take root. Dig them out. You do have the right and the necessary native ability to learn and grow and pursue your artistic dreams.

- *"Wherever you go, there you are."* You cannot escape the fact that you want to be involved in art in some way. Figure out *how* you want that involvement, and you will already be closer to getting it.

- Learn to think about your failures as something to build upon. That way they don't seem like a bad thing. Thomas Edison had multitudes of failed experiments before he found the one thing that worked. Could he have gone directly to that one thing? Of course not. Foundations of failures are what we build on. Persistence is a great intangible tool. Work on persistence. It pays.

- Be eternally grateful for the beauty and richness art adds to your life.

- Inch by inch is easy. Be content with every tiny step you take. You are on the long road.

- Don't worry about each and every drawing/painting being your best. That can never happen because when your drawing reaches that "best" level every day, then that level becomes your every day level. Then a new level will be attained containing a new "best." It is called simply, GROWTH.

- And finally, Work!

Like all lists, that one is certainly incomplete, but it has worth nonetheless, and it goes without saying it can be used for all goals in life. In the territories of life where you feel confident, competent and in charge, you have already managed the necessary steps taken to feel that way. In areas where you know you have work to do, you will find good use for the items on that list. The last item, *Work,* is the surest way to achieve your artistic and non artistic goals.

My high school art teacher was a hero of mine. His name was James Lauver, and he worked me hard. As I've mentioned previously, by the time I was a senior I had my schedule arranged so I could spend four hours a day in the art room. The art room was Mr. Lauver's kingdom. I was certainly a serious student, though not one with the most obvious talent. At the end of the school year I asked Mr. Lauver to sign my annual. He found his picture in the faculty section, and then right across his face with black ink, he scrawled these words: "Work, Work, Work, Work, Work." At the time I was most aggravated at him for destroying his picture in my beautiful book.

Many years later, teaching classes myself, I found I always told my students to "Work, Work, Work," not even realizing where that had come from. Then one day while looking at my old annual with an old friend...there it was, scribbled across his face. I knew he had taught me many things, but until that moment I hadn't given him credit for reinforcing one of the most profound lessons I'd ever learn. Work.

~

No mater what the goal, *working* steadily on it gives purpose to your everyday life. Is that enormous? I do believe it is.

BUT I'M NOT SURE? ## HOW BIG CAN I GO?

Sometimes people have a difficult time getting their goals concretely in their mind in the first place. This is why it is often impossible for people to visualize themselves as a person who really goes after and attains goals. Their self image may never have been that of a "go-getter." I believe it's because they don't actually know what their goals are. This seems pretty basic, even self explanatory, but often people I meet in my workshops have never truthfully *thought* about goal setting regarding their fantasies involved with art. Unrecognized, unclaimed or unnamed fantasies have a sneaky way of solidifying permanently in our lives as just that ~ fantasies. They are made of fluff and stuff. As such they can flit around somewhere on our horizon on beautiful gossamer wings taunting and tempting us but perpetually out of reach. They are neither named or claimed (to use words I've used all through this book). Therefore, not much ever actually happens, and if it does, it's by default. This is a fairly common condition among us humans. What can we do to change that little self-defeating habit? Well, perhaps that can now be part of your history. Leave it behind and in the dust.

The first move of course, is to consciously recognize a fantasy and see if it can be turned into a real goal. What would it take? Set small ones and big ones.

Set little goals all along the road to the *Big One*. Guess what? You don't have to buy anything or sell anything. But you do have to *think*. There's that word again ~ *Think*.

Yes, I do believe *thinking* is a real big deal. We do it every single day rarely recognizing the incredible power tool or the immeasurable gift it actually is.

If you know how to name and claim a goal, you're not common. However, I'll step out on a limb here and say I bet most of you, my readers, have not actually done the assignment of listing your goals as directed. Am I right?

I challenge you then to do that little exercise now. It costs you nothing, and it may help you acquire the incredible *goal setting tool* for your art tool box. If this seems like a crazy idea to you, then I'm pretty sure you have *not* done it. It has everything to do with knowing yourself. It's how you stamp your name in big gold letters on your own goals. It is part of your purpose. It is not just a crazy idea.

"As a man thinketh ~

so shall he become."

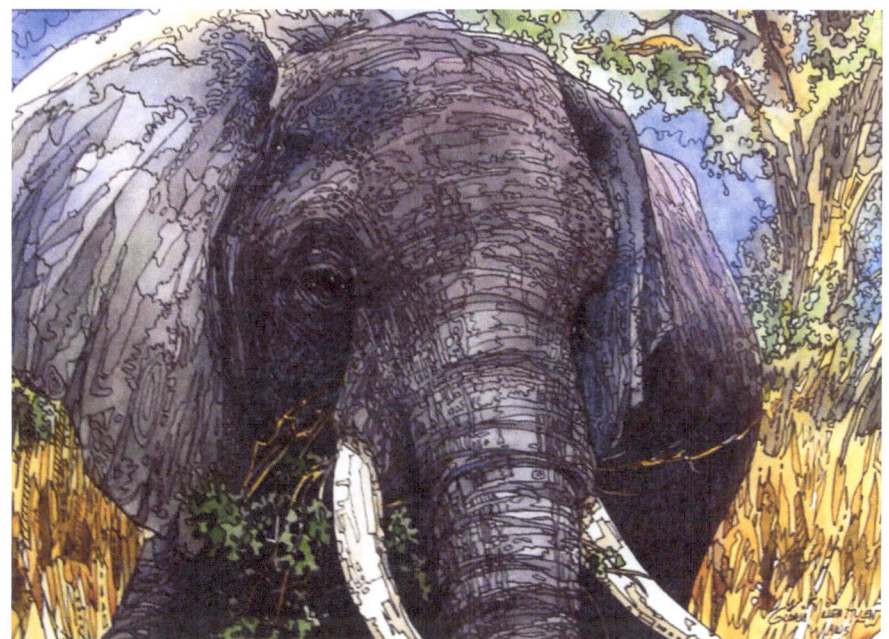

Amboseli Giant's Lunch'   *watercolor and ink*   *10 x 14*

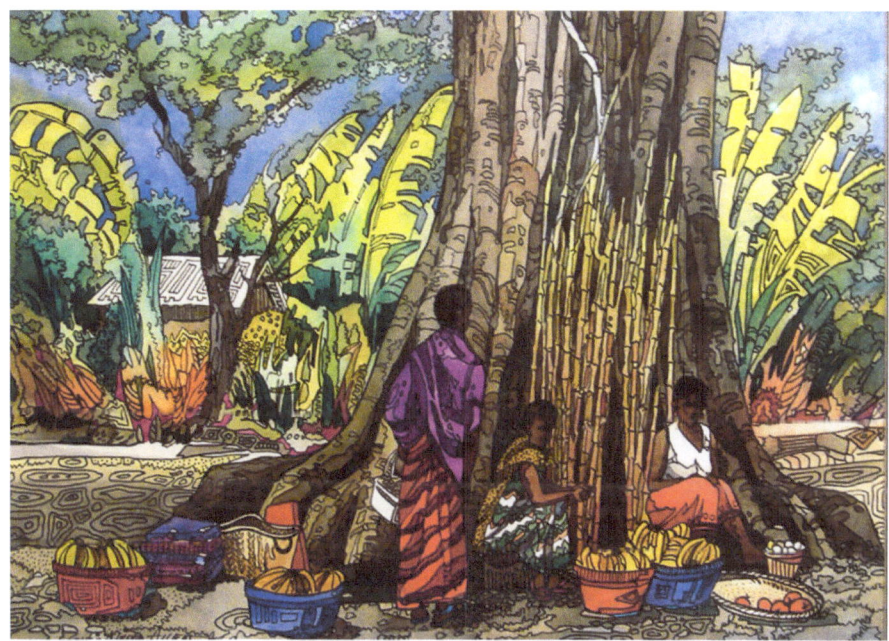

Sugarcane and Bananas   *watercolor and ink*   *10 x 14*

FINDING YOURSELF ON THAT ROAD

People go around in life trying to find themselves, trying to find out what their purpose in life is, and why they were born. These are big questions we have all heard before, but they really are *big* questions. More importantly, we've all tried to answer them at one time or another. Here's one more big question.

"Why do I want to do this art thing anyway?"

That certainly deserves some time and thought and self examination, too. Every one of us will have very personal answers for that one. It would be wise to begin to answer it for yourself. As for the other big questions, here are some of my answers that I would share:

- ♦ I believe we are exactly what we make ourselves to be with the raw materials given us.
- ♦ I believe we choose our purposes by ourselves.
- ♦ I believe purposes are free, and we can have as many or as few as we want.
- ♦ I believe nobody else can give us a purpose, and we wouldn't like it much if they did.
- ♦ I believe art not only gives me a purpose, but it also gives me contentment and energy. I can not imagine *not* pursuing it. It's like a big carrot out in front of me. It keeps me going.
- ♦ I believe purpose gives meaning to life.
- ♦ I believe in life.

How does all that relate to my life as an artist? It relates completely. *Think* about it. How does it relate to yours?

I hope this little book has been a pleasure to read and to look at. It has been one of my own *goals*. As I come to the end, I believe more than ever:

"I THINK ~ THEREFORE I ART"

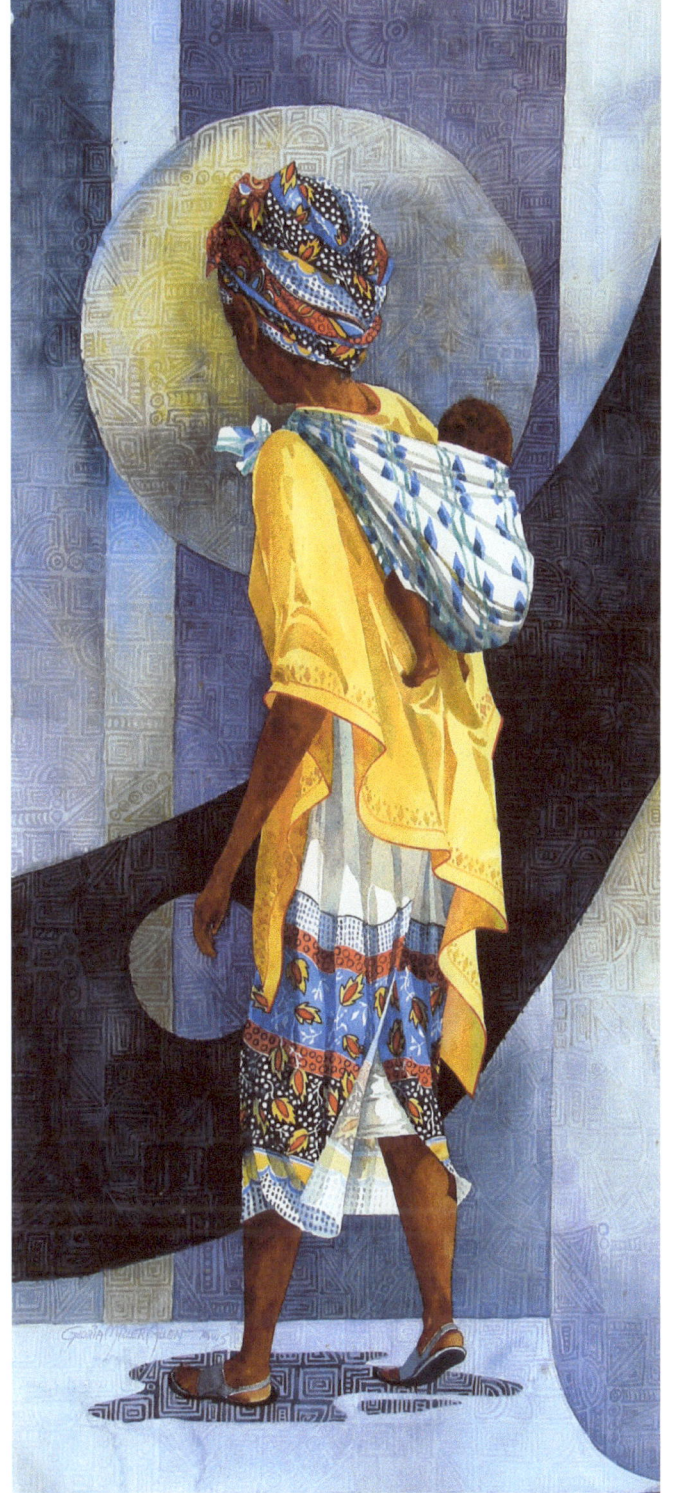

Tanzania ~ Africa Facing the Future Series   oversized watercolor   38 x26

"The ancestor of every action is a thought."

Ralph Waldo Emerson

INDEX OF PAINTINGS

ABOUT THE AUTHOR

Gloria Miller Allen is what she calls, "a lifer" - meaning she has been drawing and painting her entire life. She was born in Kansas, raised in the mid-west, and has lived in Idaho since 1974.

To date, Gloria has been juried into over 55 National and International exhibits, winning her fair share of awards. She holds signature membership in the American Watercolor Society, the Transparent Watercolor Society of America, Watercolor West, and the Northwest Watercolor Society as well as several state societies.

Gloria's paintings have been represented in galleries around the western states for over 20 years, including galleries in Carmel, CA; Sedona and Scottsdale, AZ; Boise, ID; Santa Fe and Taos, NM. Her work is currently found in the Lawrence Galleries of OR; The Juniper Sky and Datura Galleries in Kayenta Art Village, UT; and Gallery West in Bellingham, WA.

Gloria teaches workshops around the country. She holds the self image of being a perpetual student and knows from firsthand experience that giving yourself academic studies and thousands of hours spent at the drawing board or easel is an invaluable part of being an artist—no matter the lack of or the abundance of a formal art education. She believes art is simply a way of life for many people. In her workshops she makes no apology for pushing her students in academic studies dealing with the basics. Her workshop is very structured and is titled *"Power Tools for Powerful Paintings."*

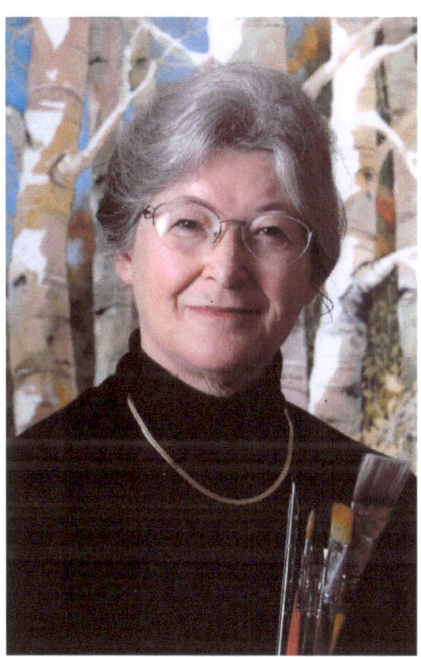

Her own artistic career grew slowly but steadily while raising a family and being an active member of her community. Art was a hobby in the beginning but grew into a career reaching in many directions. She is a life member of the Eagle Rock Art Guild in her town of Idaho Falls. She is a charter member and signature member of the Idaho Watercolor Society. She spent 10 years on the steering and building committee that saw the completion and opening of the Art Museum of Eastern Idaho. She exhibits on the national and international level. She served as Artist in Residence in Zion National Park for one glorious month in 2010. She has begun participating in invitational plein aire painting events. She has always been a poet.

Photo by Kort Duce

www.ingramcontent.com/pod-product-compliance
Lightning Source LLC
Chambersburg PA
CBHW050719180526
45159CB00003B/1075